Inari Sámi Folklore

INARI SÁMI FOLKLORE

STORIES FROM AANAAR

August V. Koskimies
and
Toivo I. Itkonen,
revised by Lea Laitinen

Edited and translated by
Tim Frandy

The University of Wisconsin Press

The University of Wisconsin Press
728 State Street, Suite 443
Madison, Wisconsin 53706
uwpress.wisc.edu

Gray's Inn House, 127 Clerkenwell Road
London EC1R 5DB, United Kingdom
eurospanbookstore.com

Originally published as *Inarinlappalaista kansantietoutta* (Helsinki: Suomalais-Ugrilainen Seura, 1978)

English translation and scholarly apparatus copyright © 2019 by the Board of Regents of the University of Wisconsin System

All rights reserved. Except in the case of brief quotations embedded in critical articles and reviews, no part of this publication may be reproduced, stored in a retrieval system, transmitted in any format or by any means—digital, electronic, mechanical, photocopying, recording, or otherwise—or conveyed via the Internet or a website without written permission of the University of Wisconsin Press. Rights inquiries should be directed to rights@uwpress.wisc.edu.

Printed in the United States of America

This book may be available in a digital edition.

Library of Congress Cataloging-in-Publication Data
Names: Koskimies, Aukusti Valdemar, 1856-1929, author. | Itkonen, T. I. (Toivo Immanuel), 1891-1968, author. | Laitinen, Lea, editor. | Frandy, Tim, editor, translator.
Title: Inari Sámi folklore: stories from Aanaar / August V. Koskimies and Toivo I. Itkonen, revised by Lea Laitinen; edited and translated by Tim Frandy.
Other titles: Inarinlappalaista kansantietoutta. English
Description: Madison, Wisconsin: The University of Wisconsin Press, [2019]
| Originally published as Inarinlappalaista Kansantietoutta (Helsinki: Suomalais-Ugrilainen Seura, 1978). | Includes bibliographical references and index.
Identifiers: LCCN 2018013082 | ISBN 9780299319007 (cloth: alk. paper)
Subjects: LCSH: Folk literature, Sami—Finland—Inari (Lapin lääni) | Folklore—Finland—Inari (Lapin lääni) | Sami (European people)—Finland—Inari (Lapin lääni)—Folklore. | Sami (European people)—Finland—Inari (Lapin lääni)—Music. | Folk music—Finland—Inari (Lapin lääni) | Inari Sami dialect—Texts.
Classification: LCC GR201.I63 K6713 2019 | DDC 398.2094897/7—dc23
LC record available at https://lccn.loc.gov/2018013082

ISBN 9780299319045 (pbk.: alk. paper)

For all people who work to revitalize and strengthen Indigenous cultures, in Aanaar, in Sápmi, and beyond.

Koccáá juo viljažam!
Peäiváž juo vaarijd páštá,
Kuđhiih juo kuodduužij mield ruotadeh,
Lode ruoja juo peeljijd vaaldij,
Káálguh juo nuotijdis čihteh,
Kálláh juo keävuidis vuorkkiistileh,
Párnááh juo sieratávgááiguim sierih.
Mikko Aikio, "Bear Song"

Contents

List of Illustrations	xv
Preface	xvii
Acknowledgments	xxiii
Introduction	xxv
Storyteller Biographies	xxxvii
Glossary of Frequently Used Sámi Terms	xlix
Index of Significant Place-Names	li

1	SONGS	3
	Joik Songs	5
	Cradle *Livđe*	5
	Bear Song	5
	Reindeer Song	6
	Raven *Livđe*	6
	The Tawny Owl	7
	Whitefish *Livđe*	8
	Trout	8
	The Old Man	8
	Hæænda-Maati *Joik*	9
	Taavvad-Piera	9
	Listrőm	10
	Aila-Jussa	10
	Ristnáá-Piätár	10
	Eerki-Piera	11
	Other Songs	11
	Stuorravuona (Isovuono) Market Song	11
	The Girl's Song	12
	This and That	12
	Väinämöinen's Nephew	12

I Saw	13
Daughter and Mother Song	14
The Fiancée's Beauty	15

2 ANIMAL TALES — 17

The Fox's Tale	18
The Fox's Tale, Version 2	19
The Fox and the Fisherman	21
The Story of the Fox's Blindness	22
The Man and the Bear	23
The Bear and Fox's Wild Reindeer Hunt	24
The Mouse and the Cat	25
The Raven and the Fox	26
The Horse and the Wolf	27
The Fox and the Hare	28
The Wagtail and the Dipper	28
The Story of the Moose and the Bear	29

3 FAIRY TALES — 31

The Poor Boy and the King's Daughter	34
The Great Lord's Son-in-Law	37
The Boy and the Golden Birds	41
Acorn Finding	44
Endless Discontent	46
The Reindeer Calf's Hooves	48
Mattias the Fearless and the Devil & Mattias the Fearless	50
The Man Who Lashed His Fortune	53
The Story of Three Girls	54

4 SHORT TALES — 56

The Resourceful Boy	57
The King and the Bank Thief	59
A Merchant	61
God's Miracles	65
Meniš-Antti's Life Story	67
The Poor Boy's Wedding Luck	69

5 HUMOROUS STORIES AND ANECDOTES — 71

The *Noaidi* Axe	72
The Travels of the Čuđit	73

The Wife's Stupidity	74
Shingle-Stick	77
The Story of the Girl's Spinning Rack	80
The Girl and Her Suitor	80
The Fool's Doorposts	81
Three Lazy People	82
Good Day—Axe Handle	82
It Is Truly True	83
The Butter Churn	83
The Wild Reindeer Hunters	83

6 BELIEF LEGENDS — 85

Etiological Legends — 86
- Aaččan, Who Tarred the Moon — 86

The *Stállu* — 87
- The *Stállu*, Version 1 — 88
- The *Stállu*, Version 2 — 89
- The *Stállu*, Version 3 — 93
- The *Stállu*, Version 4 — 94
- The *Stállu*, Version 5 — 94
- Andras Pejvi — 95

Gufihtarat — 97
- The Maker of Seven Churches — 97
- *Gufihtar* — 98

Čáhálig—Treasure Guardians — 98
- *Čáhálig* — 99
- *Čáhálig*, Version 2 — 99

Giants — 100
- A Giant Fights with Small Men — 100
- Two Giants — 101

The *Sieidi* — 102
- The *Sieidi* Root Cluster — 102
- A Story about Äjjih Island — 103
- The *Sieidi* of Ij-jävri — 104

Noaidi Tales	105
The Old Man *Noaidi*	106
Skolt Sámi *Noaiddit*	108
The *Noaidi* Wife	108
The Moose Skiers	109
Two Jealous People	110
Shape-Shifting Tales	110
The Whitefish Daughter-in-Law	111
The Whitefish Daughter-in-Law, Version 2	112
The Skolt Sámi and His Bear-Wife	112
The Bear Daughter-in-Law	113
Ghost Hauntings	114
Sárnoo Kurrâ (Speaker's Gorge)	114
The Haunting of the Old Deceased *Noaidi*	115
The Haunting of the Old Deceased *Noaidi*, Version 2	116
The Pastor and the Sexton	117
7 HISTORICAL AND REGIONAL LEGENDS	118
Siggá's Legend	119
Siggá's Weeping Strait	120
The Cannibal Vuolliǯ of Ij-jävri	120
The Maiden Hannaaǯ's Decapitation Story	121
The Dead Constable	123
The Fight of the Constables	124
The Late Raassaǯ	125
Piäjååǯ	125
Famed Antt-Piättâr's Eelliǯ, Fiancé-Waiter	126
She Who Went to Sleep as a Maiden and Woke as a Wife	127
8 STORIES ABOUT ČUĐIT	130
The Čuđit on the Move	131
A Story from the Time of Čuđit	132
The Boy Who Hunted with a Bow	133
The Boy Who Hunted with a Bow, Version 2	134
The Death of the Čuđit	134
Futile Fear	135
The Disobedient Daughter	136

The Čuđit Fall into a Ravine	137
The Čuđit Drown in the Rapids	138
The Čuđit Die of Hunger	139
The Čuđit Drown in Lake Aanaar; Hundred Pine Island	140
Hundred Pine Island, Version 2	141
Laurukåž Kills Čuđit with a Sword	142

9 PEEIVIH-VUÅLÅPPÅŽ — 143
About Peeivih-Vuålåppåž's Father, Peeivih — 144
Peeivih-Vuålåppåž Burns a *Sieidi* — 145
Peeivih-Vuålåppåž Burns a *Sieidi*, Version 2 — 146
The Capstone — 147
Peeivih-Vuålåppåž on the Sea Shore — 148
Peeivih-Vuålåppåž on the Sea Shore, Version 2 — 149
Peeivih-Vuålåppåž Fighting — 149
Peeivih-Vuålåppåž Fighting, Version 2 — 150
Peeivih-Vuålåppåž Hunting Wild Reindeer — 151
Peeivih-Vuålåppåž's Race with a Draught Reindeer — 151

10 STORIES ABOUT THE SKOLT SÁMI — 153
Scaring the Skolt Wife — 154
Scaring the Skolt Wife, Version 2 — 155
Scaring the Skolt Wife, Version 3 — 156
Scaring the Skolt Wife, Version 4 — 157
Scaring the Skolt Wife, Version 5 — 159
Scaring the Skolt Wife, Version 6 — 159
Scaring the Skolt Wife, Version 7 — 161
Kååššå — 162

11 HUNTING STORIES — 163
The Late Haannuž's Bear and Wild Reindeer Hunt — 164
A Draught Reindeer as a Wild Reindeer — 165
The Bear Hunter — 166
The Soddy Root Ball as a Bear — 167
Meniš-Antti's Bear-Hunting Stories — 168
A Bear Story — 169
The Bear Hunters — 170
The Girls and the Bear — 170
The Bear and the Women — 171

The Squirrel Hunters 171
The Wild Reindeer Skiers 171
The Moose Hunters 172
Irján-Ánná and -Antti on a Fishing Excursion to Lággujävri
  (Lankojärvi) 172
The Ermine Hunters 172

12 PERSONAL EXPERIENCE NARRATIVES 174
The Life of One Aanaar Sámi 175
An Aanaar Marriage and Life Story 176
Some Misfortune 177
The Old Man of Soađigil's (Sodankylä's) Forest Memories 177
The Autumnal Wild Reindeer Hunt in Aanaar 179
Vuávnum (Vuongunta), or Hunting Wild Reindeer in
  the Spring 180
Juoŋâstim (Juomustus) and Netting under the Ice 181

13 PROVERBS AND FIGURES OF SPEECH 183

Proverbs 184

Figures of Speech 194

14 RIDDLES 200

15 OMENS AND SIGNS 206
About the Dipper Giving Luck 210

Appendix A 211
NORTH SÁMI *JOIKS* 211
  Juhan Vesta's *Joik* 211
  Meniš-Irjan 212
  Mihkkus-Áslak 212
  Let Us Leave 212
  Pulju 212
  Ninka-Ůla Kāre 212
  Pike 213
  Burbot 213
  Perch 213
  Kaapi, Kaapi 214

STORIES	214
The Lazy One	214
Skolt Sámi Story	214
LETTERS	215
Appendix B	217
Introduction to the 1978 Edition by Lea Laitinen	217
Introduction to the 1917 Edition by A. V. Koskimies	218
Bibliography	237
Index	241

Illustrations

Map of northern Fenno-Scandinavia, with place-names highlighted along the route of Koskimies's travels and from selected stories	xxvi
The Piälppáájävri church in Aanaar, 2004	xxvii
Paulus Valle's widow, Elin Mattstytär Aikio, grinding roasted pine bark with a pestle on a reindeer hide in 1914	xxx
Map of Aanaar, with significant place-names from stories	I
Heikki Mattus and Santeri Valle on the steps of the Aanaar parsonage, 1912	27
Santeri Valle next to his fish-drying rack, 1914	136
Yrjänä Sarre's home in the early 1900s	146
Ceavccageađgi, near Unjárga, 2004	148
Lââutâž (*njollâ*) storehouse near Gárasavvon (Karesuvanto), 2018	178
Santeri Valle demonstrating pine-bark peeling in 1914	189

Preface

This project began for me in the summer of 2015, while working at the University of Wisconsin–Madison. I had read much of this collection in Finnish years before as a graduate student, and—thinking it might be useful for future publications or teaching—I decided to begin translating stories into English. Only after making surprising progress during a short span of three weeks between other projects did I seriously consider publication of this work. I am therefore particularly grateful to the children and grandchildren of Toivo Itkonen—Kerttu Itkonen, Marja Itkonen-Kaila, and Markus Itkonen—who hold copyright to this material and allowed me to pursue the publication of this collection.

Inarinlappalaista kansantietoutta (*Inari Sámi Folklore*) was first published in 1917 by August Koskimies and Toivo Itkonen and revised into a new edition in 1978 by Lea Laitinen. This edition, *Inari Sámi Folklore: Stories from Aanaar*, is faithful to the 1978 edition in organization and content, but I have made some important modifications in order to center the storytellers and Aanaar (Inari) Sámi community in this work. The new subtitle of this work—*Stories from Aanaar*—reflects the different approach to this work. The original title is in the colonial language of Finnish and literally translates to "Inari Lapp Folk Knowledge." Yet Inari is the Finnish word for Aanaar, Lapp is now widely considered a pejorative term, and the term "folk knowledge" is used as a somewhat circumlocutious way of saying "story." At heart of this new edition is the concern of what these stories meant to the individuals who told them. While this work still exists in relationship to *Inari Sámi Folklore*, it also works to rewrite this material as *Stories from Aanaar*.

Although this edition parallels Laitinen's 1978 edition, I have made several changes that expand the work and reflect changes to the field of folklore studies over the past forty years. I have reincluded most of the materials omitted from the 1978 edition in appendix A, including North Sámi *joik*s, a story in Skolt Sámi, a missing story, and an additional *joik* from Koskimies's manuscripts included in neither version. I saw no reason to omit them, since—coming from Aanaar Sámi people—they merit inclusion and serve as testament to the cultural exchange Aanaar Sámi had with their neighbors. I did not, however, include the

Bible translations (Psalms 103, 137, 146; Matthew 5:1) omitted from the 1978 edition, since they are faithful translations. Interested readers can easily find the source material in English. I reconnected one story that was broken apart for the purpose of its classification according to the Aarne-Thompson Tale Type Index in the 1978 edition ("Mattias the Fearless and the Devil" and "Mattias the Fearless"). I omitted one variant of a tale ("The Wagtail and the Dipper"), which matched virtually word for word (and even more so after its translation) the printed version here. I also made minor changes to the divisions of chapters and subchapters, although the tales are included in the same order—excluding the two above examples—as the 1978 edition for ease of cross-reference. To better facilitate cross-referencing, I have opted to generally keep the existing structure and organization of the work the same rather than give new titles to tale variants or eliminate multiple short anecdotes compiled under a single title.

I have also included Aarne-Thompson-Uther and Christiansen's Migratory Legends classification numbers, where applicable. They are indicated as ATU and ML beneath the tale title. Interested readers can use this reference tool to cross-reference these tales with other known variants of these stories—many of which are easy to locate online by using the ATU number. Stories without classification numbers do not neatly conform to preexisting tale types, and I have opted to leave them blank rather than assign a tale type that is at best an uncomfortable fit.

Additionally, in line with a person-centered approach to the study of folklore, I have included biographical sketches for each of Koskimies and Itkonen's storytellers, by cross-referencing church records, historical documents, scholarship, and a variety of personal genealogies posted online. Some of the more prominent individuals have reasonably extensive information written about them, while for others we still lack even basic information like first names and date of birth. I hope that this initial legwork will be valuable in sparking further work in understanding the relationships between the stories herein and the storytellers themselves.

Further, because many of the legends reference local place-names, I have created maps and an index that highlight place-names used in the stories and places of residence of some of the storytellers. Although these maps are of insufficient size and scale to feature every place-name referenced herein (and some place-names are not easily identifiable), they at least begin to map a living cultural landscape of the Aanaar community.

The most significant change to this work is that I have included editorial interpretation that helps to contextualize these works in their time and place.

Most notably, I have included brief chapter introductions that offer light background information on the genre of stories to follow, highlighting a few key themes that emerge from the collected stories. These short introductions at best merely scratch the surface of more than a century of scholarship on these different oral genres. They are selective in their approach, and their purpose is more to provide some food for thought to general readers and undergraduate students than to serve as comprehensive literature reviews for scholars. The introductions, along with other interpretive notes in the text, also offer some contextualization to some of the more challenging aspects of the texts. How did people regard the *noaidi* in Aanaar in the 1880s? What is a *gufihtar*? Why are Skolt Sámi women represented as so fearful? What is the connection between Peeivih-Vuâlåppâჳ and St. Olaf? I hope this light interpretation assists the reader in making sense of how these stories reflect social values or were used purposefully in the community, without getting in the way of the stories themselves.

I used both Finnish and Aanaar Sámi in preparing this translation, although my proper Sámi language instruction is entirely in North Sámi, which is considerably different from Aanaar Sámi. Fortunately, Itkonen's Finnish translations are of extraordinary quality, both accurate and inclusive of the subtle tones of the original Aanaar Sámi texts. Unfortunately, many of the subtleties—like the abundant and understated humor—in Sámi and Finnish simply do not translate well into English. I have opted to make this translation enjoyable for an English speaker to read, and therefore often stray from word-for-word translation, particularly in terms of sentence organization, figures of speech, and humor. Still, I have not tried to ornament the language into something it is not. Orally communicated stories are different from written stories, and I have translated this collection to reflect the verbal artistry and the aesthetics of the oral poetics of our different storytellers.

Because of the linguistic distance between Sámi and English, some concepts do not translate very well, or at least efficiently. Sámi reindeer terminology, for example, is rich and varied, with dozens of frequently used terms for reindeer. The quick distinctions between *kodde* (a wild reindeer), *puásui* (a semi-domesticated reindeer), and *ergi* (a reindeer used to pull Sámi sledges) becomes clunky in English, when someone mistakenly shoots an *ergi* thinking it is a *kodde*. In Sámi, the foolishness of such a deed is reflected in the words themselves; for a non-reindeer-owning English speaker, the nature of such an offense perhaps requires some additional contextualization.

Translating social life is no simpler. The frequently used terms *išševed* and *emend* are often translated as "master" and "matron," two terms that not only sound antiquated in American English but also bear uncomfortable connotations of a master-slave relationship that the Sámi terms do not really reflect. Although "female head of the household" and "male head of the household" might be accurate substitutions, because of their bulk, I have worked around these as much as possible, employing numerous substitutions (farm-master and farm-wife, husband and wife, for instance) that imperfectly convey the intersections of social standing, economic class, age, and Sámi-specific gender roles present in the original Sámi.

I have tried to give privilege as best I can to Sámi personal names and place-names. In general, I have tried to use the Aanaar Sámi for my own voice and for Sámi speakers but Finnish names in, for example, Koskimies's Finnish-language correspondence. I have tried to use the original spellings and orthographies of personal names, but provided Finnish-language alternatives if persons might be known by alternative names outside of the community. Stories, for instance, of Peeivih-Vuåláppåǯ (Päivän Olavi), Laurukåǯ (Laurukainen), or Garen-Ovla (Kaarin-Uvla, Karen Ovlla) are known widely in the north, and these name variations assist in cross-referencing.

Many place-names in Sápmi are known by different Finnish, Norwegian, and a few different Sámi names. For instance, although the coastal town called Vadsø in Norwegian is Čáhcesuolu in North Sámi and Vesisaari in Finnish, in Aanaar Sámi it is written as Čäc-suollu or Čäcisuollu in 1978, and today as Čäcisuáloi. And in certain contexts it might be important that the English translation of this place is Water Island. Even the standard Finnish has changed since the time of Koskimies's travels (Iivalo became Ivalo; Näytämö became Näätämö). I have provided alternative place-names for reference of the reader, where relevant, as sometimes these locations are essential components of stories, and reading alongside a map can be enlightening. Alternate names, contemporary units of measurement, and other short clarifiers are noted in parentheses in the main body of the book; however, in the previous introductions found in appendix B, I have used brackets for my own voice to distinguish them from the parenthetical remarks of Laitinen and Koskimies.

To further complicate matters, some Sámi words that are culturally significant concepts are already actively in use in English-language writings (*Sámi, lávvu, noaidi, goahti*). Most commonly today in English, these loan words are written in North Sámi (although formerly South Sámi was more common). Even the word *Sámi* is a North Sámi word (written in Aanaar Sámi as *Sämi*). Yet, given the abundance of English variations on the term already in use (Sami, Sámi, Same, Saami), I thought it best to conform to an already-accepted endonym in English rather than add another one into our vocabulary.

Following my drafting and cleanup of these manuscripts, native Finnish speaker and linguist Ilkka Posio carefully and thoroughly reviewed my translation alongside the Finnish for any errors—for which I am extraordinarily grateful. Ilkka not only corrected errors in translation (and even in my original English) but also offered important guidance in the interpretation of particularly challenging, unclear, and vague passages.

Translation is difficult, and I hope that I have been able to honor the storytellers and their descendants with this effort, in an attempt to assist in revoicing Aanaar Sámi narratives to a wider audience. Sámi people are still here, they still face adversities as colonized peoples in colonial Nordic states, and this reclaiming of Sámi cultural histories is part of the bigger process of securing Sámi futures.

Acknowledgments

This book comes to fruition through the support of many individuals who have come together to help make it happen. I would like to thank the children and grandchildren of the brilliant ethnographer Toivo Itkonen—Kerttu Itkonen, Marja Itkonen-Kaila, and Markus Itkonen—who held copyright to this material and generously granted me permission to translate and publish it in English. I hope this work might live up to the high standard that Itkonen sets, both in terms of scholarly merit and in terms of ethical integrity, working in alliance with communities to advocate for their best interest.

I'm also indebted to the linguist Ilkka Posio, who as a native speaker of Finnish generously agreed to review this translation alongside the Finnish-language texts. Ilkka's thoroughness helped ensure the manuscript was as accurate a rendering as possible in English, for which I am extraordinarily grateful.

I would also like to extend thanks to my mentor and former graduate advisor Thomas DuBois, who assisted with a variety of matters with this text, as well as served as my principal language instructor in Finnish and Sámi languages. I also thank my other teachers, in particular Jim Leary, whose efforts to bring primary texts to wider audiences in part inspired this collection, and my numerous Sámi teachers, mentors, colleagues, and friends over the years who have been supportive of my work, including Krister Stoor, Veli-Pekka Lehtola, Elina Helander-Renvall, and Outi Länsman.

I would also like to extend my gratitude to Amber Rose for her generous support from the University of Wisconsin Press, to Scott Mueller for his thorough copyediting, to Joel Chapman for his review of the manuscript and work in preparing suitable maps, and to Krister Stoor and John Lindow for their helpful comments on my manuscript. The enthusiasm and support of a number of other individuals helped push this project forward, including Ellen Marie Jensen, Marcus Cederström, Colin Connors, and Elizabeth Reuter.

Finally, I would like to acknowledge the storytellers themselves (twenty named and several unnamed) and their descendants. I am deeply grateful that they were generous enough to share a bit of themselves with Koskimies and

Itkonen so we can today see a piece of their world. I humbly hope that I have been able to honor them with this small project, and that this work can, at least in a slight way, serve the community of Aanaar well.

Introduction

August Valdemar (Forsman) Koskimies[1] (1856–1929) set off to travel to Sápmi—the Sámi homeland region—in the summer of 1886, upon the recommendation of Professor Otto Donner, then spokesperson for the Finno-Ugric Society and Professor of Sanskrit and Comparative Indo-European Languages at the University of Helsinki. Koskimies was tasked to collect samples of the Aanaar (Inari) Sámi language for use in linguistic research. Such fieldwork had become valued throughout Europe during the nineteenth century as part of a broader national romanticist project. Not only did the study of rural and seemingly isolated "folk" cultures offer valuable information about regional cultural history, but it also legitimized the authority of the emergent nation-states in Europe at that time by supposedly demonstrating a perceived unity of the peoples that the state governs. In this spirit, university-educated scholars (like Jacob and Wilhelm Grimm, Charles Perrault, or Elias Lönnrot) conducted and helped orchestrate massive projects to collect stories and songs from distant communities, attempting to discover what they believed to be relics of antiquity and the authentic spirit of the nation. Although this approach proved to be deeply problematic in many regards, it did produce large collections of folkloric materials that continue to offer us important insights into the complexities of life from generations past.

After a brief and intensive period of language study, Koskimies departed the Finnish city of Vaasa on June 11, 1886, traveling by ship to Sundsvall and then journeying over land to Trondheim, where he took another ship to Čácisuáloi (Vadsø), in northern Norway. From there, he proceeded from Njiävđám (Näätämö) to Aanaar, walking 50 km (30 miles) overland and then taking another inland boat trip of an additional 80 km (50 miles). He arrived in Aanaar a few days after the Juhannus midsummer celebration held on June 26. Koskimies took lodging in a small cottage that had previously served as a temporary parsonage, during the construction of the proper parsonage. The actual parsonage was occupied, at the time, by pastor Viktor Alfred Virkkula (1854–1932), and it was located on site of the old Piälppáájävri (Pielpajärvi) church. Neither parsonage remains standing today.

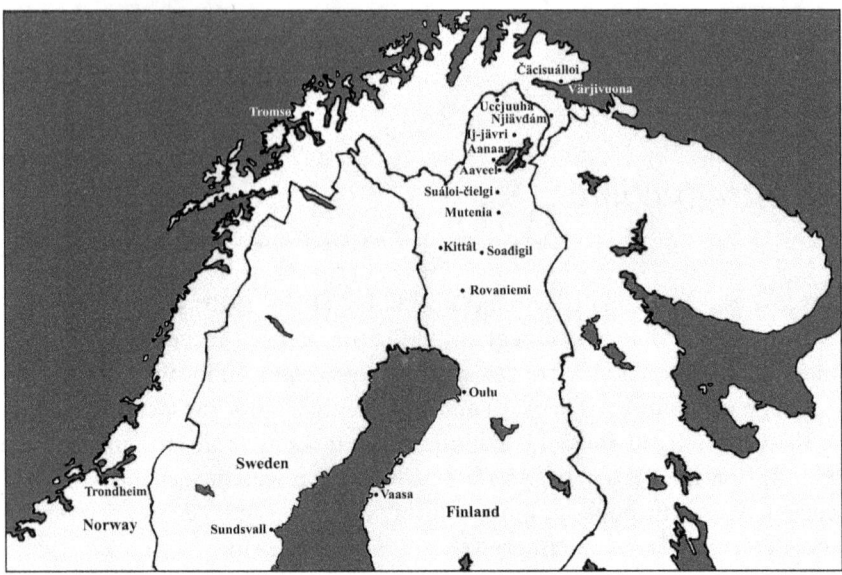

Map of northern Fenno-Scandinavia, with place-names highlighted along the route of Koskimies's travels and from selected stories. Image: Joel Chapman and Tim Frandy.

In the late nineteenth century, the Piälppáájävri church was relatively distant (about 5 km) from the principal settlements in the area. The church was constructed between 1646 and 1648 at the site of a Sámi winter camp, which fell into disuse in the 1700s because of changes in reindeer pastures and a shortage of firewood in the environs. A larger church was constructed at the same site in 1760 (and renovated in 1846), and this building remains at that site to this day.[2] In those days, Sámi people did not attend church on a weekly basis. Instead, they were required to attend church three times a winter and once in the summer, and it was at church that official state functions would occur—including tax-paying, court, marriage, and baptisms (Inarin Seurakunta n.d.). In Aanaar, like in many other Sámi communities, families would erect small cabins, suitable for short-term stays, in what amounted to a temporary village near the church. For approximately two and a half months, Koskimies worked out of the small cabin in which he resided, mostly collecting these language samples from individuals who had close associations with the church or with the recently emerged municipal government.

Inspired by other story collectors, ethnographers, and linguists of the day, including Elias Lönnrot, M. A. Castrén, and J. Qvigstad and G. Sandberg, Koskimies's language samples consisted mostly of stories and other recognized oral

The Piälppáájävri church in Aanaar, 2004. Photo: Tim Frandy.

genres; or, as Koskimies explains, "100 fairy tales, ancient legends and stories, about 200 proverbs and sayings, about 75 riddles . . . , twenty or thirty charms and omens plus twenty-some shortish or entirely short poems and songs." In the absence of recording technology, the stories were dictated to him by nearly two dozen different storytellers in Aanaar Sámi, which he wrote by hand—to the best of his ability—in Aanaar Sámi in his notebooks. This challenge certainly must have been monumental for Koskimies, after only months of language study. As evidenced in his introduction to the 1917 edition of this text (see appendix B), Aanaar Sámi resources were scarce at the time—and in fact still are today—and early orthographies were needlessly complex (DuBois 1995, 66). His ability to produce hundreds of pages of comprehensible texts reflects his great linguistic talents.

The Aanaar Sámi community has historically existed as a smaller population within a continuum of Sámi languages, cultural practices, and economic strategies. By the nineteenth century, several distinct cultural aspects helped define Aanaar Sámi from its neighboring Sámi communities. In addition to the language differences, these distinctions included their economic strategy (based on fishing and farming), their sociopolitical structure (having adapted Finnish governance systems at an early date[3]), and their embracing of Lutheranism (DuBois 1995, 64; Nickul 1977; Siida Museum n.d., "Culture"). Different Sámi communities negotiated the encroachment of a colonial state in different ways. Thomas DuBois notes that "the forest Saami of the Suenjel *siida*, for example, retained traditional modes of land use and migration into the twentieth century, while many other coastal, forest, and mountain groups underwent various cultural transformations in response to colonization, border regulations, resource depletion and relocation" (1995, 64). These distinctive responses to these economic, social, environmental, and cultural challenges—most notably the increased presence of Finnish settler-farmers moving farther north into Sámi territories—helped shape the distinctive identity that many Aanaar people maintained in the nineteenth century as devout Lutheran farmers and fishermen.

The Aanaar Sámi language is one of some nine Sámi languages living today, depending on how one distinguishes between a language and a dialect (with at least three Sámi languages having gone extinct). As part of the Finno-Ugric language family, Sámi is extremely different from Norwegian and Swedish (in the Indo-European language family), but it bears many similarities to Finnish, Karelian, and Estonian, some relationships with languages like Komi and Mari, and distant connections to Hungarian, Nenets, and Khanty. In 1886 Koskimies estimated there to be 650 Aanaar Sámi speakers; today, the number is estimated to be between 300 and 400, with the greater ethnic community around 700–900 in number (Lehtola 2004, 64). The language itself exists on a continuum between North Sámi (20,000 speakers) and the now-extinct Kemi Sámi (which died in the nineteenth century). The next closest language to the east is Skolt Sámi.

Aanaar Sámi traditionally occupied the territories surrounding the great inland Aanaarjävri (Lake Inari), a lake of 1,040 sq. km (402 sq. miles; 257,000 acres) and maximum depth of 96 meters (315 feet). The sheer volume of water tempers the nearby climate, allowing the growth of pine forests in its basin, which struggle to grow in colder and birch-dominated forests and tundra-fjells beyond its reach. The lake was at the center of much of Aanaar life, serving as a major economic resource and a central means of transportation. Fishing—in particular for the lake's abundant whitefish, pike, salmon, perch, and grayling—has long been an important fixture of the Aanaar Sámi economy. The pine forests sustained by the lake create different foraging habits and cycles for the reindeer than those found in other Sámi territories. Additionally, the inner-pine bark, an edible product that can be dried, roasted, and ground into flour, was also an important food source and annually harvested around midsummer before it later took on associations with poverty and fell out of favor among local residents

(Bogdanova 2016, 1). The more temperate climate around the lake also helped support the adoption of small-scale farming (grain cultivation and livestock rearing) in the community in the early 1800s. Many Aanaar Sámi were farming as early as 1810—following the establishment of some Finnish farms in the area in the mid-1700s—and agriculture further expanded in the 1830s, after the potato was brought to Aanaar in 1828 as a government initiative sponsored by the Oulu Household Association of Ostrobothnia (DuBois 1995, 65; Kent 2014, 29, 237). The shift toward agriculture at that time caused a shift toward the growth of more permanent settlements, contributing to the slow decline of seasonal camps based around food production, along with the traditional *siida* governance structure. Still, the long arctic winters and occasional summertime frosts kept agriculture small in scale, and the community employed a diversity of strategies (fishing, hunting, trapping, reindeer herding, gathering, farming) in a mixed economy to best maximize its own security.

Because of a variety of environmental and economic factors, Aanaar Sámi did not adopt the large-scale, extensive reindeer-herding practices as early as North Sámi, who grew the size of their reindeer herds in the 1600s, likely in response to increased taxation. Instead, Aanaar Sámi practiced so-called *intensive* herding, keeping small numbers of reindeer close to the community for purpose of transportation, and not following the reindeer as did their mountain Sámi neighbors (Nickul 1977). Wild reindeer were abundant in the area until the end of the eighteenth century or early nineteenth century. Several stories in this collection speak of seasonal hunting excursions for the purpose of communal meat procurement as an economic mainstay. The collapse of wild reindeer populations represents a major economic shift for the community. The reasons for this collapse are complex, but they likely involve a variety of factors. While older theories suggest excessive hunting and trapping were to blame for the collapse, more recent scholarship has looked toward the emergence of extensive herding in the region (which tends to absorb wild reindeer into owned herds) and the encroachment of settler communities from the south, which burned forest lands to transform them to pastures (Kent 2014, 30).

The community in Aanaar experienced another dramatic shift in response to border closings, first in 1852 (between Norway-Sweden and Russia-Finland) and again in 1889 (Russia-Finland and Sweden). These closings disrupted reindeer migration routes and forced Sámi to choose which side of the border they wanted to live on. In consequence, a great influx of North Sámi moved into Aanaar between 1870 and 1900, bringing their practice of larger-scale reindeer herding with them (Lehtola 2004, 36–37). The rise of this kind of extensive reindeer herding in the region caused further diminishing of Aanaar Sámi intensive

Paulus Valle's widow, Elin Mattstytär Aikio, grinding roasted pine bark with a pestle on a reindeer hide in 1914. Photo: Toivo Itkonen. Image courtesy of the Finnish National Board of Antiquities.

herding. Some Aanaar Sámi shifted into extensive herding practices—although the reindeer herds in the forests of Aanaar have never been as large as in the mountains.

Because of the adoption of farming and more stationary lifeways, the strong connection to the Lutheran church, and the enthusiasm of adopting Finnish governance structures, even in the nineteenth century, many felt that Aanaar Sámi were something between Finns and Sámi people. The Aanaar vicar Jakob Fellner writes, "The Inari inhabitant, who is able to read, lives to a great extent among other Lapps, without, however, adopting their customs" (qtd. in Nickul 1977, 16). Or, Johan Bartholdi Ervast notes that "the people of Inari, although they live distant from us by a far-away lake, are most flexible and disposed to abandoning all pertaining to their forefathers' ways and religion, and for this reason are to be placed before all others" (Siida Museum n.d., "Culture"). Aanaar Sámi educator Matti Morottaja has, for instance, suggested that the humility, peaceful nature, and deference to authority ultimately harmed the community, hesitant to stand up for their own best interests (Lehtola 2014, 64). Although some might attribute these changes to a process of assimilation to a dominant

Finnish culture, it is perhaps better understood as a selective adaptation to ensure cultural survival as cultures came into contact. After all, Aanaar Sámi still have their language today, many fixtures of their economy (fishing, reindeer-work, farming), and a distinct cultural identity from other neighboring peoples.

Koskimies identifies nearly two dozen different storytellers with whom he worked, who naturally do not represent the community in totality. Most prominent among them are Mikko Aikio, Juho Petteri Lusmaniemi, Iisakki Mannermaa, Heikki Mattus, Uula Morottaja, Matti Sarre, Paavali Valle, and P. Valle. As any experienced fieldworker knows, fieldworkers can only work with individuals they have access to, and those individuals also must *want* to work with that particular fieldworker. Most of Koskimies's storytellers were seemingly quite pious and devout, many were community leaders and officials—hardly surprising given his residency at the Piälppáájävri church—and nearly all of them were men. Unfortunately, only two women are present in this collection, identified without names as "an elderly woman from Juutua" and "some woman from Paatsjoki," and each contributes only one selection to the collection. The former involves a group of women fighting off a bear; the latter tells of a Skolt Sámi daughter who finds herself transformed into a bear and caught in a struggle between her shape-shifting father-in-law and a hunting party of his sons—perhaps a reflection, of sorts, of women struggling for agency in a male-dominated family setting.

Koskimies was much a product of his times, in terms of his near-exclusive focus on conducting ethnographic work with men. The devaluation of women's folklore was chronic at the time and remains a problem even today. For the most part, stories that definitively centralize women's experiences are absent from this collection—stories that deal with courtship and sexuality from women's perspectives, the burdens of women's working life, family or church pressures on women, or the resistance to patriarchal norms and expectations. Such stories were no doubt in existence, and this collection suffers from their absence. Of course, Koskimies may also have faced great hurdles to collect such materials at that time, since he was a community outsider, a man, and closely connected with the patriarchal institutions of the church and municipal governance. Simply put, women's stories told in the safe company of close women confidants are not going to be the same as stories told in close company to a pastor.

We might similarly note the tendency of Koskimies to work with churchgoers and community leaders. Despite a few exceptions, the collection mostly avoids morally compromising bawdy tales or other crass materials—though these materials were undoubtedly present in the community. Similarly, pre-Christian religion and the *noaidi* (a Sámi shaman) are presented in careful and condemning terms, and their presence is often only referred to in neighboring Sámi communities. Sámi contemporaries further north or west—as evidenced in J. Qvigstad and R. Sandberg's collection *Lappiske Eventyr og Folkesagn* or Johan and Per Turi's *Sámi Deavsttat*—more openly engaged in discourse about the *noaidi* arts, with some stories even reflecting the narrator's sympathy for certain *noaiddit*. According to the Siida Museum (n.d., "Occupations") in Aanaar, one of the last *noaidi* practitioners of the region—Ison Antin Anna, or Anna Antintytär Sarre (1843–1915), lived nearby in Ij-jävri (Iijärvi). How are we to regard the condemnations that Koskimies's storytellers levy on the *noaiddit*? Were they a reflection of a portion of the community that demonized the kind of healing work people like Anna Antintytär Sarre did? Were they lip service to an outside scholar who was actively documenting potentially damaging information about the community? Or did they reflect a distinction sometimes made during that time (for instance, seen in the writings of Johan Turi) between healers who receive their powers from God (having abandoned the term *noaidi* to describe such healers) and the kind of *noaidi* who did harm to others? Although no simple answer exists to such questions, such conflicts help illustrate that Aanaar was a community with diversity within it, and they serve as a reminder that these diversities contest each other and negotiate how the community is represented to outsiders.

Although the collected selections do not fully represent the diversity of the Aanaar community, they still do offer a stunning snapshot of Aanaar in the 1880s. Stories reflect, communicate, and shape social values: they teach us how to behave and how not to; they suggest what is important in life and what is not; they shape how we are to respond to life's joys and challenges; they establish relationships, metaphors, and tropes that manifest in real-life social interactions. Within this collection, one can see varied perspectives on real-life events: the tensions between Aanaar and Skolt Sámi, the anxieties over their uncomfortable proximity to a pre-Christian past, the decline of the wild-reindeer hunt, or how communities cope with violence and tragedy. Through these stories, we can better understand how Aanaar Sámi in the 1880s viewed themselves and their world.

Personal experience narratives paint pictures of everyday life. Humorous numskull tales serve as ways to encourage cognitive awareness and normalize behavior. Origin stories and supernatural legends help illustrate historical dimensions of Sámi beliefs and cultural worldviews. Tales involving murder, rape, and violence employ differing strategies to cope with—or perhaps in some cases rationalize—such behavior. Or, the abundance of collected fairy tales—a broad pan-European genre that is sometimes excluded in discussion of Sámi oral tradition—illustrate that Aanaar Sámi were far from the stereotype of an isolated Indigenous people, but rather part of the broader systems of European cultural, capital, and intellectual exchange that has been occurring for millennia. Together, this collection paints the picture of Aanaar Sámi people as the complex society that they are and always have been.

The 1917 and 1978 Editions of *Inarinlappalaista Kansantieoutta*

Koskimies left Aanaar on September 21, traveling along a different route, south through Finnish Lapland, to his home city of Vaasa. Koskimies documented his trip thoroughly (see appendix B), as he traveled down rapids-filled rivers and hiked through roadless forests and marshlands. His compiled notes from his travels, however, sat dormant and remained unpublished for thirty-one years. In 1915 the great Finnish linguist and ethnographer Toivo Itkonen (1891–1968), who specialized in Aanaar Sámi research, lent help to ready the manuscripts for publication. Itkonen had a long history with the community of Aanaar. In 1899, when Itkonen was still a boy, his family moved to Aanaar when his father, Lauri Arvid Itkonen (1865–1925), became rector of the Aanaar church. Itkonen read through Koskimies's transcriptions, standardized the language to some extent, arranged the texts loosely by genre, and translated each selection into Finnish. He further added a few selections from his own collections to supplement the text. The volume first appeared in print in 1917 in a dual-language edition, called *Inarinlappalaista kansantietoutta* (*Inari Sámi Folklore*), published by Suomalais-Ugrilainen Seura (the Finno-Ugric Society).

In 1978 Suomalaisen Kirjallisuuden Seura published a new dual-language edition, edited by the scholar Lea Laitinen—another respected research partner of the Aanaar Sámi community. In this new version, Laitinen standardized the Aanaar Sámi orthography to the norms of 1978 (which again was updated in 1996) and considerably rearranged the chapters and selections into what is a common "genre-based" organizational structure based on the Aarne-Thompson Tale Type Index, allowing easy comparison between stories and to other collections of European oral tradition. Laitinen returned to Koskimies's original notes as the basis of her new edition, correcting some small details from the 1917 edition that had deviated from the original notes. She added some images of Koskimies's notes along with some variants and new content (nine selections in total), while removing a small collection of North Sámi joiks, a single story told in Skolt Sámi, translations of biblical texts, and an outdated Aanaar Sámi orthographical appendix.

About This Edition

Shockingly, this work might to date represent one of the most complete, if not the first, multivoiced anthologies of Sámi oral tradition translated into English. Other collections exist and will continue to emerge as Sámi studies grows as a field. Emilie Demant Hatt's anthology *By the Fire* has been translated by Barbara Sjoholm, and will be in print in 2019. Numerous other works in English draw heavily from oral tradition, including numerous ethnographic works, such as Thomas A. DuBois's (2011) recent translation of Johan Turi's *An Account of the Sámi* (formerly, *Turi's Book of Lappland*, 1910), Johan and Per Turi's multilanguage *Lappish Texts* (ed. Emilie Demant Hatt, 1920), or Emilie Demant Hatt's *With the Lapps in the High Mountains* (trans. Barbara Sjoholm, 2013). Collections of Sámi myth are also in print: Lars Levi Læstadius's *Fragments of Lappish Mythology* (trans. Börje Vähämäki, 2002), Elina Helander-Renvall's *Silde: Sami Mythic Texts and Stories* (2004), Harald Gaski and John Weinstock's translation of *The Son of the Sun's Courting in the Land of the Giants* (2003), or Leonne de Cambrey's *Lapland Legends: Tales of an Ancient Race and its Great Gods* (1926). Lauri Honko, Keith Bosley, Michael Branch, and Senni Timonen's edited collection *The Great Bear: A Thematic Anthology of Oral Poetry in the Finno-Ugric Languages* (1994) includes several Sámi selections. Harald Gaski's collection of Sámi proverbs *Time Is a Ship That Never Casts Anchor* (2006), largely based on source material found in Just Qvigstad's oral anthologies, was translated by Roland Thorstensson. Qvigstad's four-volume *Lappiske eventyr og sagn*, published side by side in Norwegian and old orthography North Sámi, has served as the source of Gaski, Solbakk, and Solbakk's *Min Njálmmálaš Árbevierru: Máidnasat, Myhtat ja Muitalusat* (2004), yet remains a crucial source of Sámi oral tradition that still remains untranslated.

Though perhaps a minor semantic difference, the nature of an anthology differs to some extent from a single-authored ethnography or a literary interpretation of Sámi oral tradition. Koskimies and Itkonen's anthology draws from nearly two dozen different storytellers, with different values, life experiences, and individual agendas. Because most are identified by name, we can recognize important patterns in each storyteller's repertoire that reflect their own personality in countless ways. We can see the schoolmaster Iisakki Mannermaa's concern with morality and forgiveness, and speculate about connections between his literacy and his broad repertoire of fairy tales suitable for younger audiences. We might notice how only Mikko Aikio shared *joik*-songs—highly condemned by the church throughout Sápmi—with Koskimies, or how Antti Kitti willingly shared stories with sexual overtones. We might look at Juho Petteri

Lusmaniemi's fascinating repertoire of stories and speculate about his stance on women's issues. Associating names with stories helps us recognize diversities within communities and remember that folklore reflects the shared and divergent relationships that individuals maintain within communities. Because such an anthology allows us to see the world from a variety of Aanaar Sámi perspectives, its rendering of the community—though imperfect—offers a kind of depth that single-voiced narratives sometimes cannot deliver.

As the presence of English-language Sámi scholarship (produced by Sámi and non-Sámi alike) increases dramatically, and Sámi cultural studies becomes quickly more integrated into the established Scandinavian studies and Indigenous studies departments across North America, the time seems appropriate to make a concerted effort to bring more primary texts into English. This effort helps, in the words of Coppelié Cocq, to "revoice" Sámi narratives and—I would add—restore traditional multivoiced narrative structures that represent Sámi communities in more traditional ways than Western-style metanarratives do (Frandy 2017, 668). I have tried to produce a work that would be equally suitable for scholars, undergraduate students, and a general audience—in particular the growing community of North Americans of Sámi descent, who have limited access to English-language materials about their heritage. Immersing oneself in primary texts—and in all the nuances, surprises, contradictions, and even unpleasantries that they sometimes present—is perhaps the best way to rekindle connections with one's culture and heritage.

With this said, I hope this completed volume at least in small part is useful, educational, and entertaining for its readers. I also hope that this work also may spur more interest to bring additional Sámi texts into English in order to centralize Sámi voices in Sámi representations. Most importantly, I hope that it might represent the community of Aanaar in a good way, and help outsiders see the value in the community and support investment into Aanaar language preservation, cultural maintenance efforts, and improved political sovereignty.

Notes

1. Like many Finns during the nineteenth century, Koskimies fennicized his surname from the Swedish Forsman.

2. The Piälppääjävri church was eventually replaced in 1895 by a new church in the village of Aanaar. The church at Piälppääjävri still stands, is purposed for occasional use, and can be easily hiked to from Aanaar.

3. The last meeting of the traditional *siida* governance structure was in the 1860s (Halonen 1969; Nickul 1977).

Storyteller Biographies

Little biographical research has been done on the storytellers with whom Koskimies and Itkonen worked. Most of them are from prominent families in Aanaar and have descendants living in the community today. However, given the roughly 175 years that have passed since many of their births, and century since their passing, many of the stories about these individuals have been lost. For that reason, and to further emphasize that these stories are told by individuals with distinct roles in the community, I have tried to the best of my abilities to assemble some basic biographical information about the storytellers.

While a few of the storytellers show up in historic documents or Aanaar Sámi research (like Heikki Mattus or Mikko Aikio), most do not. And it is for the latter storytellers that I have potentially made errors in my cross-referencing of church records with local histories, personal genealogies posted online, and scholarship referring to place-names and farmsteads.

The church records in Aanaar are readily accessible only up until 1860 (for baptisms and deaths) or 1870 (for marriage), and they are incomplete. For instance, marriage records are missing between the years 1816–24 and 1830–38. Surnames sometimes changed with undocumented moves to new locations, and spellings varied radically. Further, first names tended at that time to run in families and fluidly move between different Swedish, Finnish, and Sámi variants of the name. Distinguishing between the five different Pehr (also known by Peter, Pietari, and Pekka) Valles living in Aanaar during the mid- to late nineteenth century is not a cut-and-dried affair, much less trying to figure out who the mysterious storyteller P. Valle actually is.

Below each biography, I have included the titles and page numbers of identified contributions to facilitate further research between individual storytellers and their repertoire. The numerous unidentified tales, songs, proverbs, riddles, and omens are not included in the below index.

I have tried to clearly distinguish between where I have a good degree of certainty and where matters are unclear. I openly invite others to correct any inadvertent mistakes found herein. Such corrections ultimately serve the purpose to further honor and recognize the people and the families behind this outstanding collection.

Mikko Aikio (1837–1918)

Koskimies identifies Mikko Aikio as a farm owner who spoke in the western dialect. Marko Jouste (2011, 51) indicates, based on Anja Akujärvi's *Morottajan Suku* (1998), that he lived from 1837 to 1918 and resided in Muddusjävri. Samuli Paulaharju (1927, 314) further indicates that Mikkel Aikio (1837–1918) was a catechist in Aanaar. He was an accomplished singer, and one of the few singers who knew how to sing in the traditional Aanaar style of *joik*-singing, called the *livđe*. He married Sara Jonaantytär Sajets in 1867, and together they had eight children: Henrik (1867), Jouni (1868), Brita Maria (1871), Anna Greta (1874), Sara Kaisa (1875), Mickel (1876), Isak Martin (1877), and Abram Olaf (1879). His daughter Brita Maria was a similarly accomplished singer, and both are featured in Jouste's book *Tullâcalmaaš Kirdâččij 'Tulisilmillä Lenteliä': Inarinsaamelainen 1900-luvun Alun Musiikkikulttuuri Paikallisen Perinteen ja Ympäröivien Kulttuurien Vuorovaikutuksessa*. Represented here in Mikko Aikio's repertoire are twenty songs, three humorous stories, five belief legends, three historical legends, a Čuđit story, two stories about Peeivih-Vuáláppáǯ, and four hunting stories.

SONGS

Cradle *Livđe* (5); Bear Song (5); Reindeer Song (6); Raven *Livđe* (6); The Tawny Owl (7); Whitefish *Livđe* (8); Trout (8); The Old Man (8); Hæænda-Maati *Joik* (9); Taavvad-Piera (9); Liström (10); Aila-Jussa (10); Ristnàa-Piätàr (10); Eerki-Piera (11); Stuorravuona (11); The Girl's Song (12); This and That (12); Väinämöinen's Nephew (12); I Saw (13); The Fiancée's Beauty (15)

HUMOROUS STORIES AND ANECDOTES

The *Noaidi* Axe (72); The Fool's Doorposts (81); Three Lazy People (82)

BELIEF LEGENDS

Aaččan, Who Tarred the Moon (86); The *Stállu*, Version 1 (88); The Maker of Seven Churches (94); The *Sieidi* of Ij-jävri (104); The Haunting of the Old Deceased *Noaidi* (115)

HISTORICAL AND REGIONAL LEGENDS

The Cannibal Vuolliǯ of Ij-jävri (120); The Dead Constable (123); The Fight of the Constables (124)

STORIES ABOUT ČUĐIT

The Boy Who Hunted with a Bow (133)

PEEIVIH-VUÅLÅPPÅƷ
Peeivih-Vuålåppåƨ Burns a *Sieidi* (145); Peeivih-Vuålåppåƨ on the Sea Shore (148)
HUNTING STORIES
The Late Haannuƨ's Bear and Wild Reindeer Hunt (164); A Draught Reindeer as a Wild Reindeer (165); The Bear Hunter (166); The Soddy Root Ball as a Bear (167)

Pekka Matinpoika Aikio (b. 1840)
Little is known about Pekka Matinpoika Aikio, outside of what he says in his one autobiographical contribution to the volume. Church records suggest he was born March 23, 1840, to Matts Gabrielsson Aikio and Ingrid Petri Kuva, and married February 21, 1864, to Karin Samuelstytär Valle. As he indicates in his story, he worked as a reindeer herder and had seven children.
PERSONAL EXPERIENCE NARRATIVES
An Aanaar Marriage and Life Story (176)

Kaapin Pekka's Sons (b.??)
Kaapin Pekka, or Petter Mattsinpoika Aikio (b. 1840), was married to Karin Samuelstytär Valle (b. 1842) on February 21, 1864. He established a farmstead called Kaabi Matti (Kaapin Matti) in 1873 at the site of a former fish camp, to the northeast of the village of Aanaar (Nahkiaisoja 2016, 91; Mattus 2010, 73). His father was called Kaaperi Pekanpoika Aikio or Kaapin Matti. His sons remain unidentified but contributed two animal tales to this collection (one of which is omitted because of its close nature to another variant).
ANIMAL TALES
The Fox and the Fisherman (21); The Wagtail and the Dipper (28)

Antti Juhaninpoika Kitti (Meniš-Antti; Menes-Antti) (b. 1847?)
Not much information is known about Antti Juhaninpoika Kitti, whom Koskimies identifies as speaking the western dialect. Kitti lived on Kakšâmjävri (Kaksamajärvi), southwest of the current village of Aanaar (Mattus 2010, 76). The Siida Museum (n.d., "Koskimies") in Aanaar indicates that Antti Kitti was one of two Meniš-Anttis in the community. The other was Antti Juhaninpoika Morottaja (1853–1907), or sometimes called Karhu-Antti, whose lands were later inhabited by Jouni Aikio (Kaapin Jouni, 1875–1956) and are now annexed into the Lemmenjoki National Park (Inari Saariselkä n.d.). The Meniš-Antti Koskimies spoke with was possibly the child of Johan Andersson Riesto and

Cajsa Henrikintytär Kyrö, born November 6, 1847. He contributes a short tale, a humorous tale, a *stállu* story, and a few bear hunting stories to the collection. His contributions reflect a good sense of humor, representing some of the most immodest pieces in this collection.

SHORT TALES
Meniš-Antti's Life Story (67)
HUMOROUS STORIES AND ANECDOTES
It Is Truly True (83)
BELIEF LEGENDS
Andras Pejvi (95)
HUNTING STORIES
Meniš-Antti's Bear Hunting Stories (168)

H. Kitti (b. 1844)

Though his first name is not identified, H. Kitti is likely Henric Kitti, born to Johan Andersson Riesto and Carin Henrici Kyrö on November 2, 1844. This would possibly make him a brother to Antti Juhaninpoika Kitti, which seems probable due to the fact that H. Kitti tells a single bear story in this collection and refers casually to hunting with Antti. Brothers were known to regularly hunt bear together, since it was said that brothers who hunted bear together were less likely to be injured during the hunt. It appears that Johan and Carin (Kaisa) had six children.

HUNTING STORIES
A Bear Story (169)

Juho Petteri Lusmaniemi (b. ??)

Koskimies indicates that Juho Petter Lusmaniemi was a farm owner who spoke the eastern dialect of Aanaar Sámi, even though he lived in the western parts of Aanaar. The Lusmaniemi peninsula in Lake Paadar was known to have a farm (Nahkiaisoja), and the surname is clearly adopted from this location. At least three Johan Petters could have lived in the community in the 1880s: son of Johan Michaelsson Kyrö and Maria Christiantytär (b. 1857), son of Adam Britasson Akujärvi and Maria Nilstytär Kyrö (b. 1848), or Johan Petter Peterson Kiviniemi who married Ingrid Ericstytär Karppinen in 1856. Lusmaniemi's contributions include four fairy tales, two humorous stories, one *noaidi* tale, two shape-shifting tales, three historical legends, two Skolt Sámi stories, and two hunting stories.

FAIRY TALES
The Poor Boy and the King's Daughter (34); The Boy and the Golden Birds

(41); The Reindeer Calf's Hooves (48); Mattias the Fearless and the Devil & Mattias the Fearless (50)

HUMOROUS STORIES AND ANECDOTES

The Girl and Her Suitor (80); The Wild Reindeer Hunters (83)

BELIEF LEGENDS

Skolt Sámi *Noaiddit* (108); The Whitefish Daughter-in-Law (111); The Skolt Sámi and His Bear-Wife (112)

HISTORICAL AND REGIONAL LEGENDS

The Late Raassaǯ (125); Piäjååǯ (125); Famed Antt-Piättår's Eelliǯ, Fiancé-Waiter (126)

STORIES ABOUT THE SKOLT SÁMI

Scaring the Skolt Wife, Version 6 (159); Kååššå (162)

HUNTING STORIES

The Bear Hunters (170); The Squirrel Hunters (171)

Iisakki Mannermaa (1830–1908)

The schoolmaster Iisakki Mannermaa was born to Jon Mannermaa and Margaretha Maria Kiviniemi on November 16, 1830. He married Catherina Perhintytär Padar (Kiviniemi), and together they had seven children: Maria (1853), Karoliina (1855), Fredrika (1858), Albertiina Iisakintytär (1860), Israel Vilhelm Iisakinpoika (1862), Frans Jouni (1862), and a stillborn (1867). Koskimies identifies his death year as 1908, and indicates he spoke the western dialect. He helped teach Lauri Itkonen (the father of Toivo Itkonen) Aanaar Sámi, and assisted with his translation of Bishop J. L. Ryle's religious pamphlet *Oađáh-uv tun? (Are You Sleeping?)* (Siida Museum n.d., "Lauri Itkonen"). Koskimies identifies Mannermaa as one of his closest collaborators, and he contributes to the collection an animal tale, four fairy tales, five short stories, two humorous stories, a story about giants, a historical legend, two Cuđit stories, and a story about Peeivih-Vuålåppåǯ.

ANIMAL TALES

The Bear and Fox's Wild Reindeer Hunt (24)

FAIRY TALES

The Great Lord's Son-in-Law (37); Acorn Finding (44); Endless Discontent (46); The Story of Three Girls (54)

SHORT TALES

The Resourceful Boy (57); The King and the Bank Thief (59); A Merchant (61); God's Miracles (65); The Poor Boy's Wedding Luck (69)

HUMOROUS STORIES AND ANECDOTES

The Wife's Stupidity (74); Shingle-Stick (77)

BELIEF LEGENDS
A Giant Fights with Small Men (100)
HISTORICAL AND REGIONAL LEGENDS
The Maiden Hannaaǯ's Decapitation Story (121)
STORIES ABOUT ČUÐIT
The Čuđit Fall into a Ravine (137); The Čuđit Drown in the Rapids (138)
PEEIVIH-VUÀLÀPPÀǮ
The Capstone (147)

J. Mannermaa (b.??)

J. Mannermaa tells one *sieidi* story with P. Valle, and his identity is unclear. Seemingly, some relationship to Iisakki would be logical, but no conclusive evidence is there. Iisakki's father's name was Jon Mannermaa (1802–??), although he would be quite elderly at the time of Koskimies's visit. Alternatively, the letters *I* and *J* are pronounced similarly, and sometimes used interchangeably, and J. Mannermaa could be the name of Iisakki (although spelling Isaac with a *J* would be uncommon). Not written into church records, the Mannermaa name remains difficult to trace. According to Nahkiaisoja (2016, 66, 113), the Mannermaa name goes back to the 1700s to Juhani Morottaja, who had established the Mannermaa farm before Jakob Fellman's 1830 travels to Aanaar.

BELIEF LEGENDS
A Story about Äjjih Island (103)

Heikki Mattus (Jurmun-Henrikki) (1838–1926)

Heikki Sammelinpoika Mattus was born September 10, 1838, to poor parents (Samuel Henrik Mattus, a fisherman; Aili Isakki Paadar) in the village of Paadar in the Jurmu home. According to Rita Kangasniemi and Petra Kuuva, "There were 7 children in the family [Henrik 1838; Isaak 1842; Samuel 1844; Matthias 1847; Johan 1849; Agent 1852; Aili 1857]. They ate mostly bark soup, and in the evening their mother always recited evening prayers and the Lord's Prayer to her children, plus the Priestly Benediction. In 1856 the vicar E. W. Borg turned his attention to the gifted eighteen year-old Heikki. He became a catechist in 1858 but did not begin work in this position until 1864. He also worked as a prisoners' escort 1868–71. Heikki Mattus was chosen as parish clerk in 1871, and was appointed to the first and only official position as catechist in 1883. He gave up his job as catechist to Matti Lehtola in 1893. Heikki Mattus was involved in the signing of the founding constitution of the Inari Municipal Government in 1876, was a vice member of the municipal board from 1894 to 1899 and belonged to the first board of the Inari Primary School.

He was himself among the first students in the new Primary School" (Siida Museum n.d., "Mattus").

Heikki Mattus was an instructor to Edvard Wilhelm Borg (1830–1910), the first representative of the Aanaar church to learn Aanaar Sámi. Heikki also learned Finnish from Borg. He served as a sexton and cantor for the church, and was widely known for his beautiful singing voice. He married Anna Aikio (1842–1910) and they had seven children, four of whom died and three of whom were deaf. Heikki lived a content life with his family where the Juvduu (Juutua) River flows from Lake Paadar. Heikki Mattus contributes an animal tale, a hunting story, and three personal experience narratives to this collection.

ANIMAL TALES
The Raven and the Fox (26)
HUNTING STORIES
The Girls and the Bear (170)
PERSONAL EXPERIENCE NARRATIVES
The Life of One Aanaar Sámi (175); The Autumnal Wild Reindeer Hunt in Aanaar (179); *Vuàvnum* (*Vuongunta*), or Hunting Wild Reindeer in the Spring (180)

Heikki Morottaja (b. 1855)

Information is sparse on Heikki Morottaja, who was born August 27, 1855, to Isak Pehrsson Morottaja and Anna Henricstytär. He had two sisters, Anna (1849) and Valborg (1851). He married Anna Antintytär Morottaja (Musta) on April 2, 1893. He contributes only one short animal tale to this collection.

ANIMAL TALES
The Fox and the Hare (28)

Uula Morottaja (b. 1855)

Uula Morottaja was born September 19, 1855, to fisherman Anders Johansson Morottaja and Maria Mattstytär Valle (35 years old). He had at least one sibling, older brother Matthias (b. 1842). Coming from Pàččvei (Paatsjoki), the river flowing out of Lake Aanaar on its eastern shore, Uula Morottaja was not in direct contact with Koskimies but rather worked with Toivo Itkonen, who added his own selections as he prepared the 1917 edition. These include an animal tale, two humorous anecdotes, one *stállu* tale, a *noaidi* tale, a shape-shifting tale, two ghost stories, a historical legend, five Čuđit stories, a Skolt Sámi story, and two hunting stories.

ANIMAL TALES
The Man and the Bear (23)

HUMOROUS STORIES AND ANECDOTES
The Travels of the Čuđit (73); The Butter Churn (83)
BELIEF LEGENDS
The *Stállu*, Version 3 (93); The Moose Skiers (109); The Whitefish Daughter-in-Law, Version 2 (112); The Haunting of the Old Deceased *Noaidi*, Version 2 (116); The Pastor and the Sexton (117)
HISTORICAL AND REGIONAL LEGENDS
Siggá's Weeping Strait (120)
STORIES ABOUT ČUĐIT
The Boy Who Hunted with a Bow, Version 2 (134); The Death of the Čuđit (134); The Disobedient Daughter (136); The Čuđit Drown in Lake Aanaar; Hundred Pine Island (140); Laurukàǯ Kills Čuđit with a Sword (142)
STORIES ABOUT THE SKOLT SÁMI
Scaring the Skolt Wife, Version 7 (161)
HUNTING STORIES
The Wild Reindeer Skiers (171); The Moose Hunters (172)

Antti Sarre (b. 1861?)

Although there is considerable ambiguity on the matter, Antti Sarre may have been born in 1861 to unknown parents near Nitsijärvi (Mattus 2010, 18), placing him in the correct dialect region that Koskimies identifies him speaking. Alternatively, he may be born to Anders Henriksson Sarre and Maria Henrikstytär Valle on July 24, 1856. Koskimies refers to "Antti and Matti Sarre," suggesting they might be of close relation (Anders and Maria had another son named Matti), and indicates that they both speak the northern dialect. Antti Sarre contributes one selection about *juoŋâstim*, or fishing under the ice with nets.
PERSONAL EXPERIENCE NARRATIVES
Juoŋâstim (*Juomustus*) and Netting under the Ice (181)

Matti Sarre (b. 1858?)

Possibly a close relative to Antti Sarre, Matti Sarre might refer to a Matti Sarre born on April 14, 1858, to Anders Henriksson Sarre and Maria Henrikstytär Valle. It bears mentioning, however, that three others were born with that name in a single year's time in Aanaar, and other prominent individuals also named Matti Sarre are suggested to be born in the years 1850, 1848, 1842 (from Sulkusjärvi) (Mattus 2010, 137) and 1834 (the Hæænda-Maati *joiked* by Mikko Aikio) (Jouste 2011, 123–27). One of these Matti Sarres resided on Kuuđhânjargâ (Muurahaisniemi), on Aanaar's north shore in the early 1900s (the correct dialect zone), where he encountered Toivo Itkonen in 1910 (Mattus 2010, 146).

In the story "Peeivih-Vuȧlȧppȧʒ on the Sea Shore," Koskimies identifies the storyteller as "Matti Sarre, Paatsjoki." This kind of place-based identification is uncommon in this collection, and could suggest there are two storytellers named Matti Sarre in the collection. Alternatively, it may simply suggest the origin of this particular story or the actual birthplace of Matti Sarre (which would not be in the correct dialect zone). Despite the number of Matti Sarres in this collection, the name is linked to three animal tales, a *stállu* legend, and three stories about Peeivih-Vuȧlȧppȧʒ.

ANIMAL TALES

The Fox's Tale, Version 1 (18) and Version 2 (19); The Horse and the Wolf (27)

BELIEF LEGENDS

The *Stállu*, Version 2 (89)

PEEIVIH-VUȦLȦPPȦʒ

Peeivih-Vuȧlȧppȧʒ on the Sea Shore, Version 2 (149); Peeivih-Vuȧlȧppȧʒ Fighting, Version 1 (149) and Version 2 (150)

Yrjänä Sarre (b. 1851)

Yrjänä Sarre tells a story about Peeivih-Vuȧlȧppȧʒ that is included in this collection, and Koskimies indicates he is from the settlement at Paadar. Only one birth record meets that name, the child of fisherman Georg Johansson Sarre and Maria Johanintytär (33 years old), born March 25, 1851, five years after their 1846 wedding. An ethnographic photo of Yrjänä Sarre's waterside cottage was taken in the early 1900s. The image is included in this volume.

PEEIVIH-VUȦLȦPPȦʒ

Peeivih-Vuȧlȧppȧʒ Burns a *Sieidi*, Version 2 (146)

Martti Valle (1838–1909)

Martti Valle was born December 1, 1838, to Matts Martini Valle and Caisa Mattstytär Sarre. He was married February 21, 1864, to Anna Göranstytär. He lived 1.5 km to the northeast of Könkäänjärvi, at Martnáátupeváárááš (Martintupavaara), and in 1857 started a farm by the name of Nirrola, 1.5 km further north. It is thought that he spent winters near Martintupajärvi (Mattus 2010, 136). His wife, Helena Nilsintytär Valle, took over the farm after his passing, from 1909 to 1911, and after that their son Isak Frans Petter Mårteninpoika Valle from 1912 to 1917 (Mattus 2010, 155–56). Valle contributes one animal story to the collection.

ANIMAL TALES

The Wagtail and the Dipper (28)

Paavali Valle (1826–1906)

Paavali Valle was born in 1826 to Matts Valle (church records do not indicate his wife's name), and he married Elin Mattstytär Aikio on July 4, 1852. He lived at Čuárvinjargâ (Sarviniemi) on the north shore of Lake Aanaar's Juutuanvuono (Mattus 2010, 214). Koskimies indicates that he is a former shopkeeper, juror, and church cleric. When Aanaar was made a municipality in 1876, he was "elected chairman of both the local council and the municipal assembly" (Kent 2014, 227). As Koskimies indicates, several of Paavali Valle's selections are told with his son, Santeri Valle. Together, Paavali and Santeri contribute two *noaidi* tales, a ghost story, and five Skolt Sámi stories, in addition to one fairy tale that Paavali alone is credited for.

FAIRY TALES
The Man Who Lashed His Fortune (53)

BELIEF LEGENDS
The Old Man *Noaidi* (106); The *Noaidi* Wife (108); Sárnoo Kurrâ (Speaker's Gorge) (114)

STORIES ABOUT THE SKOLT SÁMI
Scaring the Skolt Wife, Version 1 (154); Version 2 (155); Version 3 (156); Version 4 (157); Version 5 (159)

Pekka Valle (b.??)

Pekka Valle contributes only one animal tale to this collection, and not much is known about him. The name Pekka is the Finnish version of the name Peter (Pietari; Pehr), and a relationship to Pietari Valle is certainly a possibility. Although they could be the same person, I suspect that the name Pekka was used carefully to distinguish him from Pietari. At least three Pekka Valles exist in the community at that time: Pehr Pehrson Valle (b. 1860) and his father Pehr Isaksson Valle (b.??, married 1852), and Pehr Mårtensson Valle (b.??, married 1859).

ANIMAL TALES
The Mouse and the Cat (25)

Pietari Valle (b.??)

Koskimies indicates that Pietari Valle is a lay judge from Pâččvei (Paatsjoki), who uses the eastern dialect. According to local historian Jouni Kitti (n.d.), he is said to have been involved with the founding of the Aanaar municipality in 1876. The closest identifiable records involve the marriage of Pehr Isaaksson Valle to Brita Anderstytär Sarre in 1852 and Pehr Mårtensson Valle to Kristina Mårtenstytär Sajetz in 1859, which reflect that Pietari would be of

suitable age to be a community leader by 1876 (perhaps fifty years old). Pietari Valle tells only one identifiable story in this collection, about Čuđit.
STORIES ABOUT ČUÐIT
The Čuđit Die of Hunger (139)

P. Valle (b.??)

P. Valle remains something of a mystery. Contributor of ten stories (two *sieidi* stories, one *noaidi* story, two historical legends, three Čuđit stories, one story about Peeivih-Vuálåppáǯ, and a story in Skolt Sámi), P. Valle could refer to any of the above P. Valles, or to someone else entirely. Given the diligence of Koskimies's notes, I would suspect that Koskimies uses the name P. Valle as a way to distinguish this individual from the other aforementioned Valles who share his name.

A survey of given names in Aanaar during that time suggests the name is almost certainly a version of Peter (Pekka or Pietari) or Paul (Paavali), with an unlikely chance it could be Priita (Brita). At least eight Peter or Paul Valles would have likely been in Aanaar at the time: Pehr Pehrson Valle (b. 1860) and his father Pehr Isaksson Valle (b.??); Paulus Josef Valle (b. 1859) and his father Paul Mattson Valle (b.??); Paul Andersson Valle (b. 1858); Paul Andersson Valle (b. 1856); Paul Olofsson Valle (b.??); and Pehr Mårtensson Valle (b.??). We know that P. Valle speaks Skolt Sámi quite well, telling an entire story in it, and that he has a relationship with the also-unidentified J. Mannermaa, with whom he tells a story.

BELIEF LEGENDS
The *Sieidi* Root Cluster (102); A Story about Äjjih Island (103); Two Jealous People (110); Skolt Sámi Story (214)
HISTORICAL AND REGIONAL LEGENDS
Siggá's Legend (119); She Who Went to Sleep as a Maiden and Woke as a Wife (127)
STORIES ABOUT ČUÐIT
The Čuđit on the Move (131); A Story from the Time of Čuđit (132); Futile Fear (135)
PEEIVIH-VUÁLÅPPÁǮ
About Peeivih-Vuálåppáǯ's Father, Peeivih (144)

Santeri Valle (b.??–1918)

Santeri Valle is Paavali Valle's son and served as a church warden. He worked with Toivo Itkonen as an adult in 1914, documenting the peeling of pine bark (photos are included in this volume), and it was noted that he had found an ancient stone knife in his potato field in the early 1900s. Unfortunately, I have been able to locate no other records about him. See "Paavali Valle" above for more information.

BELIEF LEGENDS

The Old Man *Noaidi* (106); The *Noaidi* Wife (108); Sárnoo Kurrâ (Speaker's Gorge) (114)

STORIES ABOUT THE SKOLT SÁMI

Scaring the Skolt Wife, Version 1 (154); Version 2 (155); Version 3 (156); Version 4 (157); Version 5 (159)

Woman, Elderly, from Juvduu (Juutua)

While no clear identifiers suggest the identity of the elderly woman from Juvduu, her residence could have been any place between the village of Aanaar along the stem of the Juvduu River up to Lake Paadar. No other storytellers are clearly identified as coming from Juvduu, the place likely refers to the fields at the mouth of the Juvduu River, the traditional family area of the Morottaja family. Nahkiaisoja (2016, 92) indicates, however, that those fields were a common farming area, suggesting that the unnamed woman may not necessarily be of the Morottaja family. One story about a bear encounter is included in this collection.

HUNTING STORIES

The Bear and the Women (171)

Woman, Unnamed, from Pååčvei (Paatsjoki)

Again, while no clear identifiers exist to identify the woman from Pååčvei, given the distance from Koskimies's residence at Piälppáájävri, one might surmise a connection to Pietari Valle or the mysterious Matti Sarre of Pååčvei (see above). She contributes one tale about shape-shifting.

BELIEF LEGENDS

The Bear Daughter-in-Law (113)

Glossary of Frequently Used Sámi Terms

Aanaar	Inari
beaska	a heavy reindeer-fur winter coat
čáhálig/čáháligeh (sing./pl.)	a spirit that protects treasure caches
čáhcehálldi	a Sámi water spirit
Čuhti/Čuđit (sing./pl.)	invading marauders who rob and murder Sámi people
geres	a sledge pulled behind a reindeer for transporting people or goods
goahti	a traditional Sámi house not meant to be moved, usually a turf hut
gufihtar/gufihtarat (sing./pl.)	an underground-living, magical being
joik	a style of Sámi song
lávvu	a temporary and moveable Sámi shelter, most commonly a conical tent
livđe	an Aanaar *joik*-song
noaidi/noaiddit (sing./pl.)	a Sámi shaman
piärtušm	a type of fence structure used to channel wild reindeer toward an opening in hunting
Sápmi	the traditional territories of the Sámi homeland
sieidi/sieiddit (sing./pl)	a site used to leave offerings to spirits, often a large stone or distinctive landscape feature
siida	a traditional Sámi local community, with its own governance and territories
stállu/stálut (sing./pl.)	an ogre-like enemy of Sámi people

Map of Aanaar, with significant place-names from stories. Image: Joel Chapman and Tim Frandy.

Index of Significant Place-Names

The following is a list of Sámi language place-names (followed by the Finnish and Norwegian names, where relevant) and the stories in which they are referenced. Most of the place-names are found in legends and personal experience narratives. Places that are clearly fictive are not listed here.

The map was generated by cross-referencing Sámi and Finnish place-names with various maps and online map services. Some of these places exist outside the scale of the map, and some have been included on the map in the introduction. Some place-names could not be located, and some of them may refer to multiple places as well.

Aaveel (Ivalo) River: The Dead Constable
Ađikku River: Siggá's Legend
Äijihjorŋâ (Ukonselkä): Laurukáž Kills Čuđit with a Sword
Äjjih (Ukko): The Sieidi Root Cluster; A Story about Äjjih Island
Ajnoluobbali (Ainolompolo): Siggá's Legend
Ákku (Akka): The Capstone
Ákšujávri: Some Misfortune
Čäcisuálloi (Vesisaari; Vadsø): Andras Pejvi; Peeivih-Vuáláppáž on the Sea Shore, Version 2
Čarmanjargâ (Tšarminiemi): The Čuđit on the Move
Ceävžuikeđgi (Ceavccageađgi): Peeivih-Vuáláppáž on the Sea Shore
Čuđeluohtâ (Vainolaislahti): The Čuđit on the Move
Čyetpecsuáloi (Satapetäjäsaari): The Čuđit Drown in Lake Aanaar; Hundred Pine Island
Deatnu (Teno; Tana): The Fight of the Constables
Eedlihjávri (Edlihjärvi) Peninsula: The Late Haannuž's Bear and Wild Reindeer Hunt
Guáláduv (Kuola): The Man Who Lashed His Fortune
Ij-jávri (Iijärvi): The *Sieidi* of Ij-jávri; The Cannibal Vuolliž of Ij-jävri
Juvduu (Juutua): The Čuđit Fall into a Ravine
Jyelgičuopâstimvaaráž (Jalanleikkaamavaara): The Čuđit on the Move

Kálbáiääpi's (Vasikkaselkä): The Čuđit Die of Hunger
Kalluudem-čuálmi (Kallosalmi): Siggá's Legend
Kalluudem-suáloi (Kallosaari): Siggá's Legend
Karvamjävri (Kiertämäjärvi): Sárnoo kurrâ (Speaker's Gorge)
Kittâl (Kittilä): The Dead Constable; About Peeivih-Vuȧlȧppȧǯ's Father, Peeivih
Konišnjargâ (Konesniemi): The Capstone
Lággujävri (Lankojärvi): Irjȧn-Ȧnnȧ and -Antti on a Fishing Excursion to Lággujävri (Lankojärvi)
Måk-koppe (Matokupa): Peeivih-Vuȧlȧppȧǯ on the Sea Shore, Version 2
Mavra (Maura): The Capstone
Mazaǯjävri (Masaǯjärvi): Scaring the Skolt Wife; Scaring the Skolt Wife, Version 3
Muddušjävri (Muddusjärvi): Peeivih-Vuȧlȧppȧǯ Burns a *Sieidi*; The Late Haannuǯ's Bear and Wild Reindeer Hunt
Myeđhituoddar (Muotkatunturi): The Late Haannuǯ's Bear and Wild Reindeer Hunt
Myerssee-keđgi (Morsiankivi): Siggá's Legend
Nestor-čuálmi (Nestorinsalmi): Siggá's Legend
Nestor-suáloi (Nestorinsaari): Siggá's Legend
Njiävđám (Näätämö; Neiden): The *Noaidi* Wife; Scaring the Skolt Wife, Version 5
Njiđggujävri (Njiđggujärvi): Siggá's Legend
Nuárjukuoškâ (Hyljekoski): The *Noaidi* Wife
Oaivipunnjâmlássá (Päänvääntämäluoto): The Čuđit Die of Hunger; Hundred Pine Island, Version 2
Pååđȧr (Paadar) siida: The Life of One Aanaar Sámi
Pȧččvei (Paatsjoki) River: The Moose Skiers
Pajalaskeđgi (Päällyskivi): The Capstone
Pännijävri (Hammasjärvi): The Dead Constable
Peäccam (Petsamo): The *Noaidi* Wife
Peecivuona (Mäntyvuono): Andras Pejvi
Piälduvyemi (Peltovuoma): She Who Went to Sleep as a Maiden and Woke as a Wife
Puásuičuopâmsuáloi (Poronleikkomasaari): The Čuđit on the Move
Reahpen (Reppänä): The Old Man *Noaidi*
Rivdul (Riutala): She Who Went to Sleep as a Maiden and Woke as a Wife
Saaveehjävri (Sivakkajärvi): Siggá's Legend
Säđisuáloi (Säisaari): The Čuđit Fall into a Ravine; The Ermine Hunters

Sieidivaarâ (Seitavaara): Peeivih-Vuâlåppåɉ Burns a *Sieidi*
Siggá's Čiärumčoalmi (Siggan itkusalmi): Siggá's Legend
Soađigil's (Sodankylä): The Old Man of Soađigil's (Sodankylä's) Forest Memories
Sompio: Two Jealous People; Sárnoo Kurrâ (Speaker's Gorge)
Suáloi-čielgi (Saariselkä): The Old Man of Soađigil's (Sodankylä's) Forest Memories
Syenjilsīida (Suonikylä): The Man Who Lashed His Fortune
Tebdokievŋis Falls (Teutoköngäs): The Čuđit Drown in the Rapids
Tuárrupec-aajâ (Tappelupetäjäoja): The Fight of the Constables
Uccjuuhâ (Utsjoki): The Fight of the Constables
Vȧrgȧȧh (Vuoreija; Vardø): The Old Man *Noaidi*; She Who Went to Sleep as a Maiden and Woke as a Wife
Värjivuona (Varanger fjord): Andras Pejvi; Peeivih-Vuâlåppåɉ on the Sea Shore, Version 2; The Lazy One; Siggá's Legend
Veskonjargâ (Veskoniemi): The Capstone

Inari Sámi Folklore

SONGS

Although Sámi music, and *joik*-singing in particular, has come to the forefront of Sámi identity in recent decades, for a long time Sámi music was held by outsiders—church authorities in particular—in extremely low regard. Sámi music has a strong emphasis on singing, with some use of instruments—for instance, a flute crafted out of the stalk of the angelica plant and hand drums (bearing particular religious significance in traditional healing systems). Despite being most known for the distinctive *joik* tradition, Koskimies's collection also reveals the commonality of lyrical songs ("The Fiancée's Beauty"), courtship and sexual songs ("The Girl's Song," "Daughter and Mother Song"), nonsense and children's songs ("This and That," "Raven *Livđe*"), and even a song about the Finnish cultural hero, Väinämöinen ("Väinämöinen's Nephew").

There are multiple *joik* traditions in Sápmi, and different regions tend to have distinctive sounds, tonalities, meters, and forms in their *joiks*. Known in Aanaar as *livđe* (in North Sámi as *luohti* and as *leu'dd* in Skolt communities), the word *joik* comes simply from an old Sámi verb, *juoigâđ*, which simply meant "to sing." Eventually, through increased cultural contact with neighboring peoples, the verb took on the meaning of singing in a Sámi style, and another verb (*lávluđ*) was borrowed in from Finnish to mean to sing in a non-Sámi style. Knowledgeable listeners can discern where traditional *joiks* are from based on their sound, cadence, melodic structure, use of language and vocables, and subject matter. Some genres of *joik* have few, if any, lyrics, while others narrate plot-driven stories. Some genres are profoundly rhythmically and melodically complex, whereas others are quite lyrical and in simple meters. *Joik* has also changed over time, having been fused with popular and world-music sensibilities of meter, melody, and key.

Outsiders have often misunderstood the *joik* and Sámi music in general.

Joiking was banned by churches, believing it to be diabolical; it has been likened to "chanting," to which it bears little resemblance, and it has been frequently compared to Native American music, a suspect claim at best. Many of these claims that regard Sámi music as separate, exotic, and distinct from other European musical traditions tend to play into Western stereotypes and fantasies of what they perceive Indigenous peoples to be, untouched ancient relics of an imagined past, instead of the culturally vibrant, modern, and cosmopolitan people that they actually are.

Sámi people often say that you do not *joik* about a thing, but rather you *joik* the thing itself. A *joik* is connected to the essence or spirit of the entity being sung, and singing the *joik* of a person, an animal, or a place is—in a sense—an act of invocation. As such, *joik* was formerly part of religious ceremonies prior to missionization. Even today, some people believe singing an animal's *joik* will call the animal to you. Performing a *joik* can also serve as an act of remembering, in particular in recalling a late relative or far-away friend. Different renderings of an individual *joik* contain in musical dialect the nature of the relationship between the singer and the *joik*'s subject.

The following transcriptions of song lyrics are at best incomplete renderings of a vibrant Sámi musical tradition. As was common for the time, lyrics to the songs were frequently perceived as of greater importance than melody, and even the earliest recording technologies (like wax cylinder recorders) were still in their infancy, not being commercially marketed until 1888. Interestingly, the only individual who shared songs with Koskimies was Mikko Aikio. The Aanaar Sámi *livđe* tradition had already declined greatly by the 1880s, most likely because of the church's stigmatization of *joik*-singing.

Be that as it may, Koskimies's collected lyrics offer a valuable glimpse into how songs were used in a variety of contexts in Aanaar. Some of the most interesting songs offered here showcase how Sámi handle poor behavior. "The Old Man" tells of a man's inability to keep wives, who apparently leave him with the backside of their trousers ripped, suggestive of either the poverty in which they must endure while living with him or—more disturbingly—potentially indicative of him being sexually violent. "Liström" tells of a capable but suicidal man, "Taavvad-Piera" is about a wolf-like reindeer thief, and "Ristnáá-Piätàr" tells about the legendary appetites of a destitute hunter, who would regularly eat two kilograms of Norwegian margarine a day or three reindeer livers and eight liters of meat soup.

Several additional "tundra Sámi" or North Sámi songs that were omitted from this chapter in the 1978 edition can be found in appendix A.

Joik Songs

Cradle *Livđe*
Mikko Aikio (A. V. Koskimies)

So I lull,
I lull my child
to sleep.
Don't you cry!
Father is coming,
he'll bring some birds,
little one, you can eat,
some bird meat to eat,
some fish eyes to eat.

Don't cry my child,
father is coming,
and he hasn't yet
died from brandy.
Yes, he's coming soon,
don't you worry,
yes he is coming soon,
he hasn't yet died from brandy.

Bear Song[1]
Mikko Aikio (A. V. Koskimies)

Wake up, my brother!
The sun is already shining onto the forested hills,

---

1. Sámi people generally regarded bears as sacred, with some communities identifying bears as a direct ancestor of Sámi people. The kinship is reflected in the term "brother," inviting the bear to not be lazy and to wake up with the late spring. Honko et al. (1994, 182, 678) reprint this song and suggest it was connected to ceremonial bear hunting rituals. This song serves as an epigraph to this book, reimagining these layered sets of meanings in a new and decolonial context.

the ants already running on the trunks of the trees,
the bird's song already echoing in our ears,
the old women already mending their seine,
the old men already putting their net shuttle[2] away,
the children already bustling about with their toy bows.

Reindeer *Livđe*
Mikko Aikio (A. V. Koskimies)

The reindeer, small, runs quietly, nana-nana, nana-nana,
antlers on its head curving,
the lasso thrown into the antlers,
strapped the neckband to the head,
the collar strapped to the neck,
the draw-straps tied to the collar,
the *geres*-sledge connected to the draw-straps,
a person sits in the *geres*,
so nice to sit in the *geres*.
You have already washed the eyes of many,
you have already greased the chin of many,
many have already had their back cleaned with
the strong soap of the birch
for the sweetness of your flesh.[3]

Raven *Livđe*
Mikko Aikio (A. V. Koskimies)

What are you carving?
I'm carving a skewer.
Why are you carving?
To shoot a raven.
Where is the raven?

---

2. A tool used to mend fishing nets.
3. Koskimies notes that this song was generally sung for entertainment when a child was in the *geres*-sledge.

In the crown of the big old pine.
Where is the big old pine?
The ax felled it.
Where is the ax?
A stone dulled it.
Where is the stone?　　　　　　(Alternatively:)
At the bottom of the lake.　　　An otter swallowed it.
Where is the lake?　　　　　　 Where is the otter?
The draught reindeer drank it up　It dove under floating ice.
Where is the draught reindeer?　Where is the floating ice?
Hung with a strap.　　　　　　 The sun melted it.
Where is the strap?　　　　　　 Where is the sun?
The sun burned it up.　　　　　The sun's in the sky.
Where is the sun?　　　　　　　Where is the sky?
It fell into the sea.　　　　　　 It fell into the sea.
Where is the sea?
A tit[4] lapped it up.
Where is the tit?
It died of foot disease.
Chirp, chirp, chirp!

The Tawny Owl
Mikko Aikio (A. V. Koskimies)

Night-bird, vulva-bird,[5] noi, noi, noi,
a head that can turn around, noi, noi, noi,
clear eye, noi, noi, noi,
mouse-eating mouth, noi, noi, noi,
colorful back, colorful back, noi, noi, noi,
sharp claw, pointed claw, noi, noi, noi,
sits atop the old pine tree, on the rotten snag, noi, noi, noi,
stalking for mice, stalking for mice, noi, noi, noi.

   4. The Siberian tit (*Poecile cinctus*) is the most common tit in the area.
   5. Both night-bird and vulva-bird were names for the tawny owl. Vulva-bird has been translated into the Finnish as the more common "cat-owl" (*kissapöllö*). According to Jakob Fellman, the eyes of the owl were said to resemble vulvas (Jouste 2011, 104).

Whitefish *Livđe*
Mikko Aikio (A. V. Koskimies)

Little fish, little fish, swimming about
big-scaled, white meat,
swimming about in the bottom of the seine,
as a small fish I knew how to get through;
now I need, now I need
to swim about in the bottom of the seine.[6]

Trout
Mikko Aikio (A. V. Koskimies)

Trout[7] was, ja-ja-jaaj-jaa-jaa,
long in the chin it was,
shimmering in the skin it was,
red in the flesh it was,
with blazing eyes darting about.

The Old Man
Mikko Aikio (A. V. Koskimies)

Old man, old man, laa-la-la-laa, laa-la-la-laa
the old man of a long *livđe*, laa-la-la-laa, laa-la-la-laa
two wives he had, laa-la-la-laa, laa-la-la-laa
both left, laa-la-la-laa, laa-la-la-laa
the backside of his wife's trousers ripped, laa-la-la-laa, laa-la-la-laa.[8]

---

6. Though the lyrics are vague, it appears the young whitefish thought it could escape but is now trapped. The song calls attention to one's technique in manipulating the seine's bottom to ensure fish do not escape.

7. The Aanaar word used here is one referring to a small trout that lives in lakes.

8. The original text is somewhat ambiguous whether his wives left him or he left his wives. The song's final line likely refers to poverty or, possibly, violence.

Songs

Hæænda-Maati *Joik*[9]
Mikko Aikio (A. V. Koskimies)

Hæænda-Maati was a rich man,
eighty were his reindeer,
two cows, five sheep,
one cat, one dog,
one and a half troughs, one and a half cups,
one and a half spoons, one and a half ladles,
one and a half cauldrons, one and a half pine-whisks,
one and a half mittens, one and a half shoes,
one and a half sledges, one and a half storehouses,
one and a half cowsheds, one and a half hovels,
one and a half slings, one and a half draw-straps,
one and a half reindeer collar straps, one and a half straps to tie goods to
    the *geres*,
one and a half lassos, one and a half carrying saddles,
a forest gentleman he was as well,
a juror he was as well,
a decent wife he had,
he lived around Pååđåår (Paadarjärvi),
now on the shore of big Aanaar.

Taavvad-Piera
Mikko Aikio (A. V. Koskimies)

Taavvad-Piera, jaaj-jaj-jaa,
he who moved with a file of reindeer bucks, jaaj-jaj-jaa,

---

9. Hæænda-Maati is a Sámi customary name, meaning Maati, son of Hæænda. Marko Jouste (2011, 123–30) identifies the subject of this *joik* as Matti Henrikinpoika Sarre (1834–1915), who worked as a forest ranger. He married Walborg Uulantytär Paadar in 1861 and had six children, two of whom died of the Spanish flu in 1920. He was said to be mischievous and quarrelsome. Jouste includes transcriptions of some melody variations in his work.

went across nine forested river valleys,[10] jaaj-jaj-jaa,
in just one night he traveled; jaaj-jaj-jaa.
Four men chased behind him, jaaj-jaj-jaa,
he swam over the Deatnu,
hanging from the reindeer buck's tail.
Behind the river he made a fire
and yelled: just try and catch me,
he yelled: just try and catch me!

Liström[11]
Mikko Aikio (A. V. Koskimies)

Liström, old man, who had learned ten languages, jaa-ja-ja-jaa-jaa
and still couldn't handle life with ten languages,
still killed himself.

Aila-Jussa[12]
Mikko Aikio (A. V. Koskimies)

Aila-Jussa, poor boy,
one bull and an empty trunk.[13]

Ristnåå-Piätår[14]
Mikko Aikio (A. V. Koskimies)

Ristnåå-Piätår, Ristnåå-Piätår, nun-nu-da-nun-nu
here and there you ramble,

    10. Traveling over nine river valleys is an expression commonly used in describing wolves. In this *joik*, it seems to suggest that Taavvad-Piera is a reindeer thief, like a wolf.
    11. Koskimies identifies Liström as a Finnish merchant living in Čäcisuáloi.
    12. Aila Jussa refers to Johannes Valle (b. 1842), and variants of its melody are transcribed in Jouste 2011, 130–35.
    13. Aikio uses a North Sámi word for "trunk" here (*pumba* instead of *čukke*).
    14. Jouste (2011, 115–22) identifies Ristnåå-Piätår as Piettar Paadar (b. 1854), a resident of the Ristinas-Pekka fields on the Virtaniemi in eastern Aanaar. He is said to have been an excellent storyteller and destitute woodsman with a legendary appetite for

he has already eaten two reindeer,
and he's got his eyes on a third.

Eerki-Piera
Mikko Aikio (A. V. Koskimies)

Eerki-Piera, jaa-jaa-jaa
he had given two rings,
both he took back, lallaa, laallaa
both he took back, lallaa, laallaa
five dollars[15] he gave
he took them all back, lal-laa-laa-laa-laa.

Other Songs

Stuorravuona (Isovuono) Market Song[16]
Mikko Aikio (A. V. Koskimies)

Now I will sing a remembrance of the Stuorravuona market.
So pleasant to walk here, among so many people.
Hard is the ground, where they walk.
They don't worry even though the place is rugged.
At the edge of the Stuorravuona market fairgrounds, there is a big ravine,
where side by side, and top to bottom, people usually meet;
when the day wears to its end, and evening approaches,

---

food, on one occasion eating eight meals and drinking 48 cups of coffee on a trip to the village. He was married to Uula Morottaja's (1892–1963) mother's sister (Leena). Jouste includes musical transcriptions of his songs and several stories about his fascinating life.

15. Dollar here refers to *riksdaler*, the official currency in Finland up until 1840 and in Sweden-Norway until 1873.

16. The Stuorravuona Market was on the Varanger Fjord, called "large fjord" by Aanaar Sámi at the time. The market ceased operations in 1760 but reopened in 1831, after which it was held at Christmastime. At the market people would trade lichen reserves for reindeer, ptarmigan, and reindeer products, and later flower, salt, and sea fish. The market ceased in 1889, with the rise of other centers of commerce (Jouste 2011, 219).

girls and boys in couples walk about there.
Don't, market boys, criticize your market sweethearts,
but rather go about and try the sweet liquor in the shops.
Don't waste, market boys, all your money,
the wide world can never be filled up.

The Girl's Song
Mikko Aikio (A. V. Koskimies)

The year before last I was a half-grown girl,
Let there be great thanks to the Lord!
Last year I slept among ten boys,
Let there be great thanks to the Lord!
This year I am already lulling my child to sleep,
Let there be great thanks to the Lord!
I didn't have time to feed my cows,
Let there be great thanks to the Lord!

This and That
Mikko Aikio, by letter (A. V. Koskimies)

I sing verses,
like the long logs of log cabins.
I recite stories,
like a sauna's logs.
I have clumps of words
like the biggest buckets full of muck,
and these words shall roll in your hearts
like goat droppings on a cliff.

Väinämöinen's Nephew[17]
Mikko Aikio, by letter (A. V. Koskimies)

Väinämöinen's brother's son
took a squirrel from a spruce,

---

17. Väinämöinen is the cultural hero at the center of Elias Lönnrot's compiled

from a pine a furry-tail,
fed it for five years with pine cones,
the squirrel changed into a stallion,
but didn't grow hooves,
but instead had sizable claws,
never slipping on slick stretches,
nor being taken down by icy patches,
the tail was long, thick mane,
its privates huge and enormous.

I Saw
Mikko Aikio, by letter (A. V. Koskimies)

This I know to be true
what I sing here in this song:
I saw the land and sky
dancing with each other
and I saw the land and the sky
once so strangely tilted,
that the sky looked like a cricket's eye
and the fish swam on the earth.
And I saw all the fishes
once holding court.
And I saw the angel Hamajeela (Haniel)
driving in a brass chariot.
And I saw old Väinämöinen
striking up a fire in the air.
And I saw steadfast Joukkavainen[18]
carving the tundra mountains.
And I saw the forest's matron[19]

Kalevala, most of which is collected south of Aanaar in Karelia. The Sámi version of the text, and Itkonen's translation, are in Kalevala-meter, parodying the style and grandiose magic and mysticism in many of the *Kalevala*'s songs about Väinämöinen.

18. Joukkavainen is another character in Elias Lönnrot's compilation, *Kalevala*, who enters into a magical singing competition with Väinämöinen.

19. In this mythical context, the forest's matron refers to a forest goddess known in Finnish as Mielikki but common in many Finno-Ugric mythologies. Mielikki has a husband (or sometimes father-in-law) known as Tapio, and children Nyyrikki and Tuulikki.

returning home from a bird hunt
so tired, that many couldn't
believe that she would ever recover.
And I saw high saints too
that they studied the wind,
that they are according to a book of music
to give up their ghosts.
And I saw still,
that it wasn't more
than a couple steps from paradise
to the hell-lords' drinking place.
And I saw an old grandfather,
finally at the market of the land of the dead
and he brought a pair of draught reindeer
intending to go to new lands.

Daughter and Mother Song[20]
unknown (T. I. Itkonen)

D: The first suitor came, hear this now, my mother.
M: How much money does he have, hear this now, my daughter?
D: A hundred and then some more, hear this now, my mother.
M: Tell the suitor to go away, hear this now, my daughter.

D: A second suitor came, hear this now, my mother.
M: How much money does he have, hear this now, my daughter?
D: A thousand and then some more, hear this now, my mother.
M: Tell the suitor to go away, hear this now, my daughter.

D: A third suitor came, hear this now, my mother.
M: How much money does he have, hear this now, my daughter?
D: A million and then some more, hear this now, my mother.
M: Tell the suitor come inside, hear this now, my daughter.

20. According to Laitinen, an audio recording exists of this song, collected on a phonograph, which is in Finland's national recorded archives.

D: Where can the suitor sit, hear this now, my mother?
M: In the chamber there is a painted chair, hear this now, my daughter.
D: What can the suitor drink, hear this now, my mother?
M: In the cellar there is red wine, hear this now, my daughter.

D: What can the suitor eat, hear this now, my mother?
M: Reindeer calf thigh and willow grouse roast, hear this now, my daughter.
D: Where can the suitor go to sleep, hear this now, my mother?
M: In the chamber there is a daybed, hear this now, my daughter.

The Fiancée's Beauty[21]
Mikko Aikio (A. V. Koskimies)

May the sun shine brightly on Oarreejävri (Orajärvi)!
If I would climb to the top of a spruce
and I would know I could see Oarreejävri,
in whose heathery valleys she is,
I would fell all these trees
which have grown up here recently;
I would chop all those branches,
which now bear green foliage.
I follow the light clouds,
which travel toward Oarreejävri.
If only I could fly there with crow wings!
Nor do I have a scaup's wings to fly there,
nor goose feet, nor beautiful feet
to make my way to you.

21. This is an old Kemi Sámi song, evidently translated together by Mikko Aikio and Koskimies into Aanaar Sámi but first documented by Olaus Sirma (c. 1655–1719). The text differs in places from the original text. According to Laitinen, the manuscript's ending is damaged, so I offer an English translation of the last three lines based off Sirma's version. Incidentally, one couplet in this song ("the boy's will—the wind's will") served as inspiration for Henry Wadsworth Longfellow's "My Lost Youth," although he uses these lines in a way that seemingly contradicts the original message about youthfulness and irresponsibility in the original song.

You have waited long,
your most glorious days.
Your eyes are warm, your heart tender.
If you should flee afar,
I would still find you soon.
What can be harder
than bands of tendons or chains
and iron shackles, which bite hard
and love entwines our heads
and wrenches all our thoughts.
The boy's will—the wind's will,
the young one's thoughts—long thoughts.
If I listen to them all . . .
[then I will turn onto the wrong road.
I have to choose a single mind
so that I may find my pathway.]

ANIMAL TALES

Set in a magical world of talking and anthropomorphized animals, often in a semimythical past, animal tales are common throughout Europe and around the world. This collection of tales straddles the lines between etiological legends (stories told to explain the origin of certain phenomena), myth (origin stories set in a time before time, before the world came to be as it is), parables (stories purposed for moral instruction), and fairy tale (obviously fictional narratives that have magical elements in them). These animal tales sometimes explain the origin of particular animal anatomies (i.e., how the bear lost its tail; anatomical features of the reindeer; why the tip of the ermine's tail is black), illustrate characteristics of an animal (the fox is clever; the wolf is greedy), or instruct where and when to locate animals (i.e., the wagtail and the dipper). Often there is a strong educational element to these tales. Although these tales might "explain" how animals came to be as they are, they are not necessarily regarded as literal truth and do not bear cosmic significance. Rather, they are perhaps more often used as tools to encode and recall knowledge about animals and their behavior.

Animal tales are well represented in the Aarne-Thompson-Uther classification system, and versions of these tales were well known throughout northern Europe. Still, many of these tales reflect more local concerns and beliefs as well. For instance, reindeer and *geres*-sledges are used for transport, the well-known Čuđit invaders are referred to as a way to cause a panic, or in "The Bear and Fox's Wild Reindeer Hunt" there are references to certain useful but easily overlooked bones that are inside reindeer. It would, of course, be somewhat surprising to see such a story told outside of the areas where reindeer actually live, and consequently it has no corresponding ATU number.

Some of these tales illustrate relatively straightforward moral lessons ("The Horse and the Wolf"), but most instead rely on the humor generated from transgressive behavior. In these contexts, greed and trickery can be funny and even prove a pathway to victory in the end ("The Fox's Tale," "The Story of the Fox's Blindness"). For that reason, these stories are among the few in this collection that contain some bawdy and crass humor. "The Man and the Bear," for instance, features a farmer who tricks a bear into castrating itself, the bear mistaking a vulva for a castration wound, and an always-timely fart joke. Many early folktale collectors did not collect such tales because they were considered indecent, and in doing so helped create the romantic stereotype that inhabitants of isolated village communities somehow lived more innocent and pure lives than we do in our own existence today.

The Fox's Tale
Matti Sarre (A. V. Koskimies)
ATU 1; ATU 2

Once there was a man walking about and a fox that was playing dead. The man found the "dead" fox and put it on his *geres*-sledge.[1] But the fox didn't stay atop top of the first *geres* in the train, nor the second *geres*, nor the third. The last *geres* was the *geres* used to carry the salmon, and the fox stopped on top of that one. The fox took up the straps connecting the sledges, biting through them, so that the *geres* with the salmon stopped on the trail. The fox began pulling the salmon out of the load. The man noticed what had happened, and he retrieved the *geres*. Then a bear came along to the fox, and it started to ask:
—Where did you get this salmon from?
—From the hole in the ice at the village.
The bear said:
—Why don't you take me there too?
The fox said:
—Sure, I'll bring you there.
So they went to an ice hole that some man had made. The fox told the bear to put his tail into the hole in the ice, and they were on the ice so long, that the bear's tail froze in place. The bear thought:
—Now the salmon are nibbling.
And the bear pulled so hard that his tail broke off. Nothing was left for him but a nub.

---

1. The sledge here refers to a *geres* (Aanaar Sámi: *kerris*), a specific type of boat-shaped sled that is pulled behind a reindeer to transport people and other goods. Often these were tied together and pulled in trains.

The Fox's Tale, Version 2
Matti Sarre (A. V. Koskimies)
ATU 5

When the bear rose from the hole in the ice, he got mad at the fox and left his poor tail behind. The fox went under the root of a pine. The bear began to dig for him, and kept biting the root. Finally, he snatched the fox by the foot. When the bear finally grabbed him by the leg, the fox said:

—Only the pine root! Only the pine root!

Whenever the bear bit the pine root, the fox said:

—Not my bones! Not my bones!

But the bear eventually got the fox out of his hole, and he took the fox into his mouth and set off carrying him. While walking through the forest, they noticed a woodpecker in a bush, which had a multicolored back. The fox said:

—Those were better days, when I decorated that shitty bird.

The bear said:

—Can you decorate me too?

The fox said:

—Why not? But it's quite an ordeal. We'll need to dig a grave, get some pine resin, build a platform, and twist up some wicker.

The bear said:

—Okay, I will help you.

So they got to it. The bear dug a grave, and they gathered up some resin-filled wood and put it in the grave. Then they propped up the perch over the resin grave, and the fox told the bear to check whether the perch was firm. The bear tested it, and it was indeed stable. They twisted up some wicker, and the fox told the bear to get on top of the platform. The fox began to tie the bear's legs with the wicker they had twisted, until the bear couldn't move his legs at all. And the fox lit the resin-filled wood, which was under the bear in the grave. Then the fox ran away. A few days later, the fox came back to check how the bear was doing. He saw that the bear had fallen from the perch. He crept closer to the grave to see whether the bear was still alive. He saw the bear had burned up. He gathered up the burned bones and put them in a sack, took it, and set off along the road with the sack of bones. After a while, he came across a person, who was walking with some reindeer. The man asked the fox:

—What do you have inside that sack?

The fox said:

—My inheritance of silver from my late father.

The person said:

—Why don't you give that to me?

The fox said:

—I can't. Not before you give me that draught reindeer and an old barren female reindeer.[2] Then I'll give it to you. But you can't peek at it until you've crossed over five or six hills.

And so the man gave the fox the reindeer, a draught reindeer, and an old female reindeer, and he took for himself the sack of burned bear bones, which he thought contained silver. He set off walking in some direction. When the man had gone over five or six hills, he started to peek in the sack the fox gave him. They looked like burned bones, and not silver at all.

The fox went with the reindeer to the banks of a river, and thought it should kill the reindeer, but wasn't able to. Then he began to shout:

—My family, my tribe, come here and kill!

Then there started to come a number of bear, wolverines, wolves, mice, and frogs. They began to shoot, the bear first. He aimed for the chin bone, where the reindeer still to this day has the bear's point. The wolverine shot at the upper chin, where there is still the wolverine's point. The wolf too shot and aimed for the shanks, where there is still a wolf arrow. The mouse shot: he aimed between the two clefts of its hoof, where there is the mouse's arrow. The frog shot. He aimed for the heart and the reindeer died. And even today there is a little bone in the reindeer's heart, whose name is the frog's arrow.

The group began to skin it: the bear, the wolf, and wolverine. The fox was wondering how he could frighten off his companions. He announced:

—Give me the stomach. I'm going to clean it up in the river.

He got the stomach and began to hit it against a bush and yelled:

—A war is coming! A war is coming! The Čuđit are coming! The Čuđit are coming![3]

His friends began to hear the strange sounds and pounding. They took fright and ran into hiding. The fox was again alone and he decided to eat the reindeer meat all by himself.

A long time after this, the man with the reindeer found the place where the fox had killed his reindeer and eaten them. He began to scold the fox:

---

2. A draught reindeer, *ergi*, was well trained to work around humans and considered the most valuable of reindeer. The barren and mature female reindeer, called a *ronno*, is of lesser value.

3. Čuđit are well-known robbers and murderers in Sámi oral narratives. A section of Čuđit stories appears later in this volume.

—Why did you deceive me so, taking my reindeer and eating them, and giving me nothing but some burnt bones?

The fox said:

—Perhaps it wasn't I who ate them alone: my family, my tribe, came and ate them. I was in the throes of illness, and I was barely able to have a mouthful. And there's one of them now, his mouth filled with fat, he said, when an ermine happened to come along.

The man grabbed a piece of burning wood and threw it at the ermine so that the burning wood struck the tip of the ermine's tail, which blackened it. And for that reason the tip of the ermine's tail is black even to this day.

The Fox and the Fisherman
Kaapin Pekka's sons (A. V. Koskimies)
ATU 1; ATU 2; ATU 3

A fisherman was driving along with his catch of fish. A fox cast himself onto the road as if he were dead. The fisherman took the fox and threw him onto a *geres*-sledge. The fox took the fish from the *geres* off to the side of the road.

The fisherman came home and told his wife:

—Go get the fish from the *geres*. Go and see: a fox is there, dead on top of the load. Now the fox can eat as many fish as it wants!

The wife went to look at the *geres*. There were no fish. Nor any fox. Well, the wife went back to the cottage and said to her husband:

—Why did you lie to me? There's no fox back there. And no fish either.

Now, the fox hid the fish along the side of the road, and he sat there eating the fish. A wolf came along and asked the fox:

—Where did you get those fish?

—I went fishing in the river.

—Tell me how I can get some for myself.

The fox said:

—Go and put your tail into a hole in the ice. Then pull it out, so you can get some more for yourself.

The wolf took his tail, put it into the river, and pulled and pulled on its tail, but couldn't get it out. The tail was frozen in place.

In the morning some women came along who were fetching water, so the wolf started to lick at its frozen tail. Well, the women darted with their yokes for carrying water pails to the ice hole, and soon they were hitting the wolf on the head with them. Well, the wolf leapt and leapt, grabbed and grabbed at its tail, and ran off.

He went to the fox and said:

—Hello, you wretched thing. I was struck, and my head is now bleeding.

The fox rubbed its head with some fat, and showed it to the wolf:

—Look, my brains are running out, but you have only a little blood on your head.

The Story of the Fox's Blindness
unknown (A. V. Koskimies)
ATU 2

Once the fox came to the shore of a river and began to yell at the fish:

—Fish, come row me across the river!

They began to come, the burbot in the front. The fox said:

—I'm not getting on your slimy back.

Along came a pike. The fox said:

—I'm not getting on your flat back.

Along came a perch.

—I'm not getting on your spiny back.

Along came a grayling.

—I'm not getting on your hard scales.

Along came a whitefish.

—I'm not getting on your ridgelike back.

Along came an arctic char. The fox said:

—Could it be you? No. Not you either.

Along came a trout.

—Could it be you? No. Not you either.

Along came a salmon. The fox said:

—Come closer. My foot is still getting wet.

And then he attacked the salmon and snapped it up into its mouth, and he brought it onto the land. He went to a *goahti* where there were no people, made a fire, and started to cook the salmon. When the salmon began to sizzle, the fox took fright and yelled:

—Someone is coming! Someone is coming!

And he bounded off, but didn't see anyone. He returned to the *goahti* and noticed that his fish-roasting spit was also sizzling. He snatched the salmon, which was cooking, and struck it against a rock, so that the fat splashed into his eyes and he burned his eyes. He set off from tree to tree pleading for new eyes. He came to a large pine tree.

—Do you have any eyes you can lend me?

The old pine said:

—I have nothing but one pair of dry eyes. And I can't afford to give them to you.

The fox walked further and came to a medium-sized pine and said:

—Don't you have some eyes to lend me?

—I don't have any, said the pine, more than one pair of resin eyes. And I can't afford to give them to you.

The fox walked further and came to a birch and said:

—Would you have some eyes to lend me?

The birch said:

—I do have some slit-like eyes I can lend.

The fox said:

—Give them to me. I'll try and see if they will work.

And the birch gave the fox the eyes. The fox put them in his head and said to the birch:

—I'll keep them forever and ever. And he ran away.

The birch threw itself at the fox, but didn't reach him, only the tips of its branches touched the fox on the end of its tail. That's how the end of the fox's tail became white.

The Man and the Bear
Uula Morottaja (T. I. Itkonen)
ATU 153

There was once a man, who was plowing a field with a horse, when along came a bear that said:

—Why is your horse so strong?

The farmer said, because he is castrated. The bear said:

—Can you maybe castrate me too?

The farmer agreed and with his knife lashed the bear's bits right off. The bear set off, saying:

—If by tomorrow I'm not stronger, I'll come back tomorrow and castrate you yourself!

The farmer didn't think it would be a good idea to go out into the fields to plow the next day. Instead he sent a worker-girl. The bear came back, enraged, and said:

—I did not, in fact, get stronger. Now I'm going to castrate you!

The girl was quite surprised:

—Maybe I've already been castrated.

The bear said:

—I won't believe it until I see it.

And the bear wrenched the girl onto her back and said:

—Oh dear, how terribly you've been castrated. I'm going to go and get some medicine.

And the bear left to gather up some pitch. He left a hare there to guard the girl so that she wouldn't go anywhere before he came back with the medicine.

The hare stayed put. Then the girl farted really loud. The hare got surprised and ran off. It ran past the bear. The bear said:

—What are you, my guard, doing over here?

The hare answered, that earlier when you saw it, it still hadn't ripped open, but now it had just started to rip. The bear began to think:

—It's something I can no longer cure, since it has ripped open even worse than it was before. And the bear went on its way.

The Bear and Fox's Wild Reindeer Hunt
Iisakki Mannermaa (A. V. Koskimies)

A bear and a fox were running in the forest. They met each other in a large grove. The fox said to the bear:

—Would you take me into your company?

The bear said:

—Sure. Let's test you and your friends' shooting skills so I can see who among you will be a shooter. I'm going to go behind those roots to watch for a wild reindeer[4] walking along the path. Then I'll jump onto the reindeer's antlers and grab it around the neck with one paw. You need to be near me and also call your friends to that place.

When the bear had said all this to the fox, he went behind the roots to watch for reindeer. After a little while, a reindeer came lumbering along the trail, which walked right past the root cluster where the bear was waiting. The bear jumped, took the reindeer by the antlers, and wrung another paw around its neck. He yelled to the fox:

—Come quickly with your gun, fox, and your friends!

The fox came, along with a wolf, a mouse, and a frog. The bear said to the fox:

—Now you need to shoot this reindeer I'm holding. That way I can assess your shooting abilities.

---

4. *Kodde* is used for wild reindeer, and *puásui* for herded reindeer. The reindeer in this story is a *kodde*, although I have abbreviated wild reindeer to reindeer for readability.

The bear himself shot first and aimed for the chin bone. At the same time the wolf shot, aiming right inside the roast of some shank meat. The mouse shot two darts inside its back leg. The frog shot and aimed right for the reindeer's heart. The reindeer immediately fell to the ground and died.
The bear said to the fox:
—Well, why didn't you even shoot?
The fox said:
—I don't have anything to shoot with.
The bear said to the fox:
—Go and leave this place! I won't bother with you, you who doesn't even have the ability to get a single bite of food for himself.
The fox became frightened by the bear's harsh words and ran off. It trotted off behind the large grove, where there was a small lake. The fox began to run around the lake and yelled as he ran:
—The war is coming! The war is coming and great Čuđit are now in sight!
Then the fox ran secretly to see what the bear and his companions were doing.
He noticed that no one was any longer eating the reindeer meat. So the fox went to eat the meat. He ate the reindeer's fat and meat as he pleased. He lit a campfire and noticed suddenly an ermine, which hadn't been in the company previously, when they were shooting at the reindeer. The fox got mad at the ermine, grabbed a burning log, and threw it at him, saying to the ermine:
—Darn fat-eater!
But his throw didn't hit anything more than the tip of its tail, which blackened, even though it used to be white.
As a memento, still, the reindeer those animals shot has notable arrows in its chin-bone, in its shank, in its heart, and back leg. They are called the bear's arrow in the chin bone, the wolf's arrow in the shank roast, the mouse's arrow between the hooves in the back leg, and the frog's arrow in the middle of the heart.

The Mouse and the Cat[5]
Pekka Valle (A. V. Koskimies)

A mouse was a tailor for a cat. The cat ordered the mouse to make a jacket, and went to go get the jacket. The mouse said:

---

5. This tale is a bit fragmented and a little difficult to understand in a literal sense. In other versions, the inexperienced mouse tailor uses fabric to try to make the requested item, botches the job, and then suggests that he make a smaller item. The cat agrees again and again, until all the fabric is wasted to nothing.

—No jacket can be made of this.
The cat asked:
—What can be made of this?
The mouse said:
—Pants.
The cat went to get the pants. The mouse said:
—No pants can be made of this.
The cat asked:
—Well, what can be made of it?
The mouse answered:
—Vests.
The cat then went to get the vests. The mouse said:
—No vest can be made of this.
The cat said:
—What can be made of it?
The mouse said:
—A hat.
The cat went to get the hat. The mouse said:
—No hat can be made of this.
The cat asked:
—What can be made of this?
The mouse said:
—A sheath.
The cat went to get the sheath. The mouse said:
—No sheath can be made of this.
The cat asked:
—What can be made of this?
The mouse answered:
—A purse for flint and firesteel.
The cat pounced onto the back of the mouse's neck, and since that time the cat and mouse have been enemies.

The Raven and the Fox
Heikki Mattus, by letter (A. V. Koskimies)
ATU 57

Once a raven found a piece of cheese and descended from the top of an old pine to eat it. But when a fox noticed this, it came to the roots of the pine, bowed to the raven, and said:

Animal Tales

Heikki Mattus and Santeri Valle on the steps of the Aanaar parsonage, 1912. Photo: Toivo Itkonen. Image courtesy of the Finnish National Board of Antiquities.

—You are a beautiful bird, the most beautiful bird in the world. But what sort of a voice might you have?

The raven couldn't bear to be quiet, even though it still had cheese in its mouth. It cawed and the cheese fell to the ground. The fox took the cheese and ran away, saying:

—Your voice is ugly, and your coat is ugly too.

The poor raven was left without its cheese, and it flew away empty-handed.

The Horse and the Wolf
Matti Sarre (A. V. Koskimies)
ATU 122J

A wolf had grown so old that it couldn't really take care of itself anymore. Finally, he thought up an idea of how to support himself, but he needed to borrow a fox's coat. And so he did. He went trotting off, hungry, and noticed a horse in a pasture and said:

—Good day, dear friend!

After that he said he was a doctor and asked:

—Is there anything you need some help with?

The horse said:

—Why yes. You happened to come along at the best possible time. I have a have a thorn stuck into the bottom of my foot. Would you be so kind and pull the thorn from my foot?

The wolf was delighted by this, and peeked at the bottom of the horse's back leg, but the horse took his back leg, and kicked the wolf in the teeth so hard that all his teeth loosened and slipped right down his throat, and the horse ran away laughing and grinning.

Evil is the payment of evil.

The Fox and the Hare
Heikki Morottaja (A. V. Koskimies)

A fox and a hare met each other. The fox said to the hare:

—No one would ever be afraid of you.

—Who would be afraid of you either? answered the hare

—Everyone fears me, said the fox. I have a long tail, and everyone thinks I'm a wolf when they see me from afar. Then they fear me. But nobody is afraid of you.

—Let's make a deal, said the hare. I'll show you that I can be fearsome.

The fox agreed to it, and the bet was on. They set off walking together. In front of them, the hare noticed a flock of lambs lying around next to a fence. The lambs got startled and began running off as fast as they could. The hare was delighted that he won the bet, and he started to laugh. He laughed so hard that his mouth split in two. Because of this, all hares have a two-sided mouth.

The Wagtail and the Dipper[6]
Martti Valle (A. V. Koskimies)
ATU 9

A white wagtail and white-throated dipper were working as loggers. They had a thrush as a log driver. As they descended the river, the wagtail would drive on top of the log, and the dipper sat the whole time on a nearby stone,

---

6. Another version of this story, told by the sons of Kaapin Pekka, was collected and published in the 1978 edition. Because the versions are nearly identical, save for a few word choices that would be scarcely noticeable after translation into English, I have not included it here.

being lazy. The wagtail again went up and down, retrieving a log, and driving it downstream. When it went past the dipper, it always jumped up a little and acted all cheerful. The dipper thought badly of this and disliked him for it.

That evening they went to get paid. The thrush didn't pay the dipper half of what it paid the wagtail. This made the dipper angry, and he said:

—All he did was go down the river on a log, and I was his supervisor! And I'm paid less than he is, when he's just descending the river.

The thrush said:

—Now we are paying you little, but if you don't improve your work, you'll be earning even less or we'll be letting you go. Today you are being given a lesson.

The dipper said:

—I'm on the rapids far more than the wagtail. I know how to do more work than him.

The next day they started to test out who could stay on the log better and who would get to supervise, and for supervising they would receive more pay. And the thrush came to watch their work.

When they left on a log into a stretch of rapids, the dipper jumped first onto the front of the log and the wagtail jumped onto the back end. It kept jumping around there on the back end and said:

—Now, it's on!

The dipper turned to look, and in turning its head, it fell. Whenever it fell, it always got back up again onto the log. When they got below the rapids, along came the thrush and drove the dipper away. It no longer got to be in the rapids during the summer. When the wagtail comes to these lands, the dipper sets off for the summer. In the fall, when the wagtail leaves here, the dipper returns to the rapids as the occupant of its former home.

The Story of the Moose and the Bear[7]
unknown (A. V. Koskimies)
ATU 157

Once while walking in the forest, a moose happened across a bear, who was digging a winter den for himself. The moose asked the bear:

---

7. The titular character here is referred to as a *jàlupeeyri* (or *jalopeura*, in Finnish), which literally translates to "noble deer" and in a biblical sense was used by Michael Agricola (1510–57) in his translating of the Bible into Finnish to refer to lions. Recent research suggests that the term was in use before Agricola and referred to moose (or, some suggest, wild reindeer). Because of the moose's short tail and facial cleft, as alluded to late in the story, I have chosen to translate the term as "moose."

—What are you doing?

The bear said:

—I'm going into hiding from man.

—Hiding from man? said the moose.—I don't believe I've ever met such a man who was worth fearing.

The bear said:

—People are frightening when they have weapons. Set off to walk along the country road there, and you'll surely find a man who you'll need to be afraid of.

The moose set off to walk along the country road. Along came a young boy. He asked:

—Are you a man?

He answered:

—I'm not a man, but rather just the beginnings of a man.

The moose went past the young boy and continued along the country road. Along came an old man. The moose asked:

—So, are you perchance a man?

The old man answered:

—I'm not a man. I have been a man, but no longer.

The moose went past him as well and continued along the country road. He walked and walked, and then came along a soldier, riding on a horse. The moose asked:

—So, are you perchance a man?

He said:

—I am said to be a man, and a man I am as well.

The moose opened its jaw and started to charge at the soldier. The soldier grabbed his rifle and struck the moose in the mouth, so that his chin bone broke. The moose turned toward his tail and started to strike the man with it, but the soldier pulled his sword from a scabbard and struck the moose so that he cut his tail in two. The moose had to flee, and it set off on the same road from whence it came. It came back to where the bear was. The bear said:

—Perhaps now you'll believe me that you need to fear men.

FAIRY TALES

Fairy tales (sometimes called magic tales, wonder tales, or *märchen*) are among the most important historical focuses of folklore research. By the nineteenth century, folklorists had noticed the similarities in these tales, and how the same stories existed in different versions across cultural lines. Further study revealed related stories that existed over vast geographical regions. One of the most famous examples, Cinderella (ATU 510), exists in thousands of variants across Europe, the Middle East, and Southeast Asia. The tales were then used to understand contact between cultures and theorize the importance of merchant routes in the transmission of oral culture. They also served to advance the Historic-Geographic Method, which through the charting of variation in tales could hypothesize where these tales were born, how they spread, and why they changed over time. Other folklorists, most notably Vladimir Propp, looked at the structural similarities between these tales, and later scholars have approached these tales from perspectives of performance, Marxist, feminist, gender, and sexuality studies. Fairy tales have been adopted into and inspired literary forms in the writings of individuals like Hans Christian Andersen, and their Disney versions have been an important focus of media and popular culture studies.

Fairy tales were in many ways the popular entertainment of their time. They have simple and relatively predictable plots, stock characters, and are enjoyed by multiple age groups. The predictability, similar plot structures, and repetitions in sets of three made it easy for children to listen and for storytellers to narrate while occupying themselves with other work. Fairy tales are always told and recognized to be fiction, set in a world of kings, servants, and magic that bears limited resemblance to lived reality. They are generally set in a just universe, where moral behavior is rewarded and wickedness is punished. Many of the stories therefore feature a rewriting of the social order, where a poor hero or heroine is rewarded in the end with the winning of wealth or a desirable spouse after facing various tests and trials. Interestingly, appearances and reality play major roles in many fairy tales. In a simplified world in which ugly people are evil and beautiful ones are good, disguises play a major role in offering social criticism about social injustices and class hierarchies.

Tellingly, there has been relatively little interest in Sámi fairy tales, as Western research has historically emphasized Sámi culture as distinct from Nordic cultures—part of a broader phenomenon in which Indigenous peoples have been exoticized around the globe. Such tales were perceived to be "borrowing" from other cultures rather than being a real and authentic part of Sámi culture, despite the fact their presence mirrors how fairy tales were transmitted and reinterpreted elsewhere in Europe. What is perhaps interesting to note is how these tales have been translated into Sámi culture. A sense of wry humor is pervasive in the tales, for instance, and there is an emphasis on fish, fishing, and even a tale featuring a *čáhceháldi*, a Sámi spirit that presides over certain waters. "Acorn Finding" is an adaptation of a tale from *One Thousand and One Nights*, which likely reached Aanaar after being published in a Finnish newspaper in Oulu, and lacking a suitable word for "sesame" found a substitute with "acorn."

Some of these tales contain some degree of disturbing violence—at least by today's standards. For instance, in "The Boy and the Golden Birds," the hero finds a sleeping and unresponsive woman, and sequentially kisses, touches, and rapes her, before stealing one of her birds. They are separated, and the woman is later quite content to marry him. As unsettling as this is in a literal sense both today and for the Sámi communities in the nineteenth century, the conventions of the genre minimize its real-world implications into a device to advance a plot. For the audience of the day, it is perhaps no more or less objectionable than the countless unwelcome sexual advances or examples of stalker-like behavior we see in media today, which are generally interpreted as more representative of intentions and motivation than to be regarded in real-world contexts. In the movies, for example, a teenager standing in the rain outside of a love interest's bedroom is a culturally acceptable way to symbolically represent an individual's emotional and mental state; in real life, such behavior would be deeply disturbing if not outright menacing. Although we certainly should not minimize the way these scenarios have served to reinforce and perpetuate sexisms and gendered violence, it is also important to recognize their use within their historical context and to use this as an opportunity to reflect on our own culturally accepted uses of violence and sexualization in entertainment that would prove unsettling by nineteenth-century standards.

Ultimately, we do not know enough about Juho Petteri Lusmaniemi to really understand why he told this tale as he did. Was he simply faithfully recounting the tale as he had heard it, or was this device important to his understanding of the story? On the one hand, the incongruities between the rape, the bird-theft, and their later marriage could also imply the tale is a hybridized version of two separate tales (an idea reinforced by the distinctive two-part plot). On the other hand, the formulaic and structured set of three visits to the girl seems to be evidence that this was at least formerly a crucial part of the story (in fairy tales, repetitions in three mark significant happenings), and the increasing unruliness of the birds appears to be indicative of the girl's escalating emotional distress. Alternatively, their later marriage could somehow imply consent, or perhaps the necessity of the course of events (i.e., in the Sleeping Beauty sense of kissing leading to curse-breaking). We might further speculate as to whether her awakening and gratitude toward the boy represents a deeply sexist trope that rationalizes unwelcome sexual advances, or whether the girl's own sexual awakening leads to her own liberation and transition into adulthood and an avenue to her escape from an abusive and controlling situation. If we accept the latter interpretation, the birds' transition from docility to agency might be read as connected to the girl's eventual assertion of her own independence. Further evidence to this latter interpretation can be found in Lusmaniemi's repertoire. His tales include several recognizable feminist motifs that are otherwise rare in this collection, like women besting or tricking men ("The Girl and Her Suitor," "The Whitefish Daughter-in-Law," "Piäjáàǯ"), or men's cruelty toward women ("The Reindeer Calf's Hooves," "Káášša"). He also tells a variant of one of the two tales told by women in this collection ("The Skolt Sámi and His Bear-Wife") that seemingly reflects women's anxieties in a male-dominated society. Such possible proto-feminist leanings and potential evidence that Lusmaniemi told women's tales might alter how we interpret what that individual scene meant to him and his audience. Understanding how this tale was told in specific contexts, how Lusmaniemi understood this tale, how women told and interpreted this tale, and how Lusmaniemi came to learn this tale would help us find more concrete answers to these difficult questions.

Storytellers like Lusmaniemi frequently alter stories to fit their own value systems. For instance, some women in the community might purposefully refuse to tell this tale, alter the sections that potentially condone sexual violence, or make the maiden's motivations and perspectives more clear in the tale in order to recraft it into something more reflective of themselves and their values. The formation of a repertoire and creations of tale variants are an important part of storytelling and help demonstrate how these tales are not simply reflections of static communal values but instead are purposed and repurposed by individuals in a diverse community to advance numerous personalized social and cultural agendas.

The Poor Boy and the King's Daughter
Juho Petteri Lusmaniemi (A. V. Koskimies)
ATU 530

There was once an old man who was rather poor. He had three sons. Two were richer and one was poor. And the old man said to his boys:

—When I die and you put me in a coffin, put it in a haystack and each of you guard it for one night.

Well, he indeed died, and they put him in a coffin and they took it to the haystack, as he had told them to do. The eldest boy's turn to stand guard came first. He didn't go, but instead he said:

—What's left of him to guard?

The youngest boy said that he would go instead. He crawled into a tar barrel and rolled around in feathers and went there like that. He was there when the midnight hour came. Then a horse came along to eat some of that hay. The boy began to wonder what he should do. He thought:

—I'll just jump onto its back.

And jump he did. The horse set off running, and it ran inside a mountain of gold. There were people there and such riches! The boy said to them:

—Oh dear, you people... Your horse got out and went to eat my father's hay. If I tell my father, then you're really going to get it!

They started to implore him:

—Please don't tell him! We will give you as much money as you can bear to carry.

He took as much money as he could carry and set off for home, where his brothers were. He hid the money. The brothers asked:

—Well, what did you see?

—Nothing.

The next day it was the middle brother's turn. He didn't want to go either. The youngest said:

—Yes, I'll go.

And he left, went inside the tar barrel and again rolled in feathers. Then he went to stand guard. He was there until midnight. Then once again the horse came along and began to eat hay. Again he jumped onto its back, and it ran into the mountain of gold. The boy said to those people:

—Oh dear, you people... Your horse got out and went to eat my father's hay. If I tell my father, then you're really going to get it!

They started to implore him:

—Please don't tell him! We will give you as much money as you can bear to carry.

He took as much money as he could carry and set off for his brothers' home, and again he hid the money. The brothers asked:

—What did you see?

—Nothing.

Then came his own turn to guard. He again went to stand guard, went in the tar barrel, rolled in feathers, and then left. It was getting to be midnight. Again the horse came to eat the hay. He jumped on the horse's back. The horse set off running again inside the golden mountain. Again the boy berated them:

—Oh dear, you people . . . Your horse got out and now it's eaten all my father's hay. If I tell my father, then you're really, really going to get it!

They started to implore him:

—Please don't tell him! We will give you this horse and all the beautiful clothing you could possibly want—since you have such ugly clothes after all.

He took the horse and the clothes that he thought to be the most beautiful.

In a nearby city, the king had a daughter who had vanished. And the boy had seen that she too was inside the mountain, but he didn't say anything. He set off galloping with the horse, hid the horse, and went to his brothers' house. The brothers asked:

—What did you see?

—Well, nothing.

The king issued a proclamation to the entire city that his daughter had vanished, and that he knew the girl had ended up somewhere inside that mountain. If anyone should have such a horse that they could gallop up and bound inside the mountain, the girl would be freed, and she would become the wife of whoever could run his horse like that.

Well, the first trial day came, and everyone who was able to find a horse in the city went there. The three brothers also went there, and the youngest boy went in secret to get the horse that he had gotten from that same mountain. He dressed in the clothes he had gotten from the mountain, and he set off galloping.

Others galloped and their horses bounded, but they didn't get anywhere. Their horses were stymied by the mountain. That boy also was galloping and bounding forth. He got to higher than anyone else. No one recognized him, since he had a gilded horse and gilded clothing. And so they ceased in their efforts.

A second day came, and again everyone from the city tried again to see if anyone could get up that mountain. The boy also was there. But no one else could get in there. The boy got higher than anyone else, but he also could not get inside the mountain, and still no one knew who he was.

The third day came. Again everyone in the city gathered, and the boy was also on his horse, which he had gotten from the mountain. The others couldn't get anywhere with their horses. And the boy bounded up the mountain and got the king's daughter from that place, and he set off galloping to the king with his daughter. The daughter cut her gold ring in two, and she gave half of it to the boy. And the boy took the daughter to the king.

Then the boy went home, hid his horse, and undressed. He put on his tar-and-feathered clothes and went to his brothers. The brothers were wondering who got the king's daughter, since no one knew him. All the city dwellers were wondering the same thing, since no one recognized the man or the horse, as it was so beautiful.

Then the king proclaimed that the person who had the other half of his daughter's ring could take her as his own. Everyone started to search. All the city folk, whoever had a gold ring, broke their own ring in two. The boy's brothers did this as well. And each tried to bring their broken ring to the king's daughter, but none of them joined together as one.

The boy waited to be the last of the lot. He said to his brothers that he too would go to the king's palace. The brothers said:

—And what will you do there? You don't even have a golden ring!

And so he left in his tar-and-feathered clothes. He went to the king and said that he had the ring-half. The king said:

—Well, if that's the case, let's try it out.

And the boy retrieved the ring-half: it joined perfectly with that piece it had been broken from. The king's daughter said that this was the other half of her ring and the man had to be the same, but the clothes were not the same. The king said:

—You now can have my daughter as your wife, since you've already gotten her from the mountain!

The boy said that he would return the following day to get the king's daughter. And he went back to his brothers. The brothers said:

—How shameless, going to meet a king in that kind of tar-and-feather wardrobe!

The boy said that he would go the following day to get the king's daughter to be his wife. The brothers said:

—What a liar you are!

Morning came, and the boy set off walking in his tar-and-feather clothing. The brothers thought that he went to go wandering about. And he went to his horse that he had gotten from the mountain, and he undressed from his tarred clothing and put on the gilded clothes he got from the mountain, and he set off driving to the king. The city folk noticed that the horse was heading toward the king. They started to watch to see what kind of man it was who drove the horse.

And he was so handsome that no one in the city had ever seen such a horse or such a man.

The king's daughter noticed the horse coming from afar, and she said that now it was her fiancé who was coming. The king's men all came to see what he was like. They saw that he was indeed quite handsome.

He came to the king, and they held a great party with drinks aplenty. When the boy's head finally cleared up after the party, he said that he was going to go home. The king said:

—You two can leave, but I too would like to go and see your home.

The boy said:

—Why not?

And so they left trotting on the back of the golden horse. And the horse ran to the gold mountain, and when the gold mountain came into sight, it changed into a city of gold. The king said to his son-in-law:

—This is your home?

He said:

—So it is.

The king was shocked. They came to the city. The king had not ever seen such beautiful houses as there were in this city. And there they drank some, and eventually the boy left to bring his father-in-law back.

When the king returned to his wife, he had been so surprised at the city's beauty that barely could a word escape his lips, and he fell into his wife: he nearly fainted. Only after he recovered could he tell his wife about his travels, and how his son-in-law had so many beautiful houses. And the son-in-law went back to his fiancée in the golden city, and there they are still today.

The Great Lord's Son-in-Law
Iisakki Mannermaa (A. V. Koskimies)
ATU 555

There was once a poor boy who often walked about in the forest and on the shores of lakes and rivers, fished for char from the shore, and played alone in the forest. Once, while he was playing on a riverbank, he noticed a great pike in the water and became surprised, for he had never before seen such a large fish the water, only little fish.

The boy tried to run away, but as he did, he heard a voice saying:

—With pike's heads, with pike's teeth, and pike's clear eyes, I say to you, poor boy, that whatever good you want in the world for yourself or for others, so it is possible.

Because the poor boy was surprised, he didn't say anything, but instead went back to his cottage where his parents were. He didn't say anything to them, and he didn't make anything of the voice that he heard from the water. He thought to himself that it might have been a *čáhceháldi*,[1] which he had heard about in stories.

Later on, the boy happened to come across the residence of a great lord. He saw the lord's daughter and he thought to himself the wonderful statement, which he had once heard from the water on the shore of a river. He tried those words, which he had heard from the water spirit, and said them aloud to see if they would have any effect:

—With pike's heads, with pike's teeth, and pike's clear eyes, let this great lord's daughter become pregnant!

And so the poor boy returned to his home.

Some time later, the poor boy went again to the house of the great lord. He arrived and sat next to the lord's house, wondering what marvels he might see. He noticed the great lord walking outside, and the lord came to the poor boy. He asked the boy:

—What did that little bird say, who sang on the roof of my cottage?

The poor boy looked up at the roof, and he saw a little bird, whose voice sang a high-pitched song. The boy said:

—That little bird told you that your daughter is pregnant.

The great lord said to the poor boy:

—It's not true. And if it is true, what you said you heard from that little bird, then let it be *you* who is the father of the child my daughter will bear.

And the lord went back inside his house. The poor boy left for home. After some time, the lord noticed that his daughter had become pregnant. He went to speak with the girl and asked her:

—Who might the father of the child be, who you're giving birth to, since it appears as if you're pregnant?

The daughter said to her father:

—The father of the child, whom I now carry underneath my heart, let it be that poor boy, who understood the voices of the birds.

The lord thought that it was the same boy, who could interpret the bird's song for him. And when that lord's daughter gave birth to the child, the lord invited the poor boy to come quickly to talk with him. When the boy received

---

1. A *čáhceháldi* (Aanaar: *čäzihäldee*) is a protector spirit of the water.

word, he went quickly to the lord's cottage and said good day, to which the lord responded:

—God grant it.[2]

The lord said to the poor boy:

—You may need to marry my daughter, since I promised you as much, when you correctly guessed the bird's shrill song.

The poor boy answered:

—I would be happy to marry her, if your daughter also wants this.

The lord called his daughter in. The girl came and the lord asked his daughter:

—Do you take this poor boy as your husband and will you love him so long as you shall live?

The girl said:

—I will take him as my husband.

The lord said to his son-in-law:

You need to build another home, and there you shall live with my daughter.

The poor boy said:

—Even though I'm poor and my parents are poor, I will nonetheless try to start building a new home.

The boy went out again, sat on some rock, and thought to himself:

—Surely that spirit-pike that I once saw from that riverbank, surely it has the power.

The poor boy said:

—With pike's heads, with pike's teeth, and pike's clear eyes, let there be born to me new, beautiful cottages on that side of the river, opposite the lord's cottages, and a sturdy bridge over the river from my cottage to the cottage of the lord.

And so the poor boy once again went to his parents' cottage, and told his father and mother how he had taken a great lord's daughter as his spouse. When the poor boy was finishing up with his visit, a young man suddenly stepped through the door of the cottage. He said good day, and they answered God grant it. The young man said to the poor boy:

—Come quickly with your parents upon the order of the great lord. Your poverty is over. New lodgings have suddenly been born—how, we don't know—and there is a sturdy bridge across the river.

The man said goodbye and went back. The boy said to his father and mother:

—Let's go quickly and move into our new cottages.

---

2. This is a customary greeting, in response to "good day," in the Sámi languages.

And they prepared and left and rejoiced. When they came to their new cottages, they saw the very beautiful preparations, both inside and out, in the same fashion as the lord's cottages. The poor boy fetched his new wife right away and spoke to his father-in-law. The father-in-law was quite happy that the poor boy was no stupid person, even though he had only begrudgingly taken the boy as his son-in-law.

The poor boy called his father-in-law and mother-in-law to visit, across the new bridge, to see their new cottages. The lord came to his bidding, and he drove along the new bridge and stepped inside with his wife. Right away he noticed better rooms and a more finely decorated interior and exterior than he even had himself. A meal was prepared, food and drinks, a complete table, the chairs ornately crafted, and they sat to eat. They ate and drank there, the great lord's and the poor boy's families. They celebrated, since God had turned their fates in a most wonderful way. They gave gifts in honor of the young couple.

After some time, the great lord began to envy the new son-in-law's good life and he invited him to talk. The son-in-law went quickly over the bridge to talk with his father-in-law. When he came inside and was greeted, the gentleman said to his son-in-law:

—Let's go sailing over the bay in the sea, just for fun.

The son-in-law said:

—Yes, let's go!

They prepared and took two farmhands along. They went in the boat and started to row from the river's mouth toward the sea's bay. They pulled up the sail and they set off sailing in a good wind. When they were sailing, the lord said to his son-in-law:

—Let's visit that island over there.

The son-in-law said:

—Let's go.

They went to the island to look for precious stones. When the lord was walking there with his son-in-law, he said:

—You go by yourself to the other end of the island to look for stones, and come back over here when you're done.

The son-in-law said:

—Sure, why not? And he set off himself on the island, walking about a little while, and he didn't find anything, and he returned to the boat, where his father-in-law was supposed to be waiting with the farmhands. When he got near the place he had disembarked, he noticed suddenly, much to his surprise, that the boat was gone from that spot. He saw a boat sailing far away, and he realized that he was alone on the island. Tears came to his eyes. He realized the gravity of his situation: it wasn't too pleasant to be on that island without food or drink. Death was perhaps not far away.

He sat on a stone and thought to himself:

—I ought to speak those words.

And he said:

—With pike's heads, with pike's teeth, and pike's clear eyes, let help come to me!

After this, he noticed a large bird flying, which descended next to him. The bird said:

—Sit on my back! I will carry you home.

The boy did so, and the bird carried him near to his home and descended to the ground.

The boy went home and called his father-in-law in to talk. The father-in-law was surprised to hear that the son-in-law was already home. He promised to come to speak to him. After coming to the cottage, he greeted him and said right away to his son-in-law:

—Everything you see here is to become your property, for you are stronger in your doings than any other human being.

The son-in-law thanked his father-in-law and said goodbye, and they lived happily until their dying day.

The Boy and the Golden Birds
Juho Petteri Lusmaniemi (A. V. Koskimies)
ATU 550; ATU 400

There once was a poor boy who went to a king, offering his services as a cowherd. Well, the king agreed: yes, he would take the boy. And he put him to tend his cows.

The boy was off shepherding and found a beautiful feather, the like of which he had never before seen. The king fell in love with the feather and said to the boy:

—If you find the bird that shed this feather, then I will give you a great reward.

The boy said he would try to look, and see what he might find. He again set off to tend the cows the next day. As he walked, he noticed a house, and he went inside. Such a beautiful house! He went inside to see who lived there. He opened the door, but there wasn't a single person there. He opened a second door and noticed those beautiful birds were there, but since there was no one there, he didn't think he should take one. He saw that still there was one more door he could go through. He went to check if there might be someone there. He opened the door and saw that there was a beautiful girl sleeping there. He said:

—Good day!

The girl didn't answer at all. The boy asked:

—Why don't you sell me one of those birds?

The girl didn't say a thing. Then the boy turned to leave and thought that he should take just one of those birds and bring it to the king. So he took one and left.

Then the thought occurred to him: Why not kiss that girl, since she was so beautiful? He turned back, returned his bird to the flock, and went and kissed the girl. And then, once again, he went out, grabbed the bird, and went out so that he could head on his way. Then he thought, why not go and touch that girl? So he turned back again, and put down his bird and went to the girl and touched her. Then he again went out and took the bird, but struggled to catch it, since it was surprised. He went out and the thought came to mind, why shouldn't he still make love to that girl, as she was so beautiful and so fine. He spun around again and went inside and set down his bird, and went to the girl and lay with her. And again he went to the birds and took one, but this time he could hardly catch one at all. In the end, he finally caught one, and he left for the king.

When the king saw the boy coming with a bird, he walked toward him. He told the boy that if he could find just one more so that he could have a pair of them, he would get as large a reward as he desired. Well, the boy promised to bring still one more, but he could no longer find that place. He returned empty-handed to the king.

The boy came to long for that girl, since he could no longer find her. He went once again to look for that place, but he still couldn't find it. He did, however, find the home of the old woman of Kieddikeäč (Kenttäpää). He said to the old woman:

—Would you, my old woman, know about the beautiful place that I once found? There were beautiful birds and a beautiful girl. I want to marry the girl, but I can no longer find her abode.

The old woman said that she didn't know about it, but she had an older sister nearby, and perhaps she would know the place.

—Oh, if I only were to find that old woman.

The old woman said:

—You will find her indeed, since I shall give you a ball of yarn. Set it so it will roll. And you, you shall run quickly behind it. It will certainly roll to the right place.

The boy took the ball of yarn and set it off rolling. And it went to the house of the second old woman. He went to the old woman's house, and explained why he was there: he could not find the house of his fiancée. The old woman said that she didn't know, but she had a sister who was still older. She might know something about it, should he ask her.

—I would like to ask, but I don't know how to find her.

The old woman said:

—I will give you a ball of yarn. Set it to roll. And run along with it quickly.

The boy took the ball of yarn and set it off rolling. It rolled so quickly that he could barely keep it in sight. And so, he came to the home of a third old woman of Kieddikeäč, and he explained that he had a fiancée and a house but couldn't locate them. The old woman said:

—I indeed might know, but you're not going to be able to get there, since it's far away, across the unfrozen sea.

—I certainly need to go there.

The old woman said:

—Since you're serious about going, then I will give you some advice and help you get there.

And she gave the boy a horse, a walking stick, and a hat, and she advised:

—When you come to the sea, hit the sea with this stick, so that the sea divides in two. And when you put this hat on your head, then no one will be able to see you.

The boy took the horse, the walking stick, and the hat, and he set off driving and came to the shore of the unfrozen sea. He took the stick and hit the sea. It parted into two and the horse walked with dry legs through the bottom of the sea, and he came to the home of his fiancée. He put the hat on his head, so that he couldn't be seen. He tied up his horse on the shore, and the horse said:

—You must not spend too much time at your fiancée's cottage.

The fiancée was at the well drawing water. Along with her there was a boy, who had been conceived earlier, when the poor boy had found that cottage with the girl sleeping inside. The boy came up next to them and peeked into the well. The child saw his father's shadow there in the water and said to his mother:

—Mother, mother, look! Father is there!

The mother said:

—I don't think you are seeing your father now. Your father is far away, and you will never see him. Not ever.

But the child said again:

—Father's there, father is there!

The girl went to the cottage and her fiancée went as well, but the girl didn't see him since he had that hat on his head.

He took the hat from his head and then the girl could see him. And the boy remembered his horse and thought he should go to it, but the girl took his hand and held him there tight, because he thought that the boy again wanted to leave. He said that he wouldn't be going anywhere far.

He went to his horse, which was upset, since it had been left there for so long. It said to the man:

—Strike me through with your walking stick!

The man barely had the heart to strike his draught horse, since it had brought him so carefully across the sea, but the horse grew even more firm in its demands:

—Strike me now!

The man had to strike it, and the horse was split right in two. The two halves were flung into the air and flew back across the sea. And so the poor boy found his fiancée, and they still remain there to this day.

Acorn Finding[3]
Iisakki Mannermaa (A. V. Koskimies)
ATU 676

There was once a man with a young boy, who often walked in the forest and looked for buried treasure, for he had heard in fairy tales that such things exist in this world. With this mind, he wandered the forest. The father and mother often asked:

—What do you expect to come of it, when you're walking in the forest and you never bring anything home, not a single bird, nor a fox, nor other forest game, even though you're walking with your rifle?

The boy said to his parents:

—Well, it's pleasant to walk in the forest.

Some time later, the boy again set off to walk in the forest. He walked there as he pleased, as he did before, like a person who had lost something and was looking for it. Suddenly, he noticed that when he looked at this one large rock

---

3. According to Laitinen, in 1834 the Oulun Viikkosanomat newspaper had a translation of the *Arabian Nights* story "Ali-Baba and the Forty Robbers," in which the word *sesame* was translated as "acorn." Apparently this story was spread into Lapland through the printed word but still underwent a number of changes.

from afar, it appeared as if it was a kind of door. The boy looked at the big rock and thought to himself:

—Indeed this is a peculiar stone. Surely, this could be the buried treasure I've been looking for, since I see a stone door before my eyes.

But no keyhole was to be found. The boy thought to himself:

—This is indeed a tricky stone.

He left his knife next to the treasure cache, under some peat, and returned to his home. The boy's father said:

—And you didn't bring home even a single bird!

The boy said to his father:

—I wasn't able to get any birds today, but perhaps tomorrow I will catch a few.

When the following morning came, the boy again went to search for his treasure, and he thought to himself as he walked:

—I wonder if I will even be able to find that place again.

Yet he found it nonetheless, and he tried to move the door, but it didn't open, since the door was quite tight. The boy went next to some large stone and sat there watching, thinking that perhaps he would see or hear some kind of miracle. Suddenly the boy heard a voice coming from the treasure cache, saying:

—Acorn open!

The boy didn't dare to move from his place until it got dark. He rose from his spot next to the stone to stand, and he went next to that large stone where he thought there was buried treasure. The boy said:

—Acorn open!

The stone door opened suddenly. The boy walked inside, saw a great sum of money, but got terribly frightened when the door boomed shut, just as it had shut before. Standing in the darkness, the boy thought:

—I wonder what I should do now. It's not too pleasant to be inside a large stone all alone.

The boy filled up the folds in his clothing with money. The thought came to mind:

—I wonder if I can get out with the same words as I got in with.

The boy yelled:

—Acorn open!

The stone door opened. The boy went hurriedly out and when he got outside, the stone door banged shut. The boy returned home, even though it was already dark, and he rejoiced that he had so much gold and silver. He came home and said to his father and mother:

—Now I've got some birds from the forest.

The father said to the boy:

—Sure you've brought some birds back. Just like before.

The boy didn't say anything about what he had found in the forest. He hid the money in a chest, unbeknownst to his father and mother. He didn't tell anybody about the money, but he was happy and he married a woman, and they lived a prosperous life.

Whenever their money was running short, he would walk to the buried treasure. With the same words the boy would open and close the chamber, as he wished. He never squandered his money. He saved it. For that reason other people didn't come to know about the hidden treasure before he became an old man, and he told his best friends about it.

Endless Discontent
Iisakki Mannermaa (A. V. Koskimies)
ATU 555

There was a man who lived near the sea shore and lived in poverty. The man was satisfied: even if he didn't have any wealth, he had his daily bread, and even though it wasn't always abundant, he could still more or less get by.

His wife was of a different mind. All this upset her and ate away at her every day, since there wasn't much food, few possessions, and no nice clothes that she saw other people wearing. Once, when she was upset and agonizing over this, she walked to the sea shore. She sat on a large stone and, just for fun, watched the large waves rolling against the cliffs of the shoreline.

Suddenly a black cloud began to rise. Thunder rumbled in the cloud, and lightning flashed here and there. She could hear heavy rain pouring, and a strong wind howling. It wasn't fun any longer for the wife to watch the great waves of the sea. She tried to get down from the rock, but suddenly she heard a voice from the great sea waves, which said:

—Wife, wife, what good you want in this world for yourself or for your husband, so it will come to pass. All you or your husband need to do in your request is to yell out from the same stone you're sitting on now. And always say it like this: By the great sea's waves, by the sea's depths, and by the sea's limitless expanses, I want this or that.

The wife said quickly:

—I already indeed want, by the great sea's waves, by the sea's depths, and by the sea's limitless expanses, to be the farmwife on a wealthy estate.

The woman didn't hear anything anymore from the waters. She went back home, which wasn't far from the sea shore. When the wife began to get near her home, she noticed that the cottages looked better than ever before. She went inside a cottage. Her husband was there in good clothes, and there were many clothes that were quite suitable for the wife. The husband said to his wife:

—I can't begin to imagine or believe how we suddenly became so rich.

The wife said to her husband:

—Yes, it seems strange to me too, but you will come to know later. It's nice to live like this nonetheless.

But the wife was still tempted by the idea that life could be even better than it was now. She went again to the sea shore and went to the stone, where she had before seen the great waves of the sea. The woman yelled:

—By the great sea's waves, by the sea's depths, and by the sea's limitless expanses, I wish that my husband would be a merchant and I a merchant's wife!

No voice came from the sea at all, though the wife carefully listened. She climbed again down from the stone, and returned home. As she came closer, the wife noticed that the cottages were still better and more in number than before. She saw her husband outside already wearing fine clothing. The cottages were many more and their possessions were many in each cottage, and of all sorts. The wife was happy and rejoiced that she got to be the wife of such a wealthy man. The wife said to her husband:

—Already our life has changed, and our poverty ended! This is the life!

The husband, who wondered if these gifts were blessings from God at all, said to his wife:

—Yes, this is the life. But are we satisfied with these riches?

For the husband knew that his wife was not a good person, and that nothing would satisfy her.

Some months later the wife walked again to the sea shore and went again to the same large stone, where she had been before. She yelled:

By the great sea's waves, by the sea's depths, and by the sea's limitless expanses, I wish that my husband were a king and I a queen!

No voice was heard from the sea, as before, even though the wife listened carefully. She climbed down from the stone to the ground, and set off back to her home. When she approached her home, she could see golden rooms shimmering from afar, great big windows, and large and beautiful doors. Ornamented horses were visible and also many people, soldiers and generals. The wife was surprised a little at first and thought to herself:

—I wonder if I dare go into those kinds of beautiful buildings at all.

The wife stood and thought:

—Since I have asked to be a queen, I will go inside.

And she went quickly to walk inside some cottage and noticed her husband there, a king. Great lords were surrounding her husband. Suddenly the wife noticed that that she was already a queen herself. The husband said to his wife:

—Perhaps now you're satisfied?

—There is no better life that this in this world, I suppose!

The husband, who didn't really believe this was a blessing from God, that which came about so suddenly, said to his wife:

—I wonder if now you're yet satisfied with your life.

After a few months, the queen set off for the sea shore, where she had gotten her luck before. She went to that stone and yelled:

—By the great sea's waves, by the sea's depths, and by the sea's limitless expanses, I wish I were God!

Then she heard from the water a voice, which yelled powerfully:

—Oh dear, you wife!

And the sea water divided and the water started to roll toward her, and it sounded like an earthquake. The wife was so scared that she started to tremble. And the wife's clothes changed suddenly into poor clothes. She set off to return, and when she came to her home, the rooms were gone. Only one small cottage remained, just as it was before when they lived in poverty. The wife came crying to her husband, who also had on poor clothes. The man said to his wife:

—What more did you want? Are you now satisfied with your life? You should be ashamed.

And so they lived in poverty to their dying day.

The Reindeer Calf's Hooves
Juho Petteri Lusmaniemi (A. V. Koskimies)
ATU 750A

There were once two brothers, one was quite poor, one quite rich. The poor one set off to beg at his brother's house. He didn't get anything. He was heading back, and he came across a man with four reindeer calf hooves in his hand. The man asked:

—Where are you off to?

—Just wandering. I went to my brother's house begging, but I didn't get anything there.

The man said:

Take these reindeer calf hooves. Put them on a table and think of what you would like. You will receive it.

The man did just that and he thought to himself:

—The best estate of them all.

So it came to be. One reindeer hoof disappeared. The man thought:
—If only I could have caretakers for this estate.
This too came to pass. A second hoof disappeared. He thought:
—If only I had all kinds of cattle.
This too came to pass. The third hoof disappeared. He thought:
—If only I had caretakers for these cattle.
This too came to pass. The fourth hoof disappeared.
The rich brother saw his riches and started to ask:
—Where did you get this kind of wealth?

The man said that when returning from his trip to see his brother, he came across a strange man, who had four reindeer calf hooves in his hand.

—He gave them to me and told me to put them on a table and think of whatever I wanted. I did just that, and then everything I wished came true.

The rich brother said that perhaps he too could find that man.

—You can find him, sure. When you visit me and set off back home, then he will come to meet you.

So the rich man went to his brother's house and went back. He came across the man, with four reindeer calf hooves in his hand. He said:

—Perhaps you'd like to give those to me?

—Sure, you can have them. Put them on a table and think of what you want, and you shall receive it.

He took and put them on a table and went outside to consider what he should think of, but he couldn't think of anything, since he already had everything he could possibly want. Meanwhile when he was outside, his wife thought:

—If only these cottages would just topple over!

Then the cottages toppled over, and one of the reindeer calf hooves disappeared. She thought:

—If only they would come to be as they were before.

The cottages returned to their original state. A second hoof disappeared. The husband came into the cottage, saw two hooves missing and said to his wife:

—Where have they gone?

The wife said that she thought that if only the cottages would topple, and then one of the hooves disappeared, and the cottages toppled.

—Then I needed to think if only they would return to how they were supposed to be. And they righted themselves and another hoof disappeared.

Well, the man got angry and thought:

—If only that hoof would fly up your ass!

Then the hoof flew up the wife's ass. She became distressed: no one could get the hoof out of there. They hired doctors and others, but no one could free the hoof. Then the man came to realize that there was still one hoof left, and he thought:

—If only that hoof would leave my wife's ass!

Then the two remaining hooves disappeared.

Mattias the Fearless and the Devil & Mattias the Fearless[4]
Juho Petteri Lusmaniemi (A. V. Koskimies)
ATU 1160; ATU 1115

There was once a cottage built for travelers on a country road. A devil lived there, and it didn't let any people get close to that cottage. Some tried to spend the night in that cottage to win bets, thinking they would be fine, but they all lost and lost the money they bet. There was even a pastor who struck up a bet and went to that cottage, but even he didn't make it.

There was one man, named Mattias the Fearless, and he had never felt fear. He went on a bet to spend a night in that cottage. He was there in the cottage, and night came. And so the old devil came and said to the man:

—Why have you come to my cottage?

The man answered:

—I might spend the night here, as you seem to be able to.

The devil said:

—Don't you fear me?

The man said:

—No. Come sit on my lap.

The devil came and settled into the man's lap. The man started to stroke the devil's beard and said:

—This is a nice beard, but it isn't really handsome yet. I know how to pretty it up tonight, so it'll be quite striking.

When the devil heard this, he was pleased with the thought, and he told the man to make his beard beautiful. The man had a large pine log in the cottage, and he split just its end and struck a wedge just into the end of the log. He said to the devil:

---

4. Itkonen divides this single tale into two separate stories, and Laitinen further separates the halves into two sections: the first section in "Humorous Stories and Anecdotes," the latter in "Fairy Tales." I have rejoined the two sections into a single tale to better reflect the original collected material.

Fairy Tales

—If you plan to make your beard look nice, just put your beard into the gap in the log. I will put wax in the gap, so the wax will stick better.

The devil did so, and he put his beard into the gap of the log. The man knocked the wedge out, and the devils beard was stuck, so that he couldn't get out of the log no matter how he tried.

The man went to the bed and slept the night there, until the day came. In the morning the devil began to implore:

—Can't you get me out of here? I can't stand this any longer.

The man said that he wouldn't be freed until the devil gave him a lot of money, since he has been bullying travelers in this cottage. The devil said that he would no longer harass any more people and that he would give the man as much money as he wanted. The man dared to free him, since it was already daytime, and he knew that the devil wouldn't dare do any more bad. He hit the wedge back into the end of the log, and that's how the devil got out.

He asked:

—How much money do you want, when you leave?

—Well, give me a pack-load of money.

And the devil brought to the man three loads of money before he left.

In the morning the bet-strikers came to see if the man was alive. He wasn't even shaken, and he had so much money that everyone took a load when they left the cottage. He also got the money from the wager. From that day onward, the devil has stayed away from that place.

Mattias the Fearless went to the city, and in the city naturally everyone had heard of the man, who had gotten so much money. There were some of the king's aldermen, who were corrupt and who had deceit in mind. He met them someplace in the city. The lords asked:

—What kind of a man are you?

He said he was Mattias the Fearless and had never before felt fear. The lords said:

—Come with us to our residence to drink. We have a name day to celebrate today.

The man said:

—Okay. Sure.

They went to the lords' residence, and they readied the drinking party. They drank and ate the whole day. The lords wanted him to stay for the night, and the man agreed. It became time to sleep. The lords gave him an elegant room. There were two beds, and one was full and the other empty for him. He was given that bed as a place to sleep.

He lay down to sleep in the bed and noticed that a spearhead had been propped up through the ceiling, just above him. He understood that this wasn't a good place to be. He got up and started wondering what he should do. He went to look at the other bed. In that bed, a corpse was under the covers. He took the body and put it in the other bed, where he had first laid down to sleep. And he then went to the other bed where the body had been. After a few moments, the spear came through the ceiling and slammed into the corpse. Morning came, and the same lords came in. They brought some young lady, hung her from the ceiling, and left again.[5]

The man began to wonder what he should do. Then the lords' servant girl came into the room, and he needed to rise from his bed. He asked:

—Where are the lords now?

The servant said:

—They went to the king for a drinking party.

He said to the servant:

—Could you help get me out of here? I will give you as much money as you want.

The servant said:

—I don't want money, but if you promise to take me as your wife, then I will get you out, for I too want to leave this place.

The man promised to take her as his wife, and he left. He went to the king's consultation room, and even though he wasn't able to get inside, they said:

—Please state your business.

The man said that he had an important matter to discuss. So he got inside. The king rose right away to ask what the man's business was. The man explained how last night had played out. The king asked:

—Do you know these lords?

The man said that yes, he knew them. And so he showed him that those lords were right over there.

The king imprisoned the man and the two lords that he indicated, and set off to look at the sleeping chambers. And there was the proof that what the man

---

5. The hanging of the woman is most likely a plot device used here to characterize the lords in the story as wicked and brutal people.

said had been true. The man was released, and the lords were kept in prison for the rest of their lives.

The Man Who Lashed His Fortune[6]
Paavali Valle (A. V. Koskimies)

There were some men from Syenjilsīida (Suonikylä) Village[7] in the forest near the city of Guáláduv (Kuola) cutting some wood they needed, and they were spending the night there. There was one poor man, who was also in their company cutting. When he was sleeping at night he began to dream that the others had already woken and went off to start cutting. He became anxious and snatched his axe and went to walk to the place where the others had gone. And when he came to them, he didn't know any one of those axmen. And he asked one:
—Who are you?
He said:
—I am that man's fortune.
He went to another and asked:
—Who are you?
He said:
—I am this or that man's fortune.
And thus, whomever he asked:
—Who are you?
So he too said:
—I am this or that man's fortune.
And he knew those men, whose fortune they said they themselves were. Finally he asked:
—Where is my fortune?
Somebody showed him: It's sleeping over there. He took a great piece of wood and went to the place of the sleeping man. He hit him and said:
—And you're sleeping while the others are doing work!

---

6. The Aanaar Sámi used here is *oasi*, and Itkonen translated it to Finnish as *onni*. Both words have a number of overlapping meanings—including luck, fortune, fate, portion, and lot in life—that suggest a connection between good fortune and prosperity. Here I have chosen to use the word "fortune," as it ambiguously implies both good or bad luck, as well as material prosperity.

7. Syenjilsīida is a Skolt Sámi community.

So he jumped up, started to blubber, and promised:
—Don't hit me. I'm getting up and starting to live.
After that the man's fortunes began to come to life and he became wealthy.

The Story of Three Girls[8]
Iisakki Mannermaa (A. V. Koskimies)
ATU 510

There were three girls living in the same house. Of the siblings, two girls set off to be servants to the king, but the third sibling wasn't taken on, even though that's what she wanted. But she still set off after her sisters. She left walking alone, following the tracks of her sisters. Then along came a cow up to those two girls and said:
—Milk me!
They said:
—We don't have time.
The cow came to the third girl and said:
—Milk me!
She said:
—Sure, I'll milk you. I have time to do so.
And she milked and the cow told her to drink the milk as payment. And she drank and again left walking after her sisters. And when those two girls were walking, along came a lamb and said:
—Sheer me!
They said:
—We don't have time.
The lamb came to the one girl and said:
—Sheer me! You'll get wool as your payment.
And she sheered the lamb and took the wool as payment.
Then along came an old man. He met the two girls and told them to kill his head lice. The girls said:
—We don't have time.
The old man went to the third girl, who was alone, and said:
—Kill the lice on my head.

---

8. This story is an Aanaar Sámi version of Cinderella. Note the older sisters, the poor dress, the catching of the prince's eye, and the matching of lost footwear to its owner.

And when the girl completed this task, the old man said to her:

—I don't have any payment to give, but I will tell you something: When you come to your workplace, you will be set to work as a shepherd in a flock of sheep. You need to search for a bird's wings under a particular stone. After you find them and then wake the following morning, take the wings and swipe them against the table and say: "Let my work be done!"

So they parted. The two girls came first to the place of service. They were put into roles as chamber servants, since they were very beautiful. The third girl came, and she was put, just as the old man said, as a shepherd. Everyone went to the church, but they left the lesser girl at home. But when the girl saw that people were going to church, she retrieved the bird's wings and said:

—Let my work be done!

And she went to church in her poor clothes, and the same she did even a second time, except with nicer clothes. When she came to the church the second time, the king's son noticed her and thought that he knew her, but he didn't know from where. When she came to church for a third time, the king's son recognized her, but didn't yet really know from where. And the girl was the first one to leave the church, so people wouldn't see her. When the girl set off, the king's son set off behind her. The girl noticed him coming closer, took off her shoes, and threw them. The boy lingered there a bit, but then began to catch up to her again. The girl threw her stockings, and when the boy still got nearer, she threw her ring. The king's son gathered it all up.

The next day, he called his servants to him and said:

—Whose shoes, stockings, and ring are these?

The two chamber maids tried them on their legs and said:

—They aren't ours.

And the poor servant girl came, and when she tried them on she said:

—These are mine.

So the king's son married that poor, sly shepherd girl and those two beautiful girls were left behind.

SHORT TALES

The following tales were separated from other folktales by Lea Laitinen in the 1978 version and labeled under the generic heading of short tales. Although these fictive tales often involve kings and riches, disguise and concealed identity, they do not bear the same emphasis on magic that is common in what is commonly referred to as fairy tales, nor the same common plot formulas that help define the genre. The tales also exhibit a great deal more humor, sexual overtones, and darker themes, like adultery ("A Merchant"), illegitimate children ("The Resourceful Boy"), and infanticide ("God's Miracles"). Interestingly, most of these tales were told by Iisakki Mannermaa, and a number of these tales also have morally upstanding overtones in their conclusions, where young poor boys are educated, and men quickly forgive their wives for adultery and infanticide—likely reflective of Mannermaa's status in the community as an educator and moral instructor of young people.

Stories do not always neatly conform to the prescribed boundaries that folklorists were once interested in categorizing them into. "Meniš-Antti's Life Story" defies all sorts of conventions. Told as a first-person narration, which could only be mistaken as truthful by the most gullible, the story itself is a bawdy tale involving Meniš-Antti's supposed trip to France, where he sneaks into the room of a princess, tricks her into sexual relations, gives her lice, gets her drunk, extorts her to hide their relations, and abandons the child after impregnating her.

While it would be easy to condemn such a tale on moral grounds, these kinds of trickster tales generally play a fairly complicated and sophisticated role in the community. On a personal level, joking about and mock-celebrating bad behavior helps people laugh at and forgive their own mistakes, and provides relief for the tensions between one's own selfish desires and the need to maintain a functional community by not always acting on them. Further, transgressive behavior (or stories of fictional transgression) test the boundaries within the social order that force a reevaluation of the legitimacy of our shared values, customs, and hierarchies. Sometimes this works to conserve existing values, sometimes to undermine them. For instance, Antti Kitti invokes the reprehensibility of his actions for conservative effect (the behavior is humorous only because the story is clearly coded as fiction and so absurdly transgressive) but at the same time deploys these episodes strategically to levy critique about class hierarchies in Europe through a fictional inversion of power (i.e., "if only we got to treat them like they already treat us"). Humor, boundary-testing, and transgressive discourses are important human social behaviors that exist within distinct spaces and contexts in which certain people are permitted to play the role of joker—within unspoken but acceptable limits negotiated by audience and prankster. The value and importance of these complicated interactions are sometimes underappreciated in our world today, if not largely unwelcome within a variety of more regimented and moralistic communities.

The Resourceful Boy
Iisakki Mannermaa (A. V. Koskimies)
ATU 921

There was once a king who set off driving to some city. On a point along the road there was a small house. The king stopped his draught horse next to the house and said to his servants:

—I shall stop here in this small cottage.

As he approached the cottage, the king looked around, but there was not a single person outdoors. The king went inside with a servant in tow. A young boy was alone in the cottage. The king, who noticed at first glance that he was brave, asked him:

—Where is your father?

The boy answered:

—My father is patching the land with trees.

—Where is your mother?

—My mother is getting much from little.

The king asked:

—Do you have brothers or sisters?

The boy answered:

—I have one brother and one sister.

The king asked:

—Where is your brother?

The boy answered:

—My brother is in the forest hunting. He kills everything he sees. What he doesn't see, he brings them home alive.

The king asked the boy:

—Where is your sister?

The boy answered:

—My sister is in the sauna paying for last year's laughter.

The king said to the boy:

—You need to explain to me what you're saying. How is your father patching the land with trees?

—He is pounding in fence stakes.

—How is your mother making much from little?

—My mother is planting turnips.

—How is your brother able to kill everything he sees in the forest and taking that which he doesn't see home?

—My brother is killing fleas.

—How is your sister paying for last year's laughter?

—She is in the sauna, on her childbed, with baby conceived illegitimately.[1]

The king said to the boy:

—You need to call your father and mother to speak with me.

—The king left the cottage with the servants. The boy went quickly to his parents and said to his father:

—Some strangers came to our home and want to speak with you.

The master of the house went quickly to talk to the guests. The boy told his mother the same thing he told his father. They went together with their mother to the house where the important guests were.

Outside the king spoke to the boy's parents, and he said:

—Because I've noticed that your boy will become a wise man, I intend to take him with me, for you aren't able to pay for his education.

The boy's father and mother, and the boy himself, were happy about this. The king took the boy along with him and put him in school. The boy had great ability for learning and a good memory, and the king put him in school after school. The schoolmasters lauded the boy for his learning and honorable behavior. And that boy became a gentleman of the king's court.

---

1. Literally translated: "She is in her childbed in the sauna because of whorishness." I've softened the sexist language yet tried to keep reproachful and sexist overtones to reflect the word's connotations in the late nineteenth century.

The King and the Bank Thief
Iisakki Mannermaa (A. V. Koskimies)
ATU 921

Long ago there was a king who heard mixed sentiments about his kingdom. He went out traveling with a poor man's draught horse, and in poor man's clothes, in poor man's shoes, and in the manner of a poor man. He came to some house and asked the husband and wife of the house:

—Would you be able to tell me anything about what people say about the king and his rule?

The husband said to the poor man, whom he didn't know was the king:

—I have heard from people that the money from the crown's treasury is diminishing, and no one knows where it's going.

The poor guest said:

—Can you tell me anything more about this?

The husband answered his guest:

—I don't know anything more about the matter.

The guest asked the wife:

—Aren't you, wife, able to tell me something about this?

The wife said:

—No. What my husband told you, I've heard the same.

The poor stranger went back home, and no one recognized him as a king.

After a while, the king adorned himself again in the same poor clothes, which he was wearing before as a stranger. And he walked around his chambers at night and stood and listened, to see if any sounds could be heard, and if he could notice anything unusual. Suddenly the king noticed a person standing behind one chamber. The king went to talk with him. The person tried to flee, but the king said:

—Don't fear me.

When the person saw that his confronter wasn't one of the noblemen, he came boldly to the king's side.

That person was a young boy, the child of poor parents. The king thought to himself:

—Perhaps this is the boy who has been visiting my vault?

For this reason, he said to the boy:

—Do you know, my boy, a way we can get into the crown vault?

The boy said to the king:

—Yes, perhaps I would know a way, if I were a great thief.

The king guessed right away from the boy's words that he might already have found the bank thief. He said to the boy:

—I too am a thief. That's why I'm now out at night as well.

When the boy heard that this strange man was of the same intentions as himself, he said boldly:

—I have lockpicks.

When the king realized that he had found his bank thief, he said to the boy:

—Let's go test the crown vault door and see if we can get it open.

And so they left to walk to the treasury's door, and they came to the outside of the door. The king said to the boy:

—Now, try the picks. Let's see if you can get into the room.

The boy pushed his lockpick into the keyhole and opened the door. The king went into the room and the boy as well. There was a lot of money in there, strewn about the room. The king said to the boy:

—Do you have a sack to scoop the money into?

The boy said:

—I have a small sack on me.

The king said to the boy:

—Hold the sack mouth open, and I'll pour it in.

The king dug up a shovel full of silver into the sack. The boy shut the mouth of the sack he was holding. The king said:

—Well, why did you shut the mouth of the sack? I can't scoop any more money into it.

The boy said to the king:

—We must not take any more money.

The king said to the boy:

—We are not going to take so little.

And he began forcefully scooping more money into the sack. When the boy noticed that his partner was violently grabbing at the sack's mouth, he said to the king:

—There are indeed many shareholders in this treasury. I've never taken much, even though I have been here before.

And the boy got mad and hit the king on the ear. The king put up with all this to get to the bottom of the matter. The king said to the boy:

—Well, since it is your wish to no longer take all this money, you can give the money sack to me, and we can get out of here.

They locked the door. The king said to the boy:

—Tomorrow we will divide the money between us.

The boy said to his companion:

—Sounds good.

And so they parted ways. When the following morning came, the king noticed when he watched from his window that same boy whom he talked with the night before. He called for him immediately. One of the king's servants invited the boy quickly inside to speak with the king. The boy was first afraid, but he came to the king nonetheless. The king said:

—I was your companion last night and I promised to share this money with you.

The boy became terribly frightened, and he couldn't get a single word to escape his mouth. The king commanded his servants:

—Seize this boy!

And they captured him and took him on the command of the king to a dark room, which was underground and used for prisoners. That boy thief was held there on the king's command for a month. After that the king again called the prisoner to talk with him, and he said to him:

—Now you are released from your imprisonment, and I will now send you to school.

And the servants did for the imprisoned boy what that king said. They set him free and sent him to school.

He was brought from school to school, and the schoolmasters noticed that he had a great capacity to learn. And the king put the boy into colleges and military academies. And all of these schools gave him good marks. When the king saw that the boy had such learning abilities and that he had behaved so honorably, he called the boy to him. According to the king's command, the boy wore his formal clothes according to his rank. He said to the boy:

—Because I have heard good evaluations of you, that you are learned and you conduct yourself with honor, I will make you the highest lord in my kingdom.

A Merchant
Iisakki Mannermaa (A. V. Koskimies)
ATU 974

Long ago there was a merchant who became rich from his trade and went to foreign lands to procure some goods. He said to his wife:

—If I am away on my trip for longer than a year or two, then in the cellar of our cottage there is a barrel with arctic raspberries in it, and there's another barrel of berries tipped over onto the cellar floor. These raspberries you cannot touch before I return from my trip!

The wife promised that they wouldn't touch those berries at all, which the husband had prohibited them from touching. The merchant took the gold ring from his hand, broke it, wrote his name on one half, and gave it to his wife, saying:

—This half of the ring you must not lose, no matter how long I am away.

The husband saved the ring's other half for himself, said his goodbyes to his wife and family, and went to his large boat with his other traveling companions. They raised the sail in a good wind and disappeared behind a large peninsula stretching into the sea.

The merchant indeed made it to foreign lands safely, where he traveled[2] from city to city, buying all sorts of goods, and he decided to head home. He didn't get too far, when he had some bad luck. A strong wind kicked up and took their large boat in a direction they didn't want to go. The boat was damaged and started leaking. The people, however, were able to make it to shore without harm. On the land there was a little house. They went to that small house. They were there many days until good weather arrived. When they were ready to leave on their trip, the merchant got sick, and he remained ill in that house for a long time. He did finally become fit enough to travel though, so that they could set off on their trip.

After they set off again on their travels, another great wind suddenly came. This storm took their boat someplace they didn't want to go, toward the open sea. Land was no longer visible in any direction. The wind no longer was so severe, but it became foggy. They weren't able to get anywhere, but drifted for a week wherever the wind blew them. They drifted about until they finally reached land. There was not a single house to be found. They went to the shore and lived there several months. A third year had already come to an end since the merchant left his village.

As the third year was coming to an end, at the merchant's home things were changing. His wife didn't think about the raspberries at all in the beginning, which her husband told her not to touch. For two years, she patiently left them untouched, but finally she thought to herself:

—What if the berries rot!

The wife went with a farmhand to check. She opened the cellar door, peeked inside, and told a farmhand to go to the bottom of the cellar to check on the raspberries. The farmhand said to the wife:

---

2. DuBois (1995) notes that the Sámi verb used here, *juuttalij*, has the connotation of "migration." DuBois reads this as a pejorative comment about the lifestyles of migrating Sámi peoples by Aanaar Sámi who had adopted more stationary agricultural economies.

—Yes, they might be starting to go bad already.

For that reason, the wife told him to bring the raspberries up to eat. The farmhand started to gather the raspberries in a dish and bring them from the cellar, and he suddenly noticed gold and silver coins. He took the berries and came up and didn't say anything to the wife about what he had seen on the floor of the cellar. The wife locked the cellar door and the cottage door and took the keys with her.

Since the farmhand knew what kind of treasure he had found, he started to flirt with the farmwife. The wife chastised him at first for his boldness. The farmhand said to her:

—If you take me as your husband, then I will tell you a secret you don't know, and which will make us much wealthier than you are now.

And the farmhand spoke with the wife about how her husband had been away on his trip already for three years, and not a word had been heard about him, so he was most likely no longer alive. The farmwife said:

—I have already considered as much. I don't know if my husband is still alive, since he has not sent me even one letter.

When the wife heard from her farmhand that he had a secret, she started to ask him:

—Couldn't you tell me your secret, not even if I paid you?

The farmhand said:

—I'm not telling you before I have your promise of marriage. Then I'll tell you.

Well, the wife promised to take the farmhand as her husband and love him just as she loved her former husband. The farmhand no longer delayed, but said to the wife:

—This is the secret I've told you about.

The wife guessed this was why the merchant had forbidden her to touch the raspberries. She said to the farmhand:

—Look at that barrel too, and see if there is any money there.

The farmhand took the berries that were at the opening of the barrels. There too he found gold and silver coins. The wife began to rejoice and said to the farmhand:

—Your secret is really true!

They came up from the cellar. The wife locked the cellar door and the door to their room and went with the farmhand to their living room. They promised to take each other as husband and wife and planned their wedding.

Eventually, the merchant came across a large boat, and on it were people going to his homelands. The merchant's purchased wares had already started to dwindle, so the travelers were able to fit themselves and their goods easily onto the boat. They went together onto the boat, raised the sail, got a tailwind, and sailed quickly and fared well. It wasn't long at all and they came to a village, which was rather close to the merchant's home village. There, the merchant heard about the news from home and told his traveling companions:

—We will leave for my home straightaway!

They left in a hurry and sailed to the other side of the peninsula, where the merchant's home was nearby. They came to land and the merchant said:

—Stay here for a bit, as I quickly visit my home.

They agreed to do so. The merchant set off for his home and took along his worst clothes. He put them on in the forest and went home. When he came and opened the door, he noticed that the cottage was full of people who were all eating and drinking. None of the people recognized him as the merchant and husband any longer. When the wife saw a strange visitor coming in, she thought that it was some poor person, but told him to sit and eat with everyone nonetheless. The husband obeyed the wife's command, even though he could see with his own eyes that this was a wedding, just as he had heard. When the wedding guests finished eating and drinking, they started giving gifts to the couple. The merchant said to his wife, who he realized didn't recognize him in the least:

—Come closer so I can give you a gift.

He grabbed his bag, took the half of the gold ring, and said to his wife:

—Here is a small gift for you.

The wife took the half of the gold ring and looked it over: on it was written her name. She became afraid. The husband told her to get the other half of the ring. The wife brought it, tried to fit them together, and saw that it was the same ring that her husband had divided upon his departure. The wife jumped right away into her husband's arms, and begged his forgiveness for her bad ways and implored:

—You should come into the other cottage!

The husband forgave everything that the wife had done mostly out of thoughtlessness. He rose quickly, took his wife by the hand, and said so that all the guests could hear:

—Now, all of you, who are invited here for a wedding, do notice that God changes matters suddenly, and for him nothing is impossible.

He went into the chamber with his wife, and he asked her the reason why she seduced a spouse for herself, before she had heard any certain information about him. She should have assumed he was alive somewhere in this world, since she had never once heard news of his death. When the wife had told her husband the entire reason why she lapsed in judgment, he called the farmhand, who had seduced his wife, to him. And he said to him:

—Now you shall leave my house. Your faithfulness and honor are at their end. Go now in shame, since you took no shame in lying to my wife!

The farmhand went out and left the estate.

The husband took the keys to the cellar and thought:

—I wonder if I still can find my money.

He opened the door, went inside, and noticed that the raspberries were taken, but a few were still left over. He looked at the uppermost layer of money on the cellar floor, which he had marked. The master noticed that the money was safe, both on the cellar floor and in the barrels. He returned to his cottage and said to his wife:

—It is very good to find my money safe.

He spoke still with his guests about this and that and advised them with God's word and warned them of the deceitfulness of this cunning world. And so they departed. The merchant's farm lived after this in prosperity.

God's Miracles
Iisakki Mannermaa (A. V. Koskimies)
ATU 762

There was once a man who was wealthy, and his son married a wealthy girl, and they lived prosperously. Near their house there also lived some poor people, who often visited the richer houses. Once, when the poor wives gathered at a rich person's house, they spoke with each other about this and that, but the wife of the house was listening, and they started saying it was better to live without children than with children in this world. The farmwife asked why being childless was better. The poor wives said:

—One can't provide for children, when there's nothing to give them for food and clothing.

The wife said:

—You are all stupid wives. Sure one can feed children, even if there are a dozen of them.

The poor wives answered:

—Easy for you to say! You'd have the means to feed children if you have them.

Later that year, when they spoke with each other and went together to the rich man's house, the wife had gotten pregnant. When the time for the birth was getting near, the husband didn't happen to be at home, and the farmwife gave birth to twelve children, who were all extremely tiny. The wife was terribly worried and said to her servant girl:

—Because these little children are so small and they are so many, I order you to carry them into the river.

The servant girl obeyed the command of the farmwife, for she supposed that her own work would increase greatly with the coming of those children. The servant took those little children, twelve in number, and set off to bring them to the river. She met the husband on the way, and he asked the servant:

—What are you transporting in that vessel?

The servant girl became alarmed about the husband's questioning, but answered the truth:

—On the orders of the farmwife, I am taking these twelve little ones, which she bore into the world last night, into the river.

The master wanted to see his children. He took a look and saw that this was the truth. He said to the girl:

—Do not, for God's sake, do this. I will take them, and don't you say a word to my wife.

The servant promised that she wouldn't tell anyone about this matter. The husband took the children and brought them to another home, where the owners received payments to provide for the children. He forbid them to tell anyone about getting payments for the children. And everyone agreed to keep the matter a secret.

The husband went home and found his wife in the childbed. He asked his wife how she was. His wife said:

—I have had a miscarriage, and that's why I'm in the childbed.

The man didn't say anything, since he knew that this wasn't the case.

The wife got better and the little children remained in the people's care for eight years. The wife didn't have any more children during this time. One Sunday the wife left for the village, which she planned to visit. Before the wife returned home, the farm's master took the small children home, all twelve of them, to whom his wife had given birth. He took them to his room and dressed them up sharply, and he told them:

—When your mother comes, six of you stand on each side of the door inside the cottage. When your mother comes inside, the boys will bow and the girls curtsy to her.

When the helpers said the wife was coming, the children gathered up as the father had instructed them in the cottage. The mother went first to the cottage and opened the door, and she noticed the small children, seven or eight years old and well dressed, six on the right and six on the left side of the cottage. And they all rose to stand together; the boys bowed, and the girls curtsied.

The wife took fright: How did those little children find their way to us? Then she asked her husband:

—Where did these children come from to visit us like this?

The husband answered:

—These small ones, which you see now with your own eyes, are our own children, the twelve that you gave birth to and which you sent your servant to carry into the river. Look now, how many people you planned to destroy. But God would not allow it.

The wife fainted and dropped to the floor. The husband became worried that he let his wife know about these matters in an untactful way. He started hurriedly to revive his wife, and other guests, friends of the husband whom the husband had also invited for this, saw what happened. They started also to help the husband revive the farmwife. The wife woke as if from a dream. The husband spoke to the wife in good words and comforted her:

—No bad is to come to you because of this. You did something in haste and thoughtlessly.

The wife took her children, greeted them like strange visitors in all humility, raised them to be God-fearing, loved them with the love of a mother, and counseled them with God's word, for her conscience had awakened.

Meniš-Antti's Life Story
Antti Kitti (A. V. Koskimies)
ATU 856

I was a grown man when mother and father died. I went off to see the world. I walked from farm to farm, from city to city, and I came to France's capital city, Paris, late in the evening.

I was terribly tired. The candles were all extinguished. I walked the city streets. Then I noticed burning candles in one building.

I went there. People were playing music there and dancing. There were a lot of people. I sat on a bench in the doorway. Then in came the king of France's daughter, and some gentleman holding her hand, walking past me. The gentleman asked:

—Do you speak English?

I didn't say anything. The king's daughter said:

—Why did this beggar come here? Yuck. Get out of here!

And she spit in my eye. I didn't say anything, but I heard and understood the French language, what they said. The gentleman said to the king's daughter:

—Since we have played and danced so long, why don't we go to sleep together?

The king's daughter said:

—Why not?

—How do we get there? said the gentleman.

—I will be on the top of the castle, on the fourth floor. When you come, take some dry sand and throw it at the window. When I hear it, I'll open the window. I have made a ladder out of leather and I'll lower it down. Come up in that fashion.

I heard that. So I went there, beneath the castle before the lord got there, and I threw sand up at the window. The king's daughter heard this and lowered the leather ladder, and I went up. The candles weren't burning, and she didn't know me from my voice.

I lay down next to her and kissed her. The king's daughter had a silk shirt on, and I—since I had long been in the same clothes—had large black lice. They began to bite the king's daughter, quite hard. She twisted and scratched herself, not knowing what was nipping at her so painfully. She lit a candle and noticed that the gentleman she spoke with earlier was not in there with her, but rather the beggar who she saw earlier. Oh how horribly angry she became. She took her sword and was ready to strike me.

—It's you who came here! You will be beheaded tomorrow!

I said:

—You yourself told me to come here.

—Get out, said the king's daughter. I didn't tell you to come. Go away right now!

—There's no hurry, I said.

She gave me three thousand dollars,[3] saying:

—Go away, now.

—I'm not leaving. I'm tired. I'll first need to stay a bit.

She gave me cigars and wine, and it went to my head. And the king's daughter drank herself, and she told me to get into her bed. And I kissed her again.

She gave me three thousand dollars more in gold and said:

—Now go away.

—I can't go now. The wine has gone to my head.

The king's daughter gave me another three thousand dollars in gold and said:

—Now go away. Before people get up and realize what we have done.

---

3. Dollar here refers to *riksdaler*, the official currency in Finland up until 1840 and in Sweden-Norway until 1873.

And I left and went to the city. There I bought noble clothes for myself, from head to toe. I was rich. The king's daughter was said to have become pregnant and she now has a child, but I don't know what name she gave the child.

The Poor Boy's Wedding Luck
Iisakki Mannermaa (A. V. Koskimies)

There was once a wealthy man who had only one daughter. Many boys desired to marry her, but she wasn't very available. The girl was honorable. She didn't want to defile herself with anyone. The girl told her father and mother the names of the suitors who pleased her, and told her father:

—You choose, my father, a spouse for me, who I can live in love with in this world.

The father promised to do what the girl wanted. The girl had named as partners for herself both the son of a great lord and the son of a poor man. The father called both to come together to his house. Both came. When they had eaten dinner with their guests, a bed was prepared for both suitors and the girl. The husband ordered his guests to sleep in the prepared place. The father said to his daughter:

—You will sleep between the two, and whoever your eyes are facing in the morning, when I come in to check on you, let him be your husband.

The girl obeyed her father's command and went to sleep between the two young men. The father locked the door, took the key along, and went with his wife to another room to sleep.

When they slept at night the poor boy woke, noticed that the girl had turned her face, and glanced toward the rich boy's side of the bed. He thought to himself:

—I won't be able to get this rich man's daughter for my spouse.

But he thought nonetheless:

—If God wants us to get married, then nothing indeed will prevent it from happening.

The boy was thinking this as he was pulled into a dream. In his dream the poor boy saw the rich man's daughter as his spouse, who slept next to him. He woke suddenly from his dream and was happy about the good dream, but it was already getting toward dawn. It started to brighten, and the boy assumed that soon the father would come to check on them. The poor boy got up but didn't leave, since the door was locked. He went to the fireplace and then returned to bed.

The rich boy heard how the boy walked to the hearth. He said to the poor boy:

—What were you doing, going to the fireplace?

The poor boy said:

—I went to the fireplace to do my business, since I can't get out. The door is locked.

The rich boy said:

—I need to go outside too. Maybe I should use the fireplace?

He got up and went to the fireplace and did his business. When he was leaving the fireplace, he dirtied his hand and went to his spot in the bed next to his fiancée, who had already fixed her gaze toward his side. But when a bad smell came to the girl's nose from the rich boy's side, the girl turned toward the poor boy, eye to eye. He had a bit of cheese that he started to chew on, and he gave a small bit to the fiancée as well, just as he had dreamed that night in his dream.

When they were nibbling on that piece of cheese, the girl's father suddenly opened the door, stepped inside, saw the guests and the girl in the bed, and noticed right away that the poor boy and his daughter were facing each other, and eating a piece of cheese. The girl's father said:

—You, the son of the poor man, will get my daughter as your wife.

And he told them to get up and come together hand in hand to his cottage. To the rich boy, the father said:

—God didn't grant you my daughter as your wife. He prevented it, and his will be done. But come nonetheless as a guest to my cottage.

Both visitors and the girl got up; the poor boy took his fiancée by the hand and they stepped side by side into the father's cottage. When they came in, the father had already prepared food and drink. He told them to sit, eat, and drink. And the father was very happy with his son-in-law. He blessed the young pair in God's name. And they live well in this world, even after the death of the father and mother. God's blessings were in their home.

HUMOROUS STORIES AND ANECDOTES

The following stories are an assortment of fictional and realistic stories, most of which involve laughing at extreme stupidity, foolishness, and laziness. Many of these tales use humor to normalize social behaviors: by laughing at one individual's laziness, it encourages other people to be industrious. In many traditional cultures, including Sámi culture, stories are often used in place of direct instruction to educate and shape social behaviors. Telling another person how to behave or how to feel is a bit presumptuous, but sharing a timely story—whether serious or comedic—allows listeners to draw their own diverse conclusions in a nonconfrontational way.

Some of these tales are known as "numskull tales," involving characters who fail to grasp even the most basic skills necessary to care for oneself. In "The Travels of the Čuđit," an interesting story that blends historical Čuđit legends about foreign marauding parties with numskull tales, the usually fearsome Čuđit cannot, for instance, recall whether or not one of their hunters indeed possessed a head before he stuck it into a bear den. Generally, these numskulls can be easily interchanged, where the fools can be swapped out for any particular group the storyteller cares to make fun of.

Unfortunately, because Koskimies collected mostly from male storytellers, the tales collected here reflect a very male-centered world. We see this reflected, for example, in the sexist tropes of the "stupid wife" tales present in this collection, like "The Wife's Stupidity" and "Shingle-Stick," both collected from Iisakki Mannermaa. These tales play into stereotypes of women's incompetence and desire to gossip, while also rationalizing men manipulating women under threat of violence. While some tales show the stupidity of male characters, they tend to point to community outsiders like Čuđit or Skolt Sámi, or young boys ("Good Day—Axe Handle," "It Is Truly True").

One can only speculate that Aanaar Sámi women likely possessed a full repertoire of tales that reflected their own frustrations with their husbands and the other men in their lives. Although told by a man, Juho Petteri Lusmaniemi, "The Girl and Her Suitor" is one example of a tale that asserts women's autonomy. In this tale a girl rejected for a minor breach of etiquette tricks a suitor to be impressed with her impossible talents and asserts her own independence in a budding relationship. It is unfortunate that these kinds of tales are so underrepresented in this collection, since their exclusion erases an important dimension of feminist history that existed in the Aanaar community in the nineteenth century.

The *Noaidi* Axe
Mikko Aikio, by letter (A. V. Koskimies)
ATU 334

There was once a man who was on a trip hunting wild reindeer. He walked long into lands unknown, and he eventually became lost and didn't know how to get back. He pressed forward, and he walked and walked, but he didn't know which way to go. Finally, he noticed a large cabin. The man's mood improved at the sight of this cabin, since people would help him regain his bearings and get back home. But when he came near the cabin, he noticed to his amazement that it had an iron door, which was larger and uglier than a typical door.

He figured he would go inside nevertheless. When he opened the door, inside there was a one-eyed man, who said:

—Since you opened it, you may as well come inside. Good day, good day, where are you from and where are you going, pray tell?

The man thought and considered carefully what he should say, but he found a way and said:

—I'm walking to the tundra[1] to heal my eye condition.

The old man said:

—Good, good. I too have eye problems. Do heal my eyes as well!

The guest said:

—I can make them better, if you have some tin. Mine has run out, as I have walked so long and done so much healing.

---

1. "Tundra" in the Sámi languages refers to a high hill that is treeless at the top because of the cold. The Sámi word *tuodâr* (North Sámi: *duodar*) is generally considered the only known Sámi word to be borrowed into English, after first being borrowed into Russian. In English, tundra bears slightly different connotations.

The old man said:

—Yes, I have tin.

The guest asked:

—Do you have a melting ladle?

—That too is in the house, nothing's missing, said the old man, and brought the tin and ladle.

The guest melted the tin and told the old man to lie on his back. The old man locked the door and lay down on his back. But the guest was planning to trick the man, and he was worried he wouldn't be able to get out of there. And when he had melted the tin, he poured it into the good eye, and then the old man jumped hurriedly to a stand, screaming. And he said:

—Thank you so much, doctor of good *and* bad eyes. What do you want as your payment?

He took a gold axe from under the bed, threw it onto the floor, and said:

—Take that as well!

The man looked at the gold axe, which shimmered on the floor, and thought that this would be nice to take, but it might be offered not with good intentions—rather bad ones. He decided nonetheless to take the axe and see for himself what sort of thing it was. He touched it with his little finger on his left hand, which immediately stuck to it. The old man began to jump around the cottage in agony from wall to wall and smashed the lock off the door. He said:

—Stop him, gold axe, stop him, wherever you can.

But the gold axe answered:

—I would stop him, yes, but the bond is not firm!

The old man started to approach the man, as the voice told him. The man had no other recourse but to pull his knife from its sheath and strike the little finger so that it sliced the tip off, and he slipped out. And so he left that horrible house and was able to get back to his home after all.

The Travels of the Čuđit[2]
Uula Morottaja (T. I. Itkonen)
ATU 1225; ATU 1260

There once were some Čuđit traveling, and they didn't have any food. They saw a capercaillie set off flying from the branch of a pine. They cut down the pine and bent up the branch so they could fit it in the cauldron. They cooked it

---

2. Itkonen notes, "Known as the 'Fool's Journey,' this story has ended up being about the fall of some oppressors. The story has apparently been influenced by the

and drank the broth. It was a bit thinner soup than they had expected—after all, it was a big capercaillie that had been sitting on that branch they just cooked.

They again set off walking. They found a bear den. They supposed that there was a bear in there. One said:

—I'm going to look. When I start to kick, then pull me out.

When he crawled inside, the bear bit him, right through his neck. Of course, he then started kicking his legs. The others grabbed at his legs, just as they were told. When they pulled him out, the head wasn't to be found anywhere. They started wondering if he had a head when he went inside the den. They were pretty sure that he had some kind of head when he drank up the capercaillie-branch broth the day before, through his red beard with a bent-stemmed ladle.

Still they continued traveling. They found a bubbling spring. They started thinking that if they put some flour in here, they would make some porridge. They wouldn't need to cook it at all. They started to put flour in the spring, but the porridge never thickened up. One thought:

—It must be sticking to the bottom. I'll go check. If I don't come back up, you should come as well.

And so he jumped in. And he didn't come back up at all. The others thought:

—He's spooning it all up for himself and leaving us without any to eat!

And they raced and jumped into the spring, and that's where they still are, eating up their porridge.

The Wife's Stupidity
Iisakki Mannermaa (A. V. Koskimies)
ATU 1381

There was once a young man who always thought to himself:

—I would take a spouse for myself, but there aren't any worthwhile girls.

He did, however, fancy one nice-looking girl, whom he got engaged to and married. Only when they started to live together did the master notice his

---

Kola Sámi variants, in which the travelers are called Čuđit." This tale is a fusion of two very distinct genres: Čuđit tales and numskull tales. Sámi people widely recognize Čuđit tales as historical legends, likely based in the realities of the earliest colonial periods. More conventional Čuđit tales can be found later in this volume, and they involve Sámi people outwitting the violent and cruel marauders. Numskull tales, on the other hand, are humorous and fictional tales that highlight absurd levels of stupidity, often of a neighboring people, as a manner of playful rivalry and teasing.

bride's stupidity, both in her labor and in her speech. The older the wife became, the more foolish she grew.

The husband often went fishing with his wife. And they walked together frequently in the forest as well. Once when they were walking in the forest, they found a buried treasure chest, in which there was a great deal of money. At the time, the husband didn't tell his wife what he found under the peat. Before they set off to return home, the husband threw a knife on top of the treasure. They returned home. The next morning the husband went alone to set the nets in the lake. On his trip, he also checked his trap lines for capercaillie. He checked his traps and got a capercaillie that was caught in his snare. He took the capercaillie along, went to his boat, checked the nets, and got some pike. Then he fastened the capercaillie from the snare to the fishing net. He went again on his rounds and got some male and female capercaillies, which were strangled in his traps. He set the pike he got from his nets into the snares and returned to his home.

The next morning, when the man and his wife woke up, he said to her:
—Let's go check our nets and our capercaillie line.
The wife said:
—Why not?
And they left. After they got to the lakeshore, the man said:
—Check those nets. I'll be at the oars.
The wife said:
—Okay, I'll check.

When they came to the first net and the wife started to check it, there was a capercaillie in the net. She didn't think this was unusual in the least. They went to the land and set off to check the capercaillie line. They came to the first line, and there was a pike in the trap. The wife took the pike out of the trap, not thinking anything of it.

On this trip of theirs, they went to the buried treasure and dug up two loads of silver. The wife asked her husband:
—How is it that this kind of wealth ends up underneath some peat?
The husband said:
—This money we have found is called a buried treasure.

Then they went back, but before they got home, they went past some cottage with their loads of money. Next to the cottage, there were some people outside. They heard a loud noise inside, which prompted the wife to think:
—I should go into the cottage to tell them what we're carrying in our load, but that husband might be beating his wife, since such a loud racket is coming from the cottage.

Nonetheless, she tried to stop at the cottage, but the man said to his wife:
—Don't go. Come with me.
And they went to their own cottage with their loads of money.

The husband hid his money in a locked trunk. When they had eaten dinner, the wife said to her husband:
—I would like to go visit that cottage.

The man said:
—Well, you could go tomorrow too.

He could guess why the wife would want to visit, for his wife really liked to gossip with others about everything she had heard and seen. After the husband forbade his wife from going to visit that day, the wife patiently slept that night in her home, but at daybreak the following morning the wife quickly readied herself and left to visit that other house. After she got there, right away she started saying:
—Me and my husband found a cache of buried treasure.

The house's husband said to his guest:
—You surely aren't serious. You are really a foolish person. Buried treasure is not simply found at the root of every bush.

The guest said:
—It is the truth. We found what we found.

She said further:
—We got a capercaillie from our fishing nets and a pike that we got from our snares.

The house's husband believed her to be lying, and said:
—You've already started to lie.

The guest said:
—True is true. Then we went to your cottage with our loads of money, and you were in your cottage beating your wife.

When the husband of the house heard such lies, he said to his guest:
—You must go, right now! What nonsense you have brought to us.

The guest rose quickly and went out. She was ashamed that no one believed her. She went to her home, told her husband everything the husband of the other house had said to her, and said that he drove her from his cottage. The husband said to his wife:
—From this point on, you no longer may tell anyone anything about these matters, about the things you've seen or heard. Otherwise, if you start to talk to people, then they will eventually start to beat you.

The wife promised her husband that hereafter she wouldn't ever tell the truth to anyone ever again, for she feared that they would beat her.

The husband and wife became rich, and they lived happily their lives through. The wife bettered her ways. Even though she was a foolish person, she never again brought the matter to light. And great fortune was in that house until the end of their lives.

Shingle-Stick
Iisakki Mannermaa (A. V. Koskimies)
ATU 1384

There was once a man whose name was Shingle-Stick. He had gotten his name because as a child he always carved pieces of wood. He was given that name by people who were teasing him. He was the child of poor parents, and after he grew up into a man, he took a woman as a partner and married her.

They built themselves a little cottage, and they lived there in poverty for such a long time that the love between them began to diminish. The wife often blamed her husband for their losses at the market. The man tried in the beginning to avoid the matter with his wife, but when that didn't help, he said to his wife:

—Take this sheep, and go to the merchant's home and make whatever kinds of purchases you would like.

The wife was very happy about this. She took the sheep and set off for the merchant's home. When she got there, the merchant gave her some brandy first. The wife started guzzling, and pretty soon she was drunk. The merchant told the wife to go to the outbuilding to sleep. In the outbuilding there was a tar-barrel, in which the wife got herself dirty. And then in her tipsiness, she fell into some feathers, which were here and there about the room.

When she woke and her head cleared, she noticed that she was in tar and feathers, and they had stuck to her clothes, so that she was like a bird of the sky. She thought to herself:

—I wonder if I'm no longer a human being, and instead a bird?

Still she thought and wondered:

—If the dog barks and the sheep bleats when I come into my cottage, then I am not a person. But if the dog doesn't bark and the sheep doesn't bleat, then I am a human, for that means they know me.

She came into her cottage and the dog barked, and the wife became afraid that she had turned into a bird. She went to the sheep's barn and the sheep began to bleat, which worried her even more that she was no longer human. She climbed onto the roof of the barn. Her husband was in the cottage. When he heard the dog barking, he went out to see what the dog was barking at. He noticed the figure of a person on top of the barn, and he couldn't tell if it was even a person at all. He went back into his cottage, took his rifle and powder horn, and went out quickly, planning to shoot at that oddity on top of the barn roof. But the voice of his wife stopped him from shooting.

—Don't shoot me. I may be some kind of human.

The man said:

—If you might be a human, come down from there right away, and come talk to me.

The wife came down and went to her husband and told everything that had happened to her on her trip to the merchant's. The man chastised her a little bit, how careless she was in the world. The wife admitted that the reason was that she hardly had thought about the sale, and wasn't able to sell even one sheep before she took a drink of brandy.

The man said to his wife:

—I will no longer suffer to see or hear your craziness and wickedness. But if I can find other wives who are just as crazy as you, then I will not divorce you, since it was you I took for my spouse. But if I do not find such wives, then I will need, however, to divorce you.

For that reason that man set off to look for stupid wives. In his travels he came to some cottage and heard a voice from the cottage. The voice sounded like there was a person in terrible distress. He opened the cottage door and stepped in. He noticed that a person stood in the middle of the cottage floor with a shirt pulled on, and the shirt collar without a hole. A woman stood there next to him with a log in her hand, and she whacked her husband in the head with the log. After saying good day, the man said:

—What are you doing, dear wife?

The wife said:

—I am making my husband a neckline for his shirt.

The guest said:

—You are quite the crazy one, you poor woman!

He took the shirt, grabbed a knife, and cut a neckline open and said to the wife:

—You have a strange way of doing this. Don't you know a better way to make clothing for your husband other that this sort of foolishness?

The man thanked his guest for his help, and the guest said goodbye and went out pleased, since he had found one foolish wife, who was just as dimwitted as his own wife.

He started to walk again and went into another cottage and greeted them.

And the wife answered, "God grant it."³ But she was also a fool, since she was carrying sunlight into the room with a sieve. The guest asked:

—Just what are you doing here? I don't understand what will come from this.

The wife said:

—I am carrying daylight into my cottage. But I am not able to get it to work. It's always the same darkness in there as it was before.

The guest realized that the wife was stupid, and he said to her:

—Well, I can tell you a good way how to get light into your cottage without carrying that sieve around.

The wife said:

—That would make you a great visitor! I would always remember you.

The guest said:

—When your husband comes home, you need to tell him to, according to my command, cut a hole into the wall. Then the sun will shine inside without having to burden you.

And the guest said goodbye and went out thinking that he had found a second wife as crazy as his own wife. He went again to walk and came into a third cottage. He said hello. The master said, "God grant it," and then he asked his wife:

—The whole field you sowed?

The wife answered:

—All of it.

The husband said:

—What kind of seed did you sow it with? Wasn't there too little seed?

The wife answered:

—I sowed what seed there was, and for the rest I put in salt.

Then the husband and guest burst into laughter and the guest said to the former:

—Now I have found a third crazy wife, whose stupidity is comparable to my own wife's.

He said goodbye and went out. He set off back home, and when he got to his wife, he said to her this:

—Now I have found that you are not the only foolish wife in the world. Three other wives I found, who were just as foolish and silly as you. After this we can live in love and patience with each other.

---

3. A customary Sámi greeting, said in response to "good day."

The wife answered her husband, saying:

—So we will, my darling, live in this world as long as we are here.

And they lived after that in understanding until their dying days.

The Story of the Girl's Spinning Rack
unknown (A. V. Koskimies)
ATU 1453

There was once a rich girl who was incredibly idle. Along came a suitor. The girl noticed him and she slipped away to spin. The suitor thought that she wasn't so lazy, since she was spinning.

The suitor left and came again after a week. When the girl saw him, she hastened again to spin. The suitor thought:

—How is it that people say she is so idle, and when I come she's always spinning?

He took some keys and put them on top of the end of the spinning rack, so that when the thatch came to an end, the keys would be found.

Then the suitor went away. He again came after a week. When the girl saw him coming, she slipped away again to start spinning. The girl said:

—We lost some keys.

The suitor asked:

—When did they disappear?

The girl said:

—They disappeared the last time you were here.

The fiancé said:

—I do happen to know where the keys are. They are on the end of the spinning rack.

So the suitor saw that the girl was in fact quite lazy, just as people said. So he rejected the girl.

And still now there are some girls like this, who don't work when people aren't around, but when guests come they always run off to spin, so the spinning wheel whirs and the peddle hums. And people always say to these kinds of girls:

—Oh dear, you're just like the girl in that story.

The Girl and Her Suitor
Juho Petteri Lusmaniemi (A. V. Koskimies)
ATU 1456

There was a girl who was trying to find a fiancé, and one suitor indeed came to visit. The girl's mother asked:

—Well, where are the places to sit?
—Well, there's a trunk under my ass.

The suitor rejected the girl, since she didn't know to say "rear end" instead of "ass." He left. The mother advised her daughter:

—When the last suitor comes back this way, take a needle and go place it someplace and start to look for it. And if the suitor comes again and asks what you are looking for, then answer, "Well, a needle."

The suitor came and the girl started to look and he asked:
—What are you looking for?
—Well, a needle.

The suitor said:
—Now, there's a fine task for you to busy yourself with.

The girl snatched up the needle and said:
—I indeed found my needle, but you won't find some kind of girl who doesn't have an ass![4]

When the suitor heard her say he wouldn't find such a fiancée, he took the girl who he formerly rejected.

The Fool's Doorposts
Mikko Aikio, by letter, March 20, 1887 (A. V. Koskimies)

There was once a man during the time of the Great Fear[5] who was called a fool because he was stupid and crazier than other people. The fool wondered what he needed to do to protect himself from the war, when the Čuđit started to come. He made a doorframe for his cottage so loose that it could be pulled out by hand, if there was an emergency or great hurry.

---

4. This line seems to be an assertion of the young woman's independence, suggesting that her suitor's standards are unreasonable, and that she is fully entitled to be her own crass self. Her tricking of the suitor, which seems to be a sign of her cleverness, also contrasts interestingly with the girl in "The Story of the Girl's Spinning Rack," in which it reflects laziness.

5. *Palo äjgin* (*pelon aika*) literally translates as "the time of fear," a rather ambiguous reference. Most likely this refers to a period of time of war between Russia and Sweden, probably in the eighteenth century, when three wars lasted a total of twenty-five years between the two nations, including the Great Wrath (1713–21). However, border wars were common at least since the late fifteenth century. *Palo äjgin* tends to be associated with the time of the Čuđit, conceptually referring to the somewhat distant, but not ancient, historical past.

Eventually, the Čuđit started to come. So the fool ran to hide with others; he grabbed the loose doorframe he made and ran to the forest and climbed up a tree with his doorframe. When the Čuđit followed him and they came to the roots of that pine where the fool was, he dropped his doorframe down and it fell on someone's head. The man died and others fled and went on their way. That's all there is to tell.

Three Lazy People
Mikko Aikio, by letter (A. V. Koskimies)
ATU 1950

Three lazy people once lived in the same cottage. Once they got some wood and each took as much as they could carry and each carried their load to the cottage. Then they stuffed their fireplace full of wood, they lit a fire, and they lay themselves down in their places in the cottage to sleep. The fire started to burn very hot since there was so much wood. One of those three lazy ones said:
—It could be that the cottage will start to burn.
The second said:
—You sure are talkative.
And the third couldn't even manage to open his mouth, instead just saying:
—Hrm.
Two of them ran out and the third burned in there.

Good Day—Axe Handle
unknown (A. V. Koskimies)
ATU 1696; ATU 1698J

There was this house somewhere, where there lived an old wife and her son. And when the old wife went to another house, she told her son to carve an axe handle and she advised her boy:
—If a guest comes along and asks where I am, then you need to say that I'm at another house. And when he asks what you are doing here, then answer that you are carving an axe handle. If again he asks if you have a boat, then tell him that it is old and leaky. And if the guest asks how many sheep you have, just say that there are ten in the pen and twenty in the pasture.
A guest came and said good day.
The boy answered:
—Axe handle! It's an axe handle I'm carving.
—Where is your mother?
—She is old and leaky.

Humorous Stories and Anecdotes

—How old are you?
—Ten in the pen and twenty in the pasture.
The boy didn't even remember the right words that his mother told him to say.

It Is Truly True
Antti Kitti (A. V. Koskimies)
ATU 1696

Some teacher had given a lesson to some boy with these words: *tot lii tuođaj tuota* (it is truly true). When the week was done, the teacher asked:
—Well, perhaps you know those words, which I gave to you as a lesson?
—I know them, yes, said the boy.
—Well, say them, said the teacher.
The boy answered:
—*Tààt lii tout kieta* (this is that hand).
He didn't even remember, even though he had been learning those words for a whole week already.

The Butter Churn
Uula Morottaja (T. I. Itkonen)

The master of some farm started to churn butter, and the churn stunk strongly, and he realized that there must be something wrong. After he finished churning, there was just a huge amount of butter. What the hell? An ermine had crept into there, and the man churned it up. He had drained his butter container and was happy that now the butter was ready. But when he lifted up the plunger, then the ermine came along with it. The man took out the ermine and threw it against the door and threw his butter out as well. He was very upset.

The Wild Reindeer Hunters
Juho Petteri Lusmaniemi (A. V. Koskimies)

Two Skolt Sámi were in the forest hunting wild reindeer in autumn. They were walking along when they saw some wild reindeer. One grabbed the dog between his legs and whispered to his companion:
—Where is the dog's muzzle?[6]

---

6. Lusmaniemi narrates the story in Aanaar Sámi but switches into Skolt Sámi for the dialogue.

—In the bag.
He didn't hear at all, and said:
—Louder! Where is the dog's muzzle?
The other said louder:
—In the bag.
He still didn't hear and blurted out quite loudly:
—Where is the dog's muzzle?
The second also yelled:
—In the bag!
Then the wild reindeer ran off.

BELIEF LEGENDS

Legends are believable narratives that test the boundaries of the unbelievable. Supernatural legends and saints' legends test an audience's belief in an often unseen world; hero legends tell of feats requiring seemingly otherworldly strength or precociousness; and contemporary or urban legends tell of gruesome happenings that we believe exist in the world but have likely not experienced ourselves. Sometimes regarded as stories that are "told as true," legends may or may not have actually happened as recounted. Many folklore scholars feel that fixating on whether a legend "actually happened" is perhaps less interesting to consider than why we tell legends, why we test the boundaries of reality, and how we perform belief and worldview in differing social settings.

Under the wide umbrella of legends there exist a number of subgenres, including supernatural encounters (stories of ghosts, spirits, fairy folk, little people), etiological stories that explain contemporary phenomena (why the bear has a short tail, why the moon turns black), hero or saints' legends that commemorate great feats (St. Patrick, Peeivih-Vuáláppáǯ), and historical legends that recount extraordinary events (see the following chapter for more details). Legends tend to not be firsthand accounts but rather something that happened to "a friend of a friend," and they often invoke historical places and people to help cement their basis as true stories. In this regard they sometimes bear similarities to rumors, whose intrigue is also fueled by their believable unbelievability. Tall tales, on the other hand, offer something of a parody of the genre, in which clearly false stories are told as true, mostly for the amusement of the teller and others already in on the joke.

Many legends operate as a conservative genre, which showcase the dangers of the unknown and try to normalize risky behaviors. In most supernatural legends, people are warned of the danger of supernatural beings, along with the risks of sojourning into the forest or onto the seas in which they reside. (In fairy tales, by contrast, such behaviors lead frequently to great rewards.) In the case of contemporary legends, cautions are levied against teenagers staying out late, going to lover's lane, or experimenting with inebriates, which inevitably lead to visits by escaped serial killers. These kinds of legends generally express our anxieties about the dangers of the world. Some contemporary legends also reflect our anxieties over our estrangement from our food's sources (disturbing substances or rodents purportedly found in fast foods) or fears over not knowing our neighbors (Halloween candy scares, drug-laced children's stickers).

The arrangement of this chapter is somewhat decontextualized from the Sámi understanding of these stories. The *gufihtar*, a benevolent, underground-dwelling, and magical halfling, was absolutely regarded as real and is so related in these stories. The *stállu*, a Sámi-eating troll-like creature, was also considered real, and stories were generally regarded as real events, although some stories told about the *stállu* sometimes take on tale structures that resemble genres better recognized as fiction. Somewhat curious is the inclusion of giant tales in this section. These tales, set in a distant world of kings, have a clear ring of fiction to them that these other legends do not share. Their inclusion suggests more about the difficulties with tale classification than about Sámi concern with giants. Because these subgenres are all quite different, I have added a short summary before each subsection in this chapter.

Etiological Legends

Existing in the gray area between mythological tales and belief legends, etiological legends explain the origin of certain phenomena in our everyday world, many of which may defy easy explanation. The one tale in this short section explains the phases of the moon and hints at a mythic and supernormal past that helped shape cosmic events of our contemporary world. The story of the moon-tarrer is relatively common among other Finno-Ugric peoples as well. This story is also referred to in the proverbs section later in this collection. Originally part of Itkonen's section on mythical beings (like *stállu* and *gufihtar*), Laitinen moved this sole story into a chapter of its own.

Aaččan, Who Tarred the Moon
Mikko Aikio (A. V. Koskimies)

Sámi people say that there was a sort of creature who looks like a human, who moved about in the darkness of night and stole things. But when the moon shone in the night, he got mad at the moon for it, and set off for the moon, taking along a tar barrel with the intention of tarring the moon.

When he got there and intended to tar it up, he took his brush, which was the crown of a tree, and reached his hand up, planning to smudge up the moon with tar; he got stuck there himself with his tar bucket and brush. And even now his image is visible in the moon, and it is still said when the moon starts waning: "Oh, Aaččan in the moon seems to have his heel worn out."[1]

The *Stállu*

The *stállu* is a well-known figure in Sámi legend. Vaguely troll- or ogre-like, the *stállu* is large and powerful, though generally somewhat dim-witted and easily outsmarted by Sámi people. In some stories the *stállu* has mastered magical abilities. The tales here, however, better reflect a different tradition, in which a *stállu* can be created or called to take revenge on one's behalf. The tales generally are violent and sexual, and many involve the destruction of a *stállu*'s penis (e.g., "Version 2," "Andras Pejvi"). Dealing with *stálut* demands exceptional and somewhat shocking violence, particularly considering that Sámi people have long prided themselves as a nonviolent people. Killing without mercy is the best remedy for a *stállu* problem.

The *stálut* like to eat Sámi people, and they sometimes carry sucking straws that they use to drink blood from Sámi people. In particular, they were known to visit at Christmas Eve, the darkest time of year, when extensive precautions were taken to ensure that they would cause no trouble. Wood piles were stacked neatly so loose wood wouldn't snag *stálut* and cause them to linger in the area. Buckets of water were put outside so if a *stállu* was thirsty, it wouldn't seek out human blood. Everyone was expected to be quiet, since the *stálut* were on the prowl. These practices endured into the middle of the twentieth century. Today, however, more pan-European Christmas traditions have taken hold, and the name Stállu simply refers to Santa Claus.

Many *stállu* tales, though none presented here, involve a young *stállu* marrying a Sámi woman, often with implications of abusive behavior or domestic violence. Generally a family will have to rescue the daughter from the dangerous

---

1. This phrase refers to which parts of Aaččan are visible during the early wane of the moon. Aaččan is further referred to in the chapter "Proverbs and Figures of Speech."

relationship. Some Sámi scholars have seen *stállu* tales as reflective of the effects of colonization, where powerful and violent outsiders come into Sámi lands and even marry into Sámi families to disastrous effect.

The *Stállu*, Version 1
Mikko Aikio (A. V. Koskimies)
ATU 1115–44[2]

There was an Aanaar Sámi man who went to fish in the sea. On the trip he came into a disagreement with some Russians and got into a fight with them. The Russians were angry with him, and they sent a *stállu* after him to take revenge on their behalf. They sent this *stállu* to him after he had returned to Aanaar. He was in a birch grove, cutting laths for a *geres*, when he heard a whistle. He stopped cutting, and he saw a person nearby in the grove where he was working. He suspected that it might not be human. The *stállu* came to him and asked:
—Are you the person in this picture?
He started to deny it:
—I am not that person.
The *stállu* said:
—You are the person.
And so he needed to admit to being the person in the picture after all. They made an arrangement and set a time and day, when and where they would wrestle.[3] They then went their separate ways, heading in different directions. As they left that place, the man recited the verses of a hymn:
—If Satan's minions come against me, with your power I will truly defeat them all.[4]
Then he went back home and waited for the time when he and the *stállu* had agreed to wrestle. In the meantime, he occasionally saw and spoke with his wrestling companion, and he heard sometimes a whistle,[5] and he could guess what it was.

---

2. Although *stállu* tales do not neatly conform to specific ATU tale-type numbers, I have hereafter indicated the broader category "Man Kills (Injures) Ogre" (ATU 1115–44) to which these tales best relate.
3. When one fights with a *stállu*, the word "wrestle" is almost always used, indicative of how contest fights were thought of in the 1800s.
4. This devotional hymn is number 317 from the hymnal of 1886.
5. The *stállu* is associated with whistling.

It was autumn, the time when people were moving from their summer places. And when the people from one house had readied their sledges and retrieved their reindeer as well, the man who had the *stállu* called on him disappeared. He had gone to wrestle with the *stállu*, and they wrestled on the shore of a river at the edge of a rapids. And they wrestled with all their might. The man won nonetheless. He killed the *stállu* and pushed him into the rapids. He did the same to the *stállu*'s dog as well, killing it and putting it into the rapids. Then he ran back around the other side of the lake, not the side he came from. And so he came back home.

People thought in former times, and it's still thought today, that there are certain supernatural beings called *stálut*. The *stállu* is a creature that people can make into their servant. People can even make them out of turf and give them life by means of magic. People of other regions aren't able to make these *stállu*, only the Russians.[6] When they happen to get into a disagreement with someone and they fight and lose, then they call a *stállu* and send him to take revenge on the person who defeated them. When someone wanted to send a *stállu* after a person, they made a picture on a piece of paper so that the *stállu* could find that person. He has a dog along on his travels as well, so that if he ends up losing, then the person who sent the *stállu* can receive word and know to create another *stállu*. For that reason the *stállu*'s dog needs to be tied up, so that the person can kill the dog when he has killed the *stállu*. The *stállu*'s dog can come back to life after this, if it is made of turf and buried in the ground, instead of being drowned in water.

The *Stállu*, Version 2
Matti Sarre (A. V. Koskimies)
ATU 1115–44

There once lived an old woman with her son. The son was a man with a rifle, and every day he went hunting. The mother said:

---

6. This is an interesting claim and a sentiment not shared by other Sámi groups. The implication is most likely that Skolt Sámi are the ones with the power to create *stállu*, which is in line with Aanaar Sámi believing the Skolt to be particularly skilled at magic. In general, the east has a mystique about it, where magic is believed to be more powerful and where animals more dangerous and wild.

—Whatever you do, don't go behind Pasevååråå (Pyhävaara; Sacred Mountain),[7] my son.

The boy went to the forest and still went behind Pasevååråå. He found a *stállu* there seining fish with three sons. The *stállu* said:

—You will come with us, my good man.

The boy said:

—I'll come along, my good man.

The *stállu* finished his seining, and went back to his *goahti*. The boy went into the *stállu*'s *goahti*. The boy was leaving, and he climbed onto the roof of the *goahti* and peeked in the smoke hole. The *stállu* said to his oldest son:

—Let's go to kill him. It's not good to have him roaming around here.

The boy started to run home, with the *stállu*'s oldest son behind him, and the *stállu* said:

—Why don't we wrestle?

The boy said:

—Why not?

They wrestled, and he killed the *stállu*'s eldest son. Then he went back to his mother's, and he brought his day's catch. They were there again that night. Morning came, and again the boy was going off hunting. The mother said:

—Whatever you do, don't go behind Pasevååråå, my son.

The boy said:

—I won't.

He went again to the forest and went again behind Pasevååråå. Along came a *stállu*, seining with two sons. The boy said:

—You are seining, my good man.

The *stállu* said:

—I *am* seining, my good man.

Again the *stállu* returned home to his *goahti*, and the boy did as well. He started again to leave for home, and he climbed onto the *goahti*, and peeked in the smoke hole. The *stállu* said to his middle son:

—Go and kill him. It's not good to have him roaming around here. You need to wrestle better, so you don't share your brother's fate, so you don't get killed.

---

7. It is worth noting that in Sámi, and more generally in Finno-Ugric, contexts, places that are identified as sacred are places that are restricted and dangerous for most people. Calling the mountain Pasevååråå indicates that the boy should not be going there, unless he has a specific and good reason to go there.

The boy descended from the *goahti* roof and headed off. The middle of the *stállu*'s sons followed behind him. He caught up to him, and said:

—Why don't we wrestle?

The boy said:

—Why not?

They wrestled. He killed the *stállu*, as he did his brother before. He returned to his mother's, and brought the day's catch. They again were there for the night, and morning came. The boy again went to the woods just as before, and his mother said:

—Whatever you do, don't go behind Pasevååråå, my son.

The boy said as he did before:

—I won't.

But as he did before, the boy went behind Pasevååråå. The *stállu* was there seining with his youngest boy and wife. The boy said:

—You're seining, my good man.

The *stállu* said:

—I *am* seining, my good man.

Again they went to his home, into the *goahti*, and the boy did as well. They were there a little while, and he left, climbed onto the roof, and peeked inside the hole. The *stállu* said to his youngest boy:

—Go and kill him. It's not good to have him roaming around here.

The boy got down from the roof of the *goahti*, and the *stállu*'s youngest boy was behind him. He said:

—Let's wrestle!

The boy said:

—Why not?

They wrestled, and he killed the *stállu*'s son. Then he returned to his mother's, and brought the day's catch. The following morning the boy again went hunting, and his mother warned him as she did before. But the boy again went behind Pasevååråå. He got there, and the *stállu* was seining with his wife. The boy said:

—You're seining, my good man.

The *stállu* said:

—I *am* seining, my good man.

Again they went to the *stállu*'s *goahti*. The boy was there a bit, went back, and climbed up to the hole. The *stállu*'s wife said to her husband:

—Go kill him. It's not good to have him roaming around here. And when you kill him, bring his dick here.

The boy got down from the *goahti* roof, and left. The *stállu* followed behind him. He said:

—Let's wrestle!
The boy said:
—Why not?
They wrestled and the boy killed the *stállu*, cut off his dick, and sooted up his own face. He then took the *stállu*'s privates along with him, and went to the *stállu*'s wife. The *stállu*'s wife said:
—Oh, oh, you won! But you've changed.
The boy said:
—I won. But barely so.
The *stállu*'s wife took the penis, put it in the soup, and set it to boil. The boy said:
—Where is our oldest boy's money?
The *stállu*'s wife said:
—Oh dear, you're so forgetful, you don't remember.
The boy said:
—My old woman, I lost my memory, since I barely survived the fight.
The *stállu*'s wife said:
—The money is over there, under the bottom of that nook.
The boy said:
—Where is our middle child's money?
The wife said:
—Over there, it's in the middle of the nook.
The boy again asked:
—Where is our youngest son's money?
—Over there in the corner of the door.
The boy asked the *stállu*'s wife:
—Where is your money?
—Over there under the door frame.
The boy said:
—Where is my money?
The *stállu*'s wife said:
—Oh dear, you don't even remember where your own money is! It's over there under the threshold.
The *stállu*'s wife went outside, so the boy started to look around to see what was in the wife's stash. He found her sucking straws,[8] lit them on fire, and

---

8. These straws are used by the *stállu* to suck the blood out of Sámi people, which is why they are destroyed here.

burned them to ash. The *stállu*'s wife came in from outside, grabbed her soup from the cauldron, and started to eat. She then said:

—What's this I'm tasting in my meat?

The boy said:

—There might be some of your husband's privates in there.

The *stállu*'s wife jumped to the other half of the *goahti*, and started to look for her sucking straws, but couldn't find a one. Then she started to cry so hard that she split in two. The boy looked for the money and took all of it, he took it with him. Then he undressed the *stállu*'s wife and put her clothes into the fire. In the end, he went and set the *stállu*'s *goahti* on fire. Then he went back to his mother's, brought the *stállu*'s money and everything he got that day, and he told his mother that he had gone behind Pasevááráá each time and that's where he got all this money from.

The *Stállu*, Version 3
Uula Morottaja (T. I. Itkonen)
ATU 1115–44

A man was once walking about when he noticed three *stálut* burning a campfire in the dark forest at night. He crept very close to them and listened to what they were saying. He heard that they were traveling to kill him. They figured that tomorrow at that time they would already be slaughtering the old man Riima. The man put his spear into the fire to warm, and when the *stálut* went to sleep, he pierced each one with a hot spear, and that's how he killed them all.

Another time he had killed two *stálut*, when along came a third, who was really large and who also had a dog. He wanted to wrestle the man. When they wrestled, the *stállu* won, and when they wrestled a second time, the *stállu* won again. The last time there was still a further stipulation: he who won got to kill the other. When they wrestled, the man read some hymn verse. The *stállu* was defeated, and that *stállu* had a lot of money.

Another time, the same man woke in the morning and set out to tend to his needs, when along came a *stállu*. And he began to challenge him to fight. The man said:

—Not now. Let's make an arrangement to do this a little later.

The *stállu* didn't agree to this, and there was no other choice but to fight. The man got mad and grabbed the *stállu* by the hair, slammed him on his side, and took him to the shore. He grabbed a stone and smashed his skull and killed him. He rolled the carcass into the lake.

The *Stállu*, Version 4
unknown (unidentified)
ATU 1115–44

There was once a man whose name was Màvnu. He went to travel with a line of reindeer. So the draught reindeer started to take fright, and he couldn't travel onward at all. He had no other choice, and he started to yell:
—Come here in front of my eyes!
So the *stállu* came to him and said that he was going to kill him. Màvnu said that he didn't have time to wrestle now. They agreed to wrestle on Sunday evening. He went back to his home, where he stayed for a while. He read the Bible until Sunday evening. In the evening he took his knife belt and set off running. He met the *stállu*, and he said that they needed to wrestle. The first time they wrestled, the *stállu* was so strong that he couldn't possibly win in any fashion. They wrestled a second time: the *stállu* wasn't quite so strong this time. Then he read a hymn verse:
—If Satan's minions come against me, with your power I will truly defeat them all.[9]
They wrestled a third time, and the *stállu* was no longer strong at all. Màvnu spun him into the ground, grabbed his knife from his sheath, and stabbed the *stállu*. Then he went back home and went with his brothers to look around. They went to look around, and there was money there. They took the money and pulled the body into the river.

The *Stállu*, Version 5
unknown (unidentified)
ATU 1115–44

Some boy was getting hay, when along came a *stállu* who wanted to wrestle. The boy said:
—Not now. Let's arrange to do this tomorrow.
And they arranged to meet at sunset. The boy went home and didn't tell anyone about the whole matter. He didn't even eat, but just went to sleep. And in the morning he woke up. He still didn't eat, but went outside and again went to sleep and asked to be woken up at sunset.
And so the boy was woken up when evening came. He grabbed his knife belt

---

9. This devotional hymn is number 317 from the hymnal of 1886.

and left. The *stállu* had already arrived at the place where they agreed to meet. The boy came to the meeting place, so the *stállu* spun around and whistled. When the boy came, they wrestled. The boy won and killed the *stállu* and hid him under the snow. He went back home and didn't tell anyone anything about it.

The head of the house began to wonder what was going on with the boy. And he went to look along the road where the boy had been. He found the murdered *stállu*. He went back and said to the boy:

—You need to hide him better, and take his money. He has money.

The boy went back, took the money, and pulled the corpse into a bend of a thawing river and sunk him there.

> Andras Pejvi
> Antti Kitti (A. V. Koskimies)
> ATU 1060–114

In Värjivuona (Varanger fjord) there was a rich mountain Sámi whose name was Andras Pejvi. He had gotten his name since he was born on Anders' Day (Andras Pejvi). He struck up a bet with the bailiff of Čácisuáloi (Vesisaari; Vadsø):

—You can't jump over this tarred boat in such a fashion that your clothes won't touch the tar.

The bailiff said:

—Sure I can. But you can't!

Andras Pejvi jumped, and his clothes didn't touch the tar boat at all. When the bailiff jumped over, his clothes got smudged with tar. The bailiff got angry and said:

—You'll once more need to use your legs, Andras Pejvi!

And since the bailiff knew that Andras Pejvi was in Peecivuona (Mäntyvuono), he took his boat, went there, and transformed himself into a shipwreck. When Andras Pejvi saw it, he thought a ship had suffered a wreckage and was now on its way into shore. When Andras started to look at it, he took on a terrible form. Andrew realized that the bailiff had transformed himself into a *stállu*.[10] And he set off running away, and heard a *stállu* whistling in front of him. He said:

—If only I had the legs of a wild male reindeer!

---

10. Though the language is a bit vague, the implication here seems to be that the bailiff sails himself to Andras Pejvi's location, and he baits Andras by transforming

He received those legs and ran for a long time. Again he heard the *stállu* whistling in from of him. He said:

—If only I had the legs of a female reindeer!

He received them, and he ran for a really long time and again heard the *stállu* whistling in front of him. He said:

—If only I had the legs of a young reindeer calf!

And he received those legs as well. Then he heard whistling behind him. There was a strait between two lakes. In the middle of the strait there was a large stone right beneath the water level, which was not visible, but Andras Pejvi knew it was there. The *stállu*, however, did not. Andras jumped first onto the rock, and from that rock onto the other shore. And he waited there for the *stállu*. When the *stállu* came to the other shore of the strait, Andras yelled:

—You can't jump across from the same spot that a no-good Sámi jumped from.

The *stállu* got mad and jumped, but he didn't get to the other side. Instead, he fell right into the middle of the strait. The *stállu* said:

—Why did you cheat me?

—I didn't cheat you, said Andras Pejvi. I jumped from there.

Andras Pejvi had a bow, and with it he aimed at the *stállu*'s chest, but he didn't hit it. The *stállu* jumped up so the arrow flew between his legs. He shot again and aimed at his forehead but still didn't hit the mark. The *stállu* dove, and the arrow went over his head. Then he aimed for the crown of his head. The *stállu* jumped up, but the arrow hit him at the base of his torso, right in his testicles.

The *stállu* said:

—Take me now and bury me. Kill my dog and go where my boat is, and take my belongings. Just don't kill my son.

Andras Pejvi killed the *stállu* and went to the boat and took his belongings. He pushed the boat and the son into the water, for the bailiff had brought his son along on the trip. Then Andras went home. After he arrived he said:

—I really am tired.

And he went to sleep. The people at the home wondered:

—What could it be that causes him to be so tired?

When he was sleeping, his brother hit the *goahti* with a log. Then Andras jumped up and said:

---

himself or his boat into a shipwreck. When Andras nears the boat, the bailiff shape-shifts again into a *stállu*.

—Ah ha! So I guessed!

He thought that the *stállu* had been revived and again was coming to his house. His brother said:

—I too thought as much.

—Well, since you figured out what was going on, I'll give you half the possessions that I got today.

Gufihtarat

The *gufihtarat* are short, benevolent, magical beings, who live underground often atop tundras or mountains and are known for their wealth (including their beautiful reindeer herds), their powerful magic, and their physical beauty. The *gufihtarat* have different names in different parts of Sápmi. *Gufihtar* is used in the north and east (cf. Swedish *goveiter*); *ulddat* further west (cf. Norwegian *huldra*); *kanji* in Lule Sámi; and even *saajve* (*sáiva*, a common Sámi adjective denoting a supernatural, holy, or spirit force). There are some differences between all these local interpretations of related supernatural beings. Although *gufihtarat* often help Sámi people, they pose dangers too: stealing infants or luring Sámi people into the underworld.

The *gufihtarat* tales in this collection are surprisingly few in number and sparse in content, compared with their importance in other collections of Sámi oral tradition (Turi, Qvigstad). Even today some Sámi will speak of encountering them or seeing their tracks in the snow. Their absence here could signify many things, but it seems quite possible that discussion of these helpful supernatural beings was stigmatized by the church, at least in Aanaar during this time. Note the stories are from unidentified narrators and by letter from Mikko Aikio, whose *joik* singing similarly transgressed social norms in the community.

The Maker of Seven Churches
Mikko Aikio, by letter (A. V. Koskimies)
ATU 504; ML 5085

There was a person who had a child who was exchanged for another while in the cradleboard, and it was thought to be a *gufihtar* child. He was lulled for some time, until people noticed that it wasn't a real child after all, since the food kettle always emptied when the child was left alone in the cottage.[11]

---

11. This implies that the *gufihtar* changeling is eating the food up when it is unwatched.

When people noticed this, they started to be careful and stand guard. When they started to dine, they cut some meat and put it into a sack, tied the mouth of the sack, and then put the sack of meat into the kettle. And when the kettle began to boil, they went out and watched from the window and door.

The changeling child rose up from the cradle and took a spit, stuck it into the meat sack, lifted it out, and started to wonder what sort of thing this was that he had never before seen, and said this:

—Seven churches I have already made, and I have never seen this kind of sausage before.

So the people realized that they didn't have a real child. They took switches and started to whip the changeling. Then an invisible voice said:

—Don't, my rag of a father, whip him. Here is your mud-child!

And they gave the real child back and the *gufihtar* child was taken away. That's how those people got their real child back.

That's all there is to say.

Gufihtar
unknown (A. V. Koskimies)
ATU 503; ML 6055

The *gufihtarat* are smaller than a normal person and live under the earth in mountains. They have great herds of reindeer. When a person stands in the middle of these herds, he can take a stone, put it in his mitten-clad hand, and throw it in four directions, and as far as the stones fly, the draught reindeer will become the person's own. The female reindeer gotten from the *gufihtarat* are called *häldee-aldužin* (spirit female reindeer).[12] They also have cows like people do, and they sometimes go on top of the earth just like their reindeer, and they can get mixed up with people's cattle, but disappear right away once they are seen. But if a person has time to throw some kind of blade (a knife or firestriker) over the *gufihtar*'s cattle, then he can take them as his own.

Čáhálig—Treasure Guardians

The *čáhálig* (*čáhkalakkis* in North Sámi) is best known in the eastern parts of Sápmi. It is a small-statured guardian of hidden treasures, who stands about

---

12. *Häldee* (Finnish: *haltija*) refers to a type of guardian spirit and is related to the word *ulda*, referring to the *gufihtar*.

half a meter high and goes about naked or with few clothes. It presides over treasures of silver and gold, sometimes its own and sometimes placed there by people. Such treasures were said to be hidden in secret caches in the wilds, where people would be unlikely to stumble across them by dumb luck. These caches and other hidden fortunes often appear in stories. Generally regarded as good-natured, a *čáhálig* is easily tricked, and its treasures easily taken. In North Sámi communities, the *čáhálig* has gold and silver in its stomach, and it must be killed to retrieve the treasure. In the eastern communities, the *čáhálig* was never killed. Many place-names in Aanaar are named after the *čáhálig*.

Čáhálig
unknown (A. V. Koskimies)
ML 8010. f.

The *čáháligeh* reside inside the earth atop mountains, and they aren't more than forty-five centimeters (one and a half feet) tall. They are naked and own many belongings, silver and gold. When a person finds their hole, he ties a white pair of shoes made of reindeer with the hair on the outside on the end of a cord, and lowers them down. The *čáhálig* will put them on his feet, and the cord will wrap around him, and then the person can pull up the *čáhálig*. And he will want to go back, but the person won't release him until he has given up all his money.

Čáhálig, Version 2
unknown (A. V. Koskimies)
ML 8010. f.

A long time ago, there was a spirit that protected caches of silver whose name was *čáhálig*. Once some Sámi people noticed a *čáhálig* when walking, and they saw where he lived. They took someone's shoes and lacings and threw them into the place where the *čáhálig* was. He took it and jammed both his feet into one shoe and got wrapped up in the string, and he got all knotted up when turning around. And so he said:

—I turn and I turn, and I get tangled up.

And he who was watching him tried to make him run off, and since both feet were bound up inside one shoe, he couldn't go anywhere. So the man got him and he pulled out all his intestines, and in his stomach there were silver coins. The man took the silver for himself and took his shoes off the *čáhálig*'s feet, and he laced up his shoes and went on his way.

And the *čáhálig* was small and naked and looked like a little child. And still today Sámi people say to their children, when they start to fool around naked:
—You are just like the naked *čáháligeh*![13]

Giants

Neither good nor evil, giants have a presence in nineteenth-century Sámi oral tradition, although their presence is not abundant in this collection. Their presence can be felt in *stállu* stories, in stories of the superhuman feats of Peeivih-Vuálåppåǯ, or—perhaps most directly—in Sámi creation myths (see Fjellner 2003). Still, the few stories here are not set locally but rather in a distant world of kings and armies—the world of the fairy tale. This suggests the stories are told more for entertainment than to educate young people how to deal with giants, should they be encountered. The two following stories represent two variations on the same basic narrative.

A Giant Fights with Small Men
Iisakki Mannermaa (A. V. Koskimies)

There was once some king who had a giant as a servant whom he trained and schooled in the arts of warfare. And the king noticed his servant was very powerful. He once told some other king about the servant's strength. The king whom he told said:
—After a week, I will come to your house with my soldiers, and I will try to see how many of my best men it will take to defeat your servant.
And so the kings parted company at that time. After a week passed, the king came with his soldiers, the best of his men, to the king who had praised his servant's strength. The visiting king said to the other:
—Now I have come to see your servant's strength. You need to ask your servant how many of my best soldiers he intends to defeat.
The king left to ask his servant, and he went to his room and said:
—Because I have noticed you are such a powerful man, I will put you to trial to see how many men you can slay of a visiting king's best soldiers.
The giant answered:
—Nine.

---

13. A variant of this saying appears in the chapter "Proverbs and Figures of Speech."

The king said to his servant:

—Oh, oh, this might now be your final day.

The king went to his room, and he told his guest, the other king:

—My servant intends to defeat nine of your best soldiers.

The visiting king said:

—You must indeed have a powerful servant. Can I see this mighty giant of yours before this difficult fight between ten men?

The king said:

—Well, I won't promise that to you or your soldiers, not before he comes out from his room to fight upon my command.

The kings agreed with each other that the visiting king could choose nine of his best soldiers, as he would like, and they had to come one after another to the door of the king's servant's cottage and to wait there until he commands his giant to go out and to start to fight. The king told his servant what time he needed to come out. When the determined time started to grow near, the servant took a big goblet of brandy, drank it, and walked and paced across the floor. As he strode, the servant suddenly opened the cottage door, sprung out, and forgot his sword. He struck his hands together and roared: three soldiers fell to the ground and fainted, since they had never before seen such a giant man in this world. The servant kicked three soldiers to death. There were three soldiers there, praying for mercy. The kings saw how mighty that giant could be in battle, even without a sword.

The kings returned to their cottage, ate, and drank, and were in understanding. The visiting king said:

—Only now do I see that you were not giving undeserved praise, though I didn't believe that you could have such a great man, whose greatness I have never before seen.

And he wanted to buy the giant for himself, but he didn't get him. Then the kings departed.

Two Giants
unknown (A. V. Koskimies)

There were once two giants used for war, who each served a king. The kings praised each of their soldiers. They agreed among themselves:

—Let's put those two mighty men to test each other, and see which of them remains alive.

The kings commanded those two strong men to fight each other. They themselves came to watch. They determined a time for them to fight. The giants went to some great room. One took up his sword in hand, and the other giant sat down, right next to his sword.

The giant who was standing brandished his sword and lashed the other giant's ear. When this giant was badly injured, he struck the other giant at the base of the ear, who stood there with a sword in his hand. This blow knocked the giant's head off, and he fell to the floor and died.

From this, the kings saw whose soldier was stronger.

The *Sieidi*

The *sieidi* is a sacred site for leaving offerings to the spirits. These are often natural features in the landscape, including stones, islands, or cliffs of distinctive visual shape, or occasionally human-crafted statues of wood. In Lake Aanaar, the towering island of Äjjih (Ukko) is a well-known site of ceremonial sacrifice, and it appears several times in these tales. Like all sacred and powerful sites, access to them was somewhat restricted, unless one followed protocol and rules to ensure one's safety. While the sites could be used to bring good fortune to a community, failure to follow protocol could cause one to have great misfortune, to get sick, or even to die.

In exchange for goods like reindeer antlers, fish, fat, or silver coins, the spirits could assist a person in hunting or fishing or with other matters. These spirits tended to be somewhat localized and not as omnipresent as major Sámi gods or goddesses, who were more difficult and dangerous to communicate with. Although many *sieiddit* were destroyed or had churches placed directly on top of them, many still exist today.

The following tales reflect the efficacy of their powers and the tensions that follow with the shift to Christianity in earlier times, both within the community and within an individual's own belief system. Offerings to spirits were still seen as effective, but Christianity had condemned such practice as ungodly. What is one to do, when one has chosen to live as a Christian but is forced to offer to the old spirits to save one's own life? These tales touch on the complex ethics of negotiating a religious shift—a process that can take centuries—in the Sámi community.

The *Sieidi* Root Cluster
P. Valle (A. V. Koskimies)

There was a man who was hunting wild reindeer in a forested area of a tundra. In Aanaar there is a steep, rocky-cliffed island, whose name is Äjjih

(Ukko; Old Man), which in earlier times was used for sacrifices. But when all this happened, people had already been baptized as Christians, and they no longer made offerings there.

The man thought:

—The old people got game when they left offerings at Äjjih, but now I'm not getting any game since I'm a Christian. I will promise to Äjjih the antlers, if I get a wild reindeer right away.

He walked a little on his travels, and he saw two great wild reindeer bucks that had tangled their antlers together. He thought:

—I wonder if I'm seeing this game because I promised the antlers to Äjjih. But I am not going to give any honor to the devil.

Suddenly the bucks separated their antlers and ran off.

The man walked along and found a really large root cluster, which was in former times used for the offering of wild reindeer antlers. He thought:

—If I again promise to offer some antlers, then I might get some wild reindeer. But I simply won't do it.

He walked on, and he walked around the mountains, around marshes. And so he eventually came to the edge of the same root cluster where he had set off from. He went once again forward, and he went around the mountains and around marshes, and he again came to the place of the same root cluster where he left from. Tears came to his eyes. He remembered thinking that if he made an offering to this root cluster, he would get some wild reindeer. And he repented greatly and prayed to God with all of his heart, and he set off again and no longer got lost. After all this, he indeed got some wild reindeer and never again promised to sacrifice to stones or root clusters.

A Story about Äjjih Island
P. Valle and J. Mannermaa (A. V. Koskimies)

In the middle of Äijihjorŋâ (Ukonselkä) in Lake Aanaar there is a mountain called Äjjih. In former times, people regarded it as their god.[14] Once some wife went to make an offering of sheep roasts to Äjjih. After she had left with her little child to row from the village, and after she got to the shores of Äjjih

---

14. This claim about Äjjih is perhaps not entirely historically accurate and is colored by Christian discourse: "god" is perhaps a misnomer for Äjjih. Instead Äjjih, whose name invokes the Sámi god of thunder, is a sacred site, a place for offerings, and a place where powerful spirits reside.

Island, she took the sheep roasts from her boat and went onto the land. Suddenly the wife saw that the boat was drifting away from the shore. She became terribly afraid, and she thought:

—What will I ever do?

Then a pagan spirit came to her mind, and she yelled:

—Do not take, Šiella,[15] a piss-covered leg, when a ram's roast is juicier![16]

When the wife had yelled this, the boat that had drifted out to the open water returned to the wife on the shore of Äjjih Island. She took the boat and tied it up to a tree. Then she took a ram's roast and left it on Äjjih, returned to her village, and told people what bad fortunes had befallen her and how a pagan spirit had helped her.

Because of the wife's story, more of the Aanaar Sámi at the time started to make offering's to Äjjih Island's spirit, named Šiella, to whom they made offerings in former times. And for sacrifices they brought wild and domesticated reindeer antlers and bones, birds, bird eggs, and sheep meat and other things. Now still Aanaar Sámi and other travelers from afar go out to Äjjih, and they can still see there the remains of those sacrifices made to the spirits.

The *Sieidi* of Ij-jävri
Mikko Aikio (A. V. Koskimies)

In the time when *sieiddit* were being destroyed, there was a *sieidi* in Ij-jävri (Iijärvi) on an island. Once there was a girl who went with her mother to the *sieidi* on that island to make a pledge to no longer come to that *sieidi* to make offerings. The *sieidi* became angry, for she/he[17] had, as we think, the power of an evil spirit. When they left the island, they pushed their boat into the water. The mother first stepped into the boat and went to the back, and then the girl

---

15. Šiella is a Sámi word meaning a ceremonial offering or gift. Here it is used as a name for a spirit that accepts sacrificial offerings.

16. This phrase is used to buy her freedom, exchanging her own lowly "piss-covered leg" for a purportedly better cut of meat. It is possible that the piss-covered leg is also a metonym for women in general, employed here to devalue her own value to the spirit.

17. Interestingly, the *sieidi* is referred to as a person, using the Sámi pronoun for he/she. This emphasizes the living nature of the site or possibly connects to Aikio regarding the site as a god. I have chosen to use the awkward pronoun she/he here, because Sámi language does not distinguish pronouns by gender, and the spirit is not clearly gendered here.

got in. But as the girl stepped into the boat, her leg stuck to the ground, and she couldn't get it loose by any other means than yelling for the *sieidi*'s help and promising to continue to sacrifice to him/her. And they yelled and said:

—Do not take, Šiella, a piss-covered leg, a ram's neck is better!

And so she got her leg free from the land, and she needed, according to her pledge, to still bring the neck of a ram to the *sieidi*.

Noaidi Tales

The *noaidi* (shaman) is an important and complex figure in traditional Sámi religion and healing practices, which connects to broader complexes of traditional Finno-Ugric religious practices and Siberian shamanism traditions. *Noaiddit* began to face extreme persecution at the behest of missionaries as early as the seventeenth century, driving many of their practices into hiding. Although *noaiddit* were extremely few in number by the beginning of the twentieth century, some of their knowledge has endured until the present day, some traditions have intertwined seamlessly into Christian practices, and some Sámi have taken interest in reclaiming lost knowledge and restoring traditional religious practices.

The *noaidi* was said to have the capacity of soul flight—the ability to release one of two human souls that reside within people—to divine information from afar, see distant events, or pass into other spiritual planes in order to negotiate with spirits. This work was considered very dangerous. When a *noaidi* fell into a trance, if the so-called free soul could not find its way back to the body, the *noaidi* risked death. A *noaidi* was, for that reason, never supposed to be disturbed or moved while in a trance state. Generally, because of the hazards of this work, soul flight was used only during periods of need: to help the community, heal the direly ill, find game or fish during times of famine, or protect the community from external threat.

Despite the notoriety of soul flight, its role in most *noaidi* stories is minor. Always accompanied by a number of spirits, *noaiddit* could perform a number of seemingly supernatural feats: stopping thieves, healing people, causing sickness or death to others, transforming people into animals, taming predatory animals, controlling the weather, and much more. Some *noaiddit* were so powerful, even thinking on a matter would set the spirits into action. For this reason *noaiddit* were often considered dangerous: people didn't want to be on their bad side.

Aanaar was decidedly Christian by the late nineteenth century, and—as is common with other nineteenth-century Sámi oral traditions—these stories reflect the anxieties over the powers of *noaiddit* and the tensions the community has with its own pre-Christian past. The *noaiddit* in these stories are presented as threatening and powerful, and—interestingly—found only in other Sámi communities, despite the fact that they existed at least as nearby as Ij-jävri (Iijärvi), home to the reputed *noaidi* Anna Antintytär Sarre (1843–1915) (Siida Museum n.d., "Occupations"). Because Koskimies worked so closely with church leaders, it is difficult to say to what extent these tales represent attitudes and beliefs about the *noaidi* beyond the scope of this one segment of the community.

The Old Man *Noaidi*
Paavali Valle and Santeri Valle (A. V. Koskimies)[18]

There was once a wealthy Sámi reindeer herder whose name was Kaarin-Uvla (Kaarinan-Uula; Garen-Ovla).[19] He was from Norway, and he was an awful, terrible man. Once in the season of summer-autumn, he was near the town of Várgáåh (Vuoreija; Vardø) with his *siida*. Their reindeer started to eat people's hay, and they also trampled the haystacks. The residents of Várgáåh began to harass him about this, and they came to steal some reindeer as compensation for the hay.[20] But Kaarin-Uvla stopped them, so the men had to return without any reindeer. But the following day, they sent soldiers to make the trip.

Kaarin-Uvla was keeping watch and saw the soldiers coming. He rose and walked to meet them. They asked:

—Where are your reindeer?

Kaarin-Uvla answered:

—Don't the lazy folks in Várgáåh have anything better to do than come here and play tricks with me like I'm a stupid boy? Go on your way!

---

18. According to Laitinen, his tale was told to A. V. Koskimies in 1886 by Paavali Valle in Finnish, and in 1916 his son, Santeri Valle, translated it into Aanaar Sámi.

19. Several stories about Kaarin-Uvla are found in Qvigstad and Sandberg's collection *Lappiske Eventyr og Folkesagn*. He was known as a powerful *noaidi*, and he is described as a kind person, although he could be cruel and mischievous if he were drunk or if someone was harassing or threatening him.

20. Disputes over reindeer and hay were common. Settlers, who often located their farms in the middle of established reindeer routes and pasture lands, often demanded payment for hay that reindeer ate, and this created numerous tensions between reindeer herders and farmers. Interestingly, the Valles' version of the story seemingly condemns Kaarin-Uvla, despite the fact he is heroically defending his *siida*'s territorial rights.

He put his thumb up on his right hand, whistled, and murmured something to himself. And he said:

—Is this the reason why you're asking? So you can steal some reindeer? Oh, you crazy boys, know that if I go down on my knee and whistle seven times, then you won't be able to do anything at all. But whoever's hay it was, let them come to me. I want to pay them, but I won't pay anything to idle dogs.

The soldiers said something, and they decided to capture him, but he jumped forward, threw his hat to the ground, and said:

—Here is a border. If you cross over this, no good will follow.

But the soldiers said:

—We will come and strike you dead.

Kaarin-Uvla said, it wouldn't be extraordinary if a Sámi's head should fall by a soldier's sword, but it also wouldn't be extraordinary if a soldier's head should fall by a Sámi's staff. And he looked around, raised his thumb upright, whistled seven times, and murmured something. Then the soldiers became startled and frightened, and they went off on their way.

That same *noaidi* had seven *noaidi* spirits, which nobody saw unless he himself put them on his thumb. Sometimes he addressed them, and he murmured when his thumb was standing upright.

Later on, after he had gotten older and was bedridden and being taken care of by some poor man in exchange for money, some young boys started to harass the old *noaidi* man. They didn't think he had any powers left. One time, some shopkeepers brought some brandy and gave the old *noaidi* some drink, so that he would get drunk. The boys thought they could now really swindle the old man, since he was so drunk. Two brothers, Kuttar and Piera Sant, went there. They weren't really drunks, but they would drink a bit. People started forbidding any bullying of the old man, because they didn't know what he could still do. The others stopped, but Kuttar began to torment and harass him again. Then the old Kaarin-Uvla's patience came to an end, and he said:

—If you don't let me be, then today you'll die with your shoes on your feet.

Kuttar said:

—Bring it on. That way I can see if you're the same kind of *noaidi* as you were before.

The old man rose onto his knees and whistled with his thumb standing upright. Kuttar tried to stop him from doing this, but the old man redoubled his efforts, his form changing even more menacingly:

—And so it is that today you die with your shoes on your feet when you are going to another's house, right when you get to the top of that hill.

The following day people went to check, and he had indeed died in the same place the *noaidi* said he would die, and blood had come from his nose and mouth, even though he was healthy in body and still unmarried. It happened a little before Michaelmas (September 29) in Reahpen (Reppänä) village. And this is a true story.

Skolt Sámi *Noaiddit*
Juho Petter Lusmaniemi, by letter (A. V. Koskimies)

In older times the Skolt Sámi had such *noaiddit* that when they would come to another's house, a day before they arrived, the head of the house would get sick. There was one house in Aanaar, which was the first in the Skolts' path. Every time the Skolts were coming, the man always got sick a day before they arrived.

In that house there lived two young boys who once had come secretly to hear the Skolts' opining that if a steel blade were put in their path, on the path they came on, then the head of the house would not become ill.

The boys remembered this, but they didn't tell anyone anything about it. Once the Skolts were again coming, and the boys hid some steel along the pathway they were coming down. Indeed, the head of the house never got sick when the Skolts came. The boys later heard the Skolts saying:

—The head of the house never even got sick. How did he get that knowledge?[21]

The *Noaidi* Wife
Paavali Valle and Santeri Valle (A. V. Koskimies)[22]

Skolt Sámi people used to live in Njiävđám (Näätämö; Neiden) village. They had winter camps near Aanaar, but otherwise they lived in Norway and were Norwegian subjects. When they lived in Norway and fished in the sea, their main place of habitation was at the mouth of the Njiävđám River below Njiävđám Falls, where the river passes through the Nuárjukuoškâ (Hyljekoski; Seal Rapids) and out to the sea. There was a wide clearing there long ago, where there was a small cottage used for a church, eight ells long and seven and a half ells wide (12 feet x 11.5 feet). They had icons in it, just like in other Orthodox churches. They lived there in the summer, but in the winter they moved to near Aanaar and fished in the lakes on the Finnish side.

---

21. Lusmaniemi delivers this last line in Skolt Sámi.

22. According to Laitinen, this tale was told to A. V. Koskimies in 1886 by Paavali Valle in Finnish, and in 1916 his son, Santeri Valle, translated it into Aanaar Sámi.

There was one man named Huáttár, whose wife was very sensitive and easily took fright,[23] and she was said to have been a *noaidi*. Some people visited her to become healed, and by using her *noaidi* arts she healed many common diseases.

If her healing practices didn't immediately work, then she would have to send part of her spirit[24] on a trip to inquire about such secret matters from the spirits. And at a determined time, she plunged herself into sleep,[25] but another person was needed to wake the *noaidi* wife up. For this, she needed someone who understood when it was the right time to wake her: not too early, nor too late. In Peäccam (Petsamo) there was another such *noaidi* wife. The two were in contact with each other, even though Peäccam is about two hundred kilometers from Njiävđám. They came together in their spirit form, and they fought bitterly with each other.

It's said that one spring the Skolt Sámi moved into Njiävđám's field. Huáttár's wife was already old, but she still needed to fight with the other *noaidi*. One night, when everyone was asleep, the wife vanished. The *siida* looked for her the whole summer, but she wasn't found until autumn, when she was found in a winter camp—a trip of 630 km (391 miles)! Some *noaidi* spirit maybe threw her so far during that quarrel with the Peäccam *noaidi*. This ended up taking her life, since the Peäccam *noaidi* was stronger than her.

The Moose Skiers
Uula Morottaja (T. I. Itkonen)

There was once a man who was hunting a moose on skis. He caught up to it and killed it. Another man was skiing after the same moose, but he didn't catch up to it until the previous man had already killed it and skinned it. The latter began to demand a portion for himself, and the first man wasn't about to give him any. Then the man got mad and answered angrily:

—Since you won't give me part of it, you won't be able to eat this meat yourself, for it will turn to stone.

And he skied away, and immediately all the meat and skins turned to stone. We still can see those stones today on the shores of the Páččvei (Paatsjoki) River.

---

23. Note that in the following chapter on Skolt Sámi stories, Skolt Sámi women easily taking fright is a common motif in Aanaar Sámi stories.
24. This refers to her "free soul."
25. This refers to her falling into a trance, in which the free soul departs from the body.

Two Jealous People
P. Valle (A. V. Koskimies)

There were once two men who were hunting wild reindeer in the pine forests of Påččvei (Paatsjoki), and they killed a moose along with its calves. They laid out the moose hides on the north shore of a wide bay in a river, on the side of a level hogback. They put the meat in a cache, and they went away. Two other men came to that same place, and they were planning to spend the night on the shore of the still water, and as they neared it, one noticed the moose hides. He said to his companion in the Sompio language:[26]
—Look, someone killed some moose.
At the same time the moose hides took on a peculiar appearance. They indeed looked like furs, but they weren't anything more than mere dirt.

Shape-Shifting Tales

Shape-shifting is a motif that appears in a great variety of oral genres, both fictional and nonfictional alike. In genres like legends, shape-shifting can teach us about human relationships with other animals, how humans understand themselves, about the fluidity between categories perceived only by the eye. Unlike many Western traditions—werewolves, possessions, curses, witches' familiars, and the like—Sámi shape-shifting tales are less likely to dismiss shape-shifting as something inherently wicked and demonic. These are not exactly stories about "losing one's humanity" through the transformation into a werewolf or gaining horrific powers through contract with a demon. While there is certainly some degree of anxiety about shape-shifting reflected in the tales (Aanaar Sámi are, after all, telling these stories about their Skolt Sámi neighbors with whom they have frequent disputes), there is sometimes a practical dimension to shape-shifting clearly reflected in the tales, like becoming a bear to hibernate through the winter.

Each tale also reflects the sense of danger that happens when people transform into animals. In part, this might connect to late nineteenth-century struggles with religious shifts, since shape-shifting was within a powerful *noaidi*'s abilities. The transformations are understood as real: they are dangerous and it is perhaps unwise to meddle in such affairs. Today, however, many of these tales have been

---

26. The Sompio language refers to Kemi Sámi. This detail is an interesting inclusion, since Påččvei is a bit north of traditional Kemi Sámi territories.

taken up as representative of how powerful Sámi people once were and the metaphysical connection Sámi people have with the animals that inhabit Sápmi—an ideal, of sorts, that some might care to return to.

The Whitefish Daughter-in-Law
Juho Petteri Lusmaniemi (A. V. Koskimies)

There was once a Skolt household that had just taken in a new daughter-in-law. One time the people went to seine, and they were starting to pull in their catch. The daughter-in-law stayed home. She started to wonder why fish go to the bottom of the net and don't just escape by swimming between the boats. She thought, then, that she would actually change herself into a fish and go to the place they were seining. When they pull in the nets, she would try to see if she could get in between the boats and not become part of the catch by going toward the bottom of the net.[27]

And she went to the fishing waters. When the others were in position to lift the nets, the daughter-in-law intended to escape the seine, but there was no longer a way out. Between the boats a fire was lit, and there was no way to get through there. So she couldn't get out. She was forced to head toward the bottom of the net, and the seiners pulled their seine into the boat, and they caught something fish-like, so large that they had never before seen such a sight.

They were really happy, and they decided they didn't need to seine any longer. They set off back home, to the new daughter-in-law, to show off the giant fish they had just caught. They landed their boat, pulled their boat onto the shore, and ran off to tell the daughter-in-law. When they came to the cottage, the daughter-in-law wasn't anywhere to be found. They stayed there, waiting for her, wherever she might be.

The daughter-in-law, who in the meantime was inside the boat in the form of a fish, started to flop about, and she got back into the lake, where she was able to turn herself back into a human. Then she went back to the people at the

---

27. There are different seining techniques that can be used. This technique involves using two boats to drag a net into a circular shape and then pulling in the nets, shrinking the size of the circle. The bottom of the net is either weighted or, with a purse seine, a bottom line can be used to close the net at the bottom. In the following story, people also wade into the water to assist with the pulling of the nets. The use of fire to keep fish from escaping a seine between the boats is seemingly not a widespread practice.

cottage. They boasted to the daughter-in-law that they had gotten such a huge fish that she wouldn't believe it. It was so huge! They said:

—Let's put the kettle on the fire!

They told the daughter-in-law to put the kettle on the fire, and they themselves went to retrieve the fish. They got to their boat, but the fish had disappeared. They became very upset, and they thought someone had stolen it. They then went back to the daughter-in-law and explained to her that the fish was gone.

The Whitefish Daughter-in-Law, Version 2
Uula Morottaja (T. I. Itkonen)

There was one Skolt Sámi woman who could run as a bear and as a wolf. Being a wolf was the worst of all, since she was always hungry. She would have to spit yellow saliva over and over. Being a fish was the best of all. One time a seine was thrown around her. She was planning to get free, as they started wading to pull in the nets. They could see that a big fish was in there. But when they started wading, a fire was started between the two boats, so she couldn't escape. She had to go to the bottom of the net and stay there. And so they pulled her into the boat, and she didn't dare to move, knowing she would be killed.[28]

The seiners went home. They went into a *goahti* to eat, and they told everyone that they had killed a giant fish. Some elderly woman started to clean the fish, and she took that large fish and thought:

—This is a roe fish. I should get a birchbark basket from my *goahti* to collect the roe. In the meantime, the fish flopped back into the lake, when the old woman was off getting her basket. So the great fish disappeared, and they didn't know where it might have gone off to.

The Skolt Sámi and His Bear-Wife
Juho Petteri Lusmaniemi (A. V. Koskimies)

There was once an old and cautious Skolt Sámi who had a wife and many sons. In the winter, he didn't dare feed himself nor his wife or sons. Instead, he and his wife changed themselves into bears for the winter, so their food stocks wouldn't diminish. In the summer, they changed themselves back into humans so they could fish.

---

28. This remark most likely refers to fish being clubbed if they are flopping about in the bottom of a boat.

Once they had again changed themselves into bears, and the sons happened to be circling[29] them to find their den for a wintertime hunt. Later that winter the sons went to kill them. They came to the den and woke one bear. The bear told his wife:

—Don't you move, as I am soon to be killed! Not until I have been brought home and skinned, my pelt spread out in the yard. Then you will have to jump over my pelt so you can become a human again.

The wife did just that. When the bear went out, they killed him and took his carcass home. They spread out the hide for the night in the yard. That night, the bear-woman ran along their tracks and came to the yard. She saw the hide spread out in the yard, and she jumped over it. But she didn't make it all the way over with her jump. So the claws on her toes didn't turn back into toenails, since they touched the pelt.

She went to her sons and said:

—Why did you kill your father?

The sleeping boys jumped up and saw that this was her mother, but her toes were like bear claws. They started to ask:

—How could this have happened?

Well, the mother had to explain the whole story, and they saw that her toes were changed into bear claws. They had to believe what she said, and the boys sent this story out to the world.

The Bear Daughter-in-Law
an unnamed woman from Pàččvei (A. V. Koskimies)

There was one elderly Skolt Sámi man who disappeared every autumn for the whole winter and in the spring came back to his home. One autumn, when he again disappeared, his daughter-in-law went to follow his tracks. She saw her father-in-law circling three times around a leaning tree. He turned into a bear. The daughter followed him still and watched where her father-in-law went to. And she circled herself around the same tree and changed herself into a bear. The father-in-law and daughter-in-law went to the same den and laid down to sleep.

So his own sons came circling them in hunt. The father-in-law said to the daughter-in-law:

—We are being circled. Well, I have indeed already lived out my life, but you have children . . . Well, when I am killed, then you must, my daughter-in-law,

---

29. Circling refers to a specific and common tracking technique to locate bear dens.

run out of the den. When I am skinned and my pelt has been stretched on the door of the *goahti*, then you need to jump over my pelt, and you will change back to a human right away.

And so the daughter-in-law jumped over the pelt and changed back into human form. But one claw touched the pelt and remained a bear claw.

Ghost Hauntings

Legends of ghosts and the walking dead exist across the globe. The following Sámi stories reflect both broader Nordic and European traditions (including the so-called midnight mass for the dead) as well as motifs more distinct to Sámi culture (namely, the powers that the *noaidi* has beyond death). The *noaidi* must be tended with extra care after death, and certain burial customs were specific for the *noaidi* that would protect the living community. In some cases, the *noaidi* is buried facedown to prevent his or her spirits from wreaking havoc on the world. In other instances, however, living *noaidi* were said to visit the gravesites of powerful *noaiddit* to retrieve knowledge and powers from beyond the grave. In the Finnish *Kalevala*, for instance, Väinämöinen seeks out a reputed Kemi Sámi *noaidi* named Antero Vipunen in the text but likely referring to Akmeeli's (Ikämieli's) Christian name of Antereeus. Believed to be a historic figure alive in the sixteenth and seventeenth century in Sompio, his grave was frequently visited for knowledge.

Sárnoo Kurrâ (Speaker's Gorge)
Paavali and Santeri Valle (A. V. Koskimies)[30]

A long time ago, when people could hunt all of the forest game freely, the Aanaar and Skolt Sámi would gather together in a place at Karvamjävri (Kiertämäjärvi), where there was formerly a large *goahti*. At one end of Karvamjävri, on the Russian side of the border, there was a big gorge. The menfolk went skiing, and two were skiing there in the afternoon, right by that gorge. One wondered aloud:

—I wonder how deep this gorge is.

The other didn't know, and the bottom of the gorge was not visible. They

---

30. According to Laitinen, this tale was told to A. V. Koskimies in 1886 by Paavali Valle in Finnish, and in 1916 his son, Santeri Valle, translated it into Aanaar Sámi.

came closer and took a look. Then they started to hear a voice from the bottom of the gorge, which said in the old Sompio language:[31]

—You skiers of mountains and forest wanderers, say these words to Ruige, that his brother has died.

The men became afraid because of the unexpected voice. They left, skiing back to the *goahti*, where the other wild reindeer hunters had gone to. They were talking about what they all had bagged, but then they asked what the two men had gotten. They explained:

—Surely reindeer have lost their lives before, but no one has ever before heard the kind of voice we heard today.

But when they explained what had happened, they suddenly heard a wail from inside the *goahti*:

—Oh no! My brother is dead!

And people saw the door suddenly open, as if an invisible spirit had run out.

After this, people started calling the gorge the Sárnoo Kurrâ (Speaker's Gorge).

The Haunting of the Old Deceased *Noaidi*
Mikko Aikio, by letter (A. V. Koskimies)

There was a man in Russia who was a *noaidi* in his life, and when he died, a poor man was paid to bring him to the graveyard. He was given ten rubles before he left.

But after he set off, he started to think:

—Even though I already collected my ten rubles for pay, I ought not transport the body of a *noaidi* . . . despite the fact that I was planning to do it.

When he drove up to the first house on his route, he said to the head of the house:

—Why don't you transport this body on my behalf?

The head of the house said he wouldn't go, but the guest offered him the ten rubles. The man, however, fancied the pay, since he would be paid before he left—ten rubles to put into his purse. So he was eager enough to get on his way.

But he just couldn't wait until morning, and instead set off that evening. He drove until it started to become dusk, and only then did it occur to him:

---

31. The Sompio language refers to the Kemi Sámi language. The following line is delivered in Kemi Sámi in Santeri Valle's translation.

—How did I wind up in such a situation? I am not going to the graveyard at night. And where can I spend the night? I shouldn't be alone with this old *noaidi* man. If only I had a traveling companion, then I wouldn't mind being in the forest for the night.

But then the man noticed, much to his terror, that the old *noaidi* was sitting upright in his coffin. He didn't know what to do, so he tied up his draught reindeer and climbed up into a spruce tree. The dead man walked to the base of the spruce and began to bite through it. But when the man started to move around in the tree, he would stop biting for a moment. But this didn't work for long. The man took a silver ruble and started to jingle the edge of the silver coin. The corpse went back into the coffin, and it was there for a long while. But eventually it rose up again and started to gnaw through the base of the spruce where the man was. The man would rattle the edge of a silver ruble, and he would always go back into the coffin. This happened for a while, since it was around Christmastime and the nights were long. Many rubles disappeared that night. The man dropped some, since his hands were trembling with fear.

But as it got toward dawn, the dead man no longer would retreat back into his coffin. The man started to shout:

—Dawn is breaking!

So the *noaidi*'s corpse again returned to the coffin, and it was there a long time. But eventually it rose yet again, and gnawed again at the spruce. In the end, the corpse didn't even heed the warning that dawn was breaking.

And they kept this up until the spruce began to lean to one side, and the day was lighting up the land. The man finally was able to descend from the tree where he had spent the night. He untied his draught reindeer, and he drove until he found a great root cluster of an old pine. He set it ablaze, and he flipped the *noaidi*'s coffin into the fire, on top of the burning stump, and he left it to burn.

So he set off driving his reindeer, and eventually he got home. When someone asked him how it all went, he simply told them that it took him a night, but he nonetheless got him to his grave. Yet he took no pleasure from those wages at all. After some years, he finally told people what kind of grave he had put the old *noaidi* in.

The Haunting of the Old Deceased *Noaidi*, Version 2
Uula Morottaja (T. I. Itkonen)

The father of a Skolt Sámi died. He didn't go himself to bring his father to the graveyard, but instead he paid another man, who went to bring his father there. This man noticed that the body was sitting upright when he was driving.

He tied up his draught reindeer and climbed up into a tree. But that dead person began to bite the spruce. The corpse's driver took a flint striker and started to strike it. The dead man hesitated to look at the spark, but eventually it didn't interrupt him from his gnawing at all. Then the driver screamed:

—Dawn is breaking!

So the dead man stopped briefly to look, but again started to gnaw, and he kept biting on the spruce until morning came. Then the man yelled again that dawn had come. Right away, the dead man jumped into his coffin so violently that the boards rattled.

From this point on, the Skolt Sámi stopped burying their dead in one place.

The Pastor and the Sexton
Uula Morottaja (T. I. Itkonen)
ML 4015

There was a graveyard around one church, and the dead could be seen at night burning candles in the church. The sexton said to the pastor that he would spend the night in the church and would be alive the next morning. The pastor didn't believe him, and they struck up a wager. The pastor took the sexton to the church and locked him inside.

The sexton took three large stones and went to the balcony. When evening came and it started to darken, the dead started to come forth and light candles. They could be heard moving toward the balcony. The sexton rolled a stone down, and then everyone vanished and all the candles snuffed out.

At midnight, the dead came out again and lit candles and started again to move toward the balcony. The sexton again rolled a large stone down. Again all of it vanished. In the morning when it was getting toward dawn, the dead came again and lit their candles. The sexton took the largest of the stones and rolled it out on the floor. Again all of it vanished.

When the pastor came to the church in the morning, the sexton was still there. The pastor said that he would also spend the night at the church, just like the sexton did. The sexton said that he wouldn't make it. And again they struck up a wager. The sexton locked up the pastor in the church. The pastor took a Bible and went to the pulpit. And when the sexton came to the church in the morning, the only thing left of the pastor was his guts pulled out and wrapped around the pulpit.

HISTORICAL AND REGIONAL LEGENDS

Like other legends, historical legends are regarded as actual happenings, although they do not generally contain supernatural elements. Commonly told about real people in recent memory, historical legends occur in places that are regionally known and even specified in detail as if to prove the truthfulness of the tale. Still, they too test the boundaries of what reality means, with encounters that are fantastical, or otherwise unbelievable.

Legends often involve some aspects of transgressions—people behaving in ways they shouldn't—and the terrible consequences of risky behavior. For this reason, legends are often told to tease us with social anxieties and cultural fears and to normalize behavior of young people. Alternatively, they also challenge people to confront these anxieties by engaging in transgressive behaviors, sometimes daring people to even visit the sites of tragic events—a practice known as legend tripping. These cultural norms are alive and well today. Teenagers still frequent graveyards or "haunted" sites to engage in all manners of illicit behaviors (drinking, smoking, sex), while telling scary stories and trying to frighten each other, all while conquering their fears and asserting their own emerging adult identity. In traditional cultural settings, the landscape itself can become something of a library: when people visit sites of historical importance, these stories are recounted and history is remembered and carried forward. This practice is common today across cultures.

These historical legends reflect both historical realities and ongoing anxieties within the Aanaar community. They reflect the dangers of having multiple love interests ("Siggá's Legend," "Siggá's Weeping Strait"), the threat of encountering violent people ("The Cannibal Vuolliǯ of Ij-jävri," "The Dead Constable"), or the consequences of poor decision-making in one's young adulthood ("The

Maiden Hannaaǯ's Decapitation Story"). On the other hand, some of these legends might be better regarded as humorous narratives ("She Who Went to Sleep as a Maiden and Woke as a Wife," "Famed Antt-Piättår's Eelliǯ, Fiancé-Waiter"). Part joke, part local legend, these stories test the boundaries between real people and the absurdity of their actions. Such unique characters in a community can be remembered for a long time in stories.

Siggá's Legend
P. Valle (A. V. Koskimies)

There was a fine woman living in Aanaar. She had two suitors, and both she thought to be good, so she didn't want to reject either of them. So the parish's elders came together to figure out whom she should turn away. They realized that there was a good place nearby that they could go to where the matter could be resolved. They set off rowing to the southern half of Lake Aanaar, and when they came to a strait the parish elders announced their decision. According to their plan, Siggá was to be placed on a stone in the middle of the strait, and the two suitors would be on each side facing each other, and they were to shoot at each other's heads with their bows. He who remained alive would get to be Siggá's husband.

The others rowed away to watch what happened. Siggá waited there in good spirits:

—Now at least I will see who will be my husband. Either one is good, whoever survives.

But when both bows were shot by each suitor, she took fright and said:

—Oh merciful sun, moon, and stars, how these matters may have gone!

The people who were in boats hurried to take Siggá from the rock. And when they went to find the first suitor, they found him lifeless with an arrow wound in his forehead. They went to the other suitor and found him just as the first. And from that day on that strait was called Kalluudem-čuálmi (Kallosalmi; Skull Strait) and the island Kalluudem-suáloi (Kallosaari; Skull Island) and the rock Myerssee-keđgi (Morsiankivi; Fiancée's Rock).

Siggá became so sorrowful that she almost lost her mind. In one boat there was a man, whose name was Nestor, who started to console Siggá as best as he was able. And when they rowed to an island, Siggá wanted desperately to go onto the land. Nestor promised to help her with anything she wanted. And that island's name is even to this day Nestor-suáloi (Nestorinsaari; Nestor's Island) and the strait Nestor-čuálmi (Nestorinsalmi; Nestor's Strait).

They came to another island, which had a peninsula, and again Siggá wanted to go onto land, and she went ashore and cried hard. Siggá didn't want to leave that island and go back to the boat, but Nestor promised he would be able to get her a husband. And so he did. When he went to Stuorra-vuona (Varanger Fjord), which was in the sea, he took Siggá along with him, and there was a good man there, who married Siggá. And she lived the rest of her life happy, fishing in the sea and in the inland lakes in the forests, in Njiđggujävri (Njidggujärvi), in Ajnoluobbali (Ainolompolo), and Saaveehjävri (Sivakkajärvi), and she built a winter dwelling along the Ađikku River, which still has a field, which is called even today Siggá's Field.

Siggá's Weeping Strait
Uula Morottaja (T. I. Itkonen)

A maiden had two suitors who were both to her liking, but she couldn't be a wife to both of them, nor could they both take the same person as a wife. For that reason they went to two sides of a strait and agreed to shoot at each other with bows at the same time. He who defeated the other, killing him, would get the maiden for his wife.

But each man struck each other, and they both died at that place. When Siggá came to hear this, she ran to that place, and she cried and mourned them for a long time.

When those men were buried, the girl was buried alive between them and people said:

—Since you couldn't reject either one of them, now you shall get both.

The place is on an island in Lake Aanaar, and its name is now Siggá's Čiärum-čoalmi (Siggan Itkusalmi; Siggá's Weeping Strait).

The Cannibal Vuolliʒ of Ij-jävri
Mikko Aikio, by letter (A. V. Koskimies)[1]

Around Ij-jävri (Iijärvi) during pagan times there was a horrible man whose name was Ij-jävri Vuolliʒ. He was so crude and bad-natured that he ate his wife and children. First he ate his wife, and then he gave the skin to his oldest son, so he could endure the cold. And he fed his boy, so he would fatten up, until he too would be ready to eat.

Once a guest was visiting, and Vuolliʒ was roasting a flank of his wife. The guest asked Ij-jävri Vuolliʒ:

---

1. According to Laitinen, this happened in 1769, as noted by I. Fellman in *Handlingar och Uppsatser III*, 198–203.

—What are you roasting?

Vuolliǯ said:

—I'm roasting what I'm roasting. It's a side of lamb I'm roasting.

Once some reindeer-herding Sámi were passing through with their reindeer herds. The oldest boy, who was wearing the skin of his dead mother, started to go to bed without undressing first. The father said:

—Why aren't you undressing?

He said, this way would be warmer. So he went to bed still wearing his coat and leggings. And when the father went to bed and had fallen asleep, the boy got up secretly during the night and set off running, following the tracks of the reindeer-herding Sámi, who had passed by earlier in the day. He ran so long that he caught up to them. So he was taken into their company and he got free from his father. His name was after that point "Pääđiist pessee Maattiǯ" (Escaped the Kettle Maattiǯ).

But Ij-jävri Vuolliǯ ate all his other children. When people realized what Vuolliǯ had done, they regarded him as evil, and they gathered up the men and went to stand guard outside his cottage by night, for Ij-jävri Vuolliǯ slept nights with an axe and a knife by his side. When they were on guard, he came out naked. They attacked him and captured him and tied him up. Then they sentenced him to carry a stone and bear it until the time that blood began to come from his mouth and nose, and he tired out and died.

The Maiden Hannaaǯ's Decapitation Story[2]
Iisakki Mannermaa (A. V. Koskimies)

There was in former times an Aanaar Sámi maiden who was beautiful and graceful and an otherwise pleasant person. Her parents indeed always warned their daughter about whorishness.[3] The daughter obeyed everything her parents told her. She was a dutiful daughter and an otherwise godly girl, but the world however seduced her into its snares so that she became a whore, and while living in that state she eventually became pregnant.

---

2. Hannaaǯ was executed for these crimes, although the actual site of execution doesn't appear to have been in Aanaar. DuBois (1995) discusses this piece in terms of wickedness coming from outside the community and the belief that Aanaar Sámi compassion is closer to a godly ideal than that presented by the Finnish criminal justice system of the day.

3. The word used in Aanaar Sámi is *huàrrà*, a cognate of "whore," which reflects Mannermaa's attitudes toward premarital sex. The implication, however, is more of unchaste behavior than actual prostitution.

The girl's parents kept watch, so that the girl wouldn't at least do away with the child. But the daughter went into the forest, gave birth to her child there, and killed it.

But when the girl went back home, two people came behind her, and they told everything that she had done in the forest. The girl confessed that she had done wrong, and they returned to their home. The girl's parents noticed right away that she had already given birth to her child. The girl didn't dare to deny anything any longer, since the strangers had seen her illicit doings.

The strangers, who had seen the maiden's terrible doings in the forest, went and told the village's constable about this matter. The constable wrote down this matter in his book, just as he had done with other issues. So one winter some magistrates came to hold court. The village constable notified the judge about the matter, that Hannaaǯ had birthed a living child into this world but killed it. Hannaaǯ came in front of the court as well as those two witnesses. The judge studied the matter and decided that Hannaaǯ was to be beheaded after three days.

The fourth day was the day of the beheading. The executioner, who had come along with the magistrates, came to Hannaaǯ's home and told her briefly who he was and what his profession was upon command of the magistrates. He dressed her up in a new white dress, took her by the hand, and walked next to her to the place of the beheading, which was a large stone within sight of the Aanaar parsonage.

As the executioner and Hannaaǯ walked to the place of the beheading, people sang a hymn in Finnish, which started like this: "For my soul came so soon / Such a heavy command."[4]

The hymn was sung through, and when it ended the executioner took his axe and went with Hannaaǯ to the stone, where the beheading was to take place. The executioner covered Hannaaǯ's eyes, put her neck on a log, and struck through her neck.

Many people were standing around the place of the beheading. Suddenly, they noticed that from Hannaaǯ's headless body there appeared something that looked like a star in the sky, which rose up into the heaven. People said to each other:

—Look, look at Hannaaǯ's soul, how it goes to God!

---

4. This hymn is number 392 from the hymnal of 1701, identified in a section for death and burials. The hymn speaks about the unexpectedness of death and how it spares no one, about Christ who is forgiving, and about the joys of heaven as opposed to the harsh life on this earth.

Some cried hard at that place. Others wondered what kind of marvel it was that they saw coming from Hannaaȝ's body. Others thanked God that her soul had gone to be with God.

So it was that this was the first and, to this date, the last person beheaded in Aanaar.

The Dead Constable[5]
Mikko Aikio (A. V. Koskimies)

People tell the following story about the late great-grandfather of the current farm master of Pännijävri (Hammasjärvi).

In Aanaar there was a man who was chosen to be a headman of the magistrates, which was called a village constable. His name was Juhanas Morottijjee (Juhani Morottaja). He was a hunter and had made an agreement with other people, who were from Kittâl (Kittilä). In those days, there were still beaver in the rivers of Aanaar, and such was the case in the Aaveel (Ivalo) River as well, the river about which the late constable had made the agreement with the men of Kittâl.

But two men of Kittâl came to the place of agreement before the constable, and they were already trapping beaver and even killed one. After a day or so, the constable came to the place of agreement and found the *lávvu* of his companions, but they weren't there. He started to look over their belongings, and he noticed that they had already killed a beaver. He took it and went away, for it was killed on the Aanaar side of the border.

When the men from Kittâl came to their *lávvu*, they noticed that a person had come into their *lávvu* and taken the beaver they killed. They became terribly angry and set off to follow the tracks where he had gone.

When they caught up to him and found his *lávvu*, upon their arrival they threatened to beat him. When the constable heard this, he became afraid and worried that they would do something bad to him. He was already asleep when they came and he heard their threats. He grabbed his rifle and shot one in the leg. The men attacked him right away, and one was planning to whip him and strip him of the beaver he took, but the other stabbed him to death with a spear.

They tied three stones to his body and took him and dragged him into the depths of the river and sunk him there. Then they left and continued their hunting and went back home, when they were ready to leave.

---

5. Kent (2014, 40) verifies this story as historical fact.

But the deceased constable's people at home waited and waited, and they didn't hear anything about their hunter. Then a woodpecker started to spend time near their home and took to pecking the wood of their *goahti* and their doorframes as well. Then the constable's son Jooanaǯ (Jouni), who was at that time a little boy, put the door ajar, and when the woodpecker started to tap on the door frame, he snatched up the woodpecker into his hand and ripped it in two, for they thought it was a bad omen for the beaver hunter, for whom they waited, sick with worry.[6]

And so the deceased constable was gone forever. People even searched for him, but he wasn't found. Eventually, they searched for him with the help of a *noaidi*, who supposedly knew how he was murdered: that people had killed him and with the help of three stones sunk him into a deep river.

They who had killed him confessed it once to a pastor that they had killed a man in the forest on a hunting trip, and drowned him in a river.

The Fight of the Constables
Mikko Aikio (A. V. Koskimies)

In olden times, just like today, people fought over territorial borders. So the story goes that in Aanaar and Uccjuuhâ (Utsjoki) there were village constables who came together with jurors to advise about borders. They did not in those negotiations come to any sort of agreement at that time. They started to argue with each other, and they grew angry. Each of them had wanted naturally to have their land be larger and to move the border farther outward, but neither would accept the other's proposals.

They got so terribly angry that they began to fight. They each had a bow, which they drew, and they were planning to shoot at each other. They started to circle around some great tree, and they circled and they shot at the same time. Each hit the other with an arrow, and both died.

People took their bodies away, cut that tree through at the height of a fathom (180 centimeters; 6 feet) from the ground, and they left the stump there. They scorched the surface so it wouldn't rot, so it would stand long as a remembrance and marker of the fact that the two village constables had killed each other here.

And the stump is still standing today on the shore of the Deatnu (Teno) River, and the name of the creek is Tuárrupec-aajâ (Tappelupetäjäoja; Fighting Pine Creek).

---

6. This woodpecker omen is mentioned in the chapter "Omens and Signs."

Historical and Regional Legends

The Late Raassaǯ
Juho Petteri Lusmaniemi (A. V. Koskimies)

There was once a man named Raassaǯ, and he usually was the winner in the wagers he struck. Once he bet some man that he could get the postman on the road to step aside for him. In those days, everyone on the road needed to stand aside for the postman.

He made himself a big bundle, stuffed his reindeer-fur coat full of mosses,[7] and set off to walk along the postal road. The postman came toward him and blurted out:

—Who is on the postal road?

Raassaǯ answered:

—I am Raassaǯ, and I will stand aside for no one, for I am carrying letters from the king and I have a heavy load.

The postman needed to stand aside as best as he could, and he even tipped his cap and said:

—Safe travels and Godspeed.

This same Raassaǯ was once hunting wild reindeer in the forest and met some hunters. They saw that he had a really long axe handle. They asked:

—Why are you holding such a long axe handle?

Raassaǯ answered:

—I am holding a fathom-and-a-half handle (275 cm; 9 feet) so I can reach a bear to strike it before it can get to me.

Piäjååǯ
Juho Petteri Lusmaniemi (A. V. Koskimies)

There was once a man, whose name was Piäjååǯ, who was summoned as a witness in the matters of a theft, and he was called in front of the court. He pretended to be crazy, walked to the edge of the judge's table, and started to roll his eyes and let his mouth drop wide open. The judge saw what kind of man he was and asked:

—Are you thinking now?

---

7. Seemingly, Raassaǯ is stuffing his coat to appear larger. Alternatively, he may be using his coat as the bundle.

—Well, I am thinking . . . am I not?

The judge couldn't do anything but order him to leave, since he was fooling him and the jurors into thinking he was crazy.

Once this same Piäjååʒ had stolen a bottle of brandy from some person. He had two fiancées, and they were unknowingly summoned as witnesses against Piäjååʒ in the matter of the bottle theft. Well, they pretended to be crazy when they were called inside. One said when she came in:

—I have come. Now all of you, kill! I have come. Kill!

The second started to repeat:

—What is this thing, this bottle? A churn, or a half barrel, or a churn, or a half barrel, or what?

She even asked the jurors:

—What is this thing, this bottle?

Then the judge ordered them to leave as well.

Famed Antt-Piättår's Eelliʒ, Fiancé-Waiter
Juho Petteri Lusmaniemi (A. V. Koskimies)

Farm master: The sounds of bells can be heard from the river.

Servant girl: Don't deceive me anymore. You have fooled me before.

Farm master: I'm not fooling, no. I'm telling the truth, I am.

Servant girl: So I too went out as well, and you really *can* hear the bells. I ran to the barn and put on the very finest apron, the very finest shawl, but when I tried to get out I realized that my hat was still poor.[8]

She went to get a little medicinal brandy. She asked someone for it, and received some, then took a little taste:

—It's all in there, and that's good enough![9]

---

8. The humor in this story lies in Eelliʒ dressing up in her finest barn clothes in anticipation of meeting a suitor.

9. The punchline in this story is unclear, but it seems to imply that even a small taste of brandy is more than Eelliʒ can handle, perhaps undermining the purpose of seeking it out for medicinal purposes.

She Who Went to Sleep as a Maiden and Woke as a Wife
P. Valle (A. V. Koskimies)

This story happened at the Aanaar church.[10] When Aŋŋel-Erkki, who was born in Piälduvyemi (Peltovuoma), was in Aanaar for confirmation as a young man, the widow of Rivdul (Riutala) had one daughter named Leena still at home. The widow wanted to get Erkki to be her son-in-law. He would get a household under his control, and he could support her as an elder of the house. Aŋŋel-Erkki had a brother named Saammal-Aŋŋel, who started to talk with Erkki so he could get to court Leena. Since the girl had an entire house ready for him, it would be suitable to live there. But Erkki bemoaned:

—How can I even begin to court her, when I have nothing more than two empty hands?

But Saammal said:

—How now . . . I will help in the beginning for my part, and fortune will take you further. It is rare to be offered a complete house. You need to take action at once. I'll even prepare an engagement party for you, if you are not able to do so for yourself.

Well, Erkki agreed to it. So they started to arrange the engagement party. But there was also a wealthy boy whose name was Irján-Kààrăǯ. He too had thought about starting to court Leena, but he hadn't been man enough to do that. He had, however, a bottle of wine he had bought on a work trip in Várgàáh (Vuoreija; Vardø) city. When Irján-Kààrăǯ got to hear what was happening on the other side of the church site, he ran to his cottage, opened his trunk, snatched that bottle, slipped it into his breast pocket, and grabbed his money purse, which contained fifty silver dollars.

After coming to the other side of the church site, he peeped with eager eyes to look around corners, where he might find Leena. After seeing some small female, he deduced that she looked enough like Leena. He went to her, embraced her, and whispered lovingly:

—We should talk, but we can't otherwise talk about such important matters, on account of all these people, unless we go into your cabin.

Leena said:

—Well, just say what you have to say.

But Irján-Kààrăǯ said:

---

10. During these times in Aanaar, the church was surrounded by temporary cabins that were used for lodging when people visited the churches, explaining why people have come from afar to Aanaar in this story.

—Not here, since there are so many people, and I have something to say that must be said among only us two. Be so kind, and let's pop into your cabin, so we can chat.

—Well, okay, let's go, agreed Leena.

So they went into the cabin and Leena asked:

—Well, what do you have to say? Out with it!

A youth ran to the outside to listen. Irján-Kààràӡ grabbed the bottle from his breast pocket and offered it to her:

—Have a taste of this first!

Leena saw how the bottle was thoroughly decorated, and she took a drink. It tasted sweet. She had never tasted something so sweet in her entire life. Irján-Kààràӡ started to caress her, and he warned her:

—Throw away that marriage business with Erkki. He is poor as an empty sack, which surely is unable to stand up on its own.

He grabbed his large money purse, lowered it onto Leena's lap, and said:

—These boys are something else! If you take me on, I give you this purse as an engagement present.

Leena tried to lift it: it was as heavy as a bag full of rocks, and she said:

—If this is all silver, then I would have money for my whole life!

Irján-Kààràӡ said:

—It's all silver, I swear by my own eyes.

—Well, good man, don't swear by your eyes, your eyes are bad as it is, said Leena. And she started to marvel at Irján-Kààràӡ's great amount of silver and riches, and the love he had for her. Even though he was a complete stranger before, he now was offering the best he had.

—I don't intend to swear, nor have I learned to, since it's not a custom in the entire parish, but I have heard it from the Finns. That's why I talk that way, but grant me pardon and guzzle from this sweet and ornamented bottle. If only you could see how beautiful the bottle's outside is!

Irján-Kààràӡ struck a match so that she could see, and Leena stated that it was pleasant in both taste and appearance. She drank more, and she started to feel good and fell asleep.

But the suitors had in the meantime made a deal and arrangement with the widow and her relatives. The spokesperson Saammal said:

—Now the matter is agreed. There's nothing else to do but invite the fiancé inside.

The fiancé was still in their company, not knowing where Leena had ended up, and he hadn't seen or heard her even after having gone to find her. The word spread through the parish that an engagement party was planned, but the bride was missing. Anyone who knew anything about her would get a reward. Then a group of boys told where Leena could be found for the reward.

They went to that place and took Irján-Kåårăž out by the neck, but Leena was passed out and had no sense left in her. Erkki carried her to the engagement cabin and set her down on the table like a dead body. The bridegroom thought:

—Indeed for this there is no remedy. I need to stop this whole undertaking.

But Aŋŋel-Saammal said:

—What about this? We are not children, so enough with the child's play! Push good Leena under the bed, and we will use a stand-in for your bride. Don't worry about your poverty, Erkki. I will give you two milking cows to start with and fortune will indeed bring a man forward.

So Leena's place was taken by her oldest sister, and the couple sat on a footstool. The speaker asked the wishes of both, and they offered their consent. So the engagement presents were given to the woman who was the stand-in. She received them. The speaker Saammal started to bless the new couple: "God has joined you, and you will no longer separate aside from death." Then people sung the hymn "Let the Lord Bless You Well," and the engagement presents were put into Leena's bag. But her sister Riitu needed to sleep with her fiancé for the night before her shift was through.

When Leena woke the next morning, she started to find it odd that she was under the bed, not knowing when or where she had crawled to. She last remembered being in the storehouse with Irján-Kåårăž. The people all were still sleeping. In the morning she took her bag, which was set next to her, opened it, and found bundles of cloth. Then she noticed her mother was also waking up, and she asked:

—Who crammed these into my bag?

The mother told everything about how the evening had gone. Leena listened closely with her mouth open and griped:

—Well, so it is. At least you, mother, were there looking out for me. I guess everybody knew what they were doing. Oh, but where are Erkki and Riitu, then?

—They are still sleeping.[11]

---

11. The humor in this punch line seemingly lies in the businesslike attitudes everyone maintains toward having a wedding ceremony and an implied sexual encounter with a stand-in for Leena.

STORIES ABOUT ČUĐIT

Čuđit (pronounced in English "choo-theet") stories are among the most common of Sámi historical legends. Set in the distant past, perhaps anytime between the Viking Age and the eighteenth century, they tell the story of bands of merciless marauders who come to Sápmi to indiscriminately murder Sámi people and steal their possessions. No one is certain who exactly the Čuđit were or what the precise historical basis of these legends is, but variations of the term *Chude* have been historically used to describe various Baltic Finnic peoples in the areas of Northwest Russia, Karelia, and Estonia. Komi people believe that Čuđit are also their own mythic ancestors, and other scholars have linked Čuđit with Veps and Seto peoples. In a Sámi context, the term *Čuđit* might best be used to describe not a specific ethnic group but rather any invaders from the south or east who come to raid Sámi camps. Around the turn of the twentieth century, many Čuđit stories use the term *Ruošša-Čuđit* (Russian Čuđit), making explicit link between Čuđit and ethnic Russians. This phenomenon is likely a product of its time and the political realities of the eighteenth and nineteenth centuries.

Čuđit stories tend to take a specific narrative form. A group of ruthless Čuđit are able to isolate an individual Sámi person (often a young adult or an older woman) whom they compel to serve as their guide to another Sámi settlement so that they may raid it. The guide uses superior knowledge of the environment to outsmart the Čuđit, usually leading to their gruesome deaths, whether leading them over a cliff, getting them to walk across unsafe lake ice, guiding them in a raft down a waterfall, or stranding them on an island.

Some of these stories feature a young heroic character named Laurukàʒ (Laurukainen). Not distinct to Sámi cultures, Laurukàʒ is well known in North and Ladoga Karelia, as well as parts of Finland (Kainuu and northern

Ostrobothnia), in particular in places that endured the numerous border wars between Sweden-Finland and Russia, when raid wars were occurring between Finns and Karelians. More than six hundred tales of this type have been collected from these regions (Sarmela 2009, 487–89).

At heart stories that depict the violence of colonialism and its threat to shared Sámi values and communities, Čuđit stories resonate deeply even today. Nils Gaup's Oscar-nominated 1987 film *Ofelaš* (*Pathfinder*) is a modern interpretation of a Čuđit story; or, on her album *Orda*, Sofia Jannok's song "Čuđit" is translated as "Colonizer." These stories will perhaps stay poignant until colonization ends in Sápmi.

The Čuđit on the Move
P. Valle (A. V. Koskimies)
ATU 968; ML 8000

In Čarmanjargâ (Tšarminiemi) there is a bay, which is called Čuđeluohtâ (Vainolaislahti; Čuđit Bay). At the base of the bay there was a summertime fishing place. People saw some thieving Čuđit coming right toward that fishing place. So they took their boat out farther, behind the peninsula. Their seine wasn't visible on the shore, since it was on the island farther out.

And as the Čuđit, whose approach was being watched by one of the men, came closer, the people no longer had time to escape anywhere. Instead, they had to take their children and also their dogs into the *goahti*. The *goahti* was built deeper in the forest, so if the Čuđit happened to come by, it wouldn't be visible from the shore.

And so it happened that the Čuđit were walking past the *goahti* and they didn't notice it, instead walking right past it until they found a boat on the shore, with which they could row their companions over the strait to the island. They thought there would be a house there, since they saw some large stones, which they mistook for cottages. It was a really small island, which had no dwellings—only some reindeer. They hung around the reindeer the whole day and eventually found some tame draught reindeer, which they tried to take with a lasso and to kill.[1] When they had killed them, they lit a fire and roasted the meat and skinned the hides, as much as they needed to get the meat. They

---

1. Killing the valuable draught reindeer for meat symbolically shows the brutality and stupidity of the Čuđit. The word "tried" implies that they struggle with even routine Sámi work.

fell asleep for the night, and they woke and roasted more meat and ate their fill. Then they set off over the strait to the mainland of Čarmanjargâ, where they came from. That island's name is still to this day Puásuičuopâmsuáloi (Poronleikkomasaari; Cut Reindeer Island).

Then they walked to a hill, where they found some more tamed reindeer. They again took some of the tamer draught reindeer from that place and killed them, but they weren't able to eat any longer, since they had eaten so much on the island. They thought:

—It was good to eat that reindeer meat, but it'll no longer do, since there was so much, that I can't bear to eat any more. We'll just have to take the legs of these ones.

So they cut up only the legs of the killed draught reindeer and they left the rest of the bodies there. That hill's name is to this day Jyelgičuopâstimvaarâǯ (Jalanleikkaamavaara; Leg Cutting Hill). And they went back from Čarmanjargâ to the south.

A Story from the Time of Čuđit
P. Valle (A. V. Koskimies)

ATU 968; ML 8000

In some household there was a head of house who had a brother as a servant, and they were hunting birds in the autumn with bows. Other people had just come home from fishing. The brothers came home when the wife was cooking the fish. They stretched themselves out on their beds for a bit, until the wife finished up the cooking.

And when the wife had finished cooking, she took the fish dishes and started to ladle up some fish, but she noticed a shadow in the pot. At that time it was not permitted to ladle up the head of a pike on its side unless it lay so in the pot too, and this itself was an omen. And so she scooped with the ladle the pike's head with the wrong side up, and showed it to the men.

So they saw that now this was serious business, since the pike head was lying on its side in the ladle. The man asked his wife what had happened. The wife showed him the smoke hole, and the husband and farmhand noticed that there was a person peeking down the smoke hole, and they saw that he wasn't a proper kind of person.[2] And since he was still staring through the hole, the husband shot at his head with his bow. He was knocked out,[3] and rolled down the *goahti*.

---

2. This is a roundabout way of saying that it was clear there was something wrong with this person.

3. Why he is only knocked out from an arrow is unclear.

They went out to look, and when he recovered, they saw that he was a Russian.[4] They said to the Russian:

—Are you alone, or do you have companions in hiding? If you speak the truth, then we won't kill you. But if you say "no," then we will kill you.

He promised to speak the truth in Russian. He had left his companions on the other side of the mountain. When they saw that there was a place of residence nearby, they stayed behind to build a fire, and they sent him to the home to see how many people were there.

They told him:

—We will tie you up until we go see if it's true, what you've said.

So they tied up the man, and they went to look where he said the group was waiting. Since it was already dark when they arrived there, the Čuđit were already burning a fire. They had a warlord-leader, whom they started to feed. When they crept closer, the group sitting around the campfire didn't see them. The man reckoned:

—I will shoot the end of that fork, right when he's giving a juicy bite to the leader.

The servant reckoned:

—You won't hit the end of the fork.

But the man said he was able to hit it. And when the server offered the leader a bite, then the man shot the very end of the fork. The fork stuck into his throat hole. The soldier fell to his death, and the others attacked the server, thinking that he was responsible for that wickedness. But the man and farmhand again shot into the group until the remaining men ran off. The place was devoid of life. Only the dead remained there, some half dead, and they then beat them, until everyone was dead. And so they returned home and told the man who was tied up there that if he intended to be loyal to them, they wouldn't kill him, but instead they would keep him as a servant.

When he heard that his companions were all already killed, he started trembling and promised to be a subject and to serve them as well as he was able. So they released him and kept him as their servant, and he was obedient to everyone.

The Boy Who Hunted with a Bow
Mikko Aikio (A. V. Koskimies)
ATU 968; ML 8000

In former times in Sápmi, there was a place where some people lived. One summer they set off to seine and the children remained at home. One of those

---

4. Russian is used interchangeably here with Čuhti.

boys had a bow, which he carried with him as he walked along the shores and shot birds. At the tips of his bow's arrowheads were the beaks of loons, so if he happened to shoot a larger bird, it too would die.[5]

Once while he was walking, he noticed Čuđit coming through a strait on the other side of the lake, where their home was. He became frightened and was about to run back home, but he started to wonder if they would perhaps do even more evil, if they followed him to his home. He ran to the lakeshore, to a place where they would need to land their boat. He drew an arrow and went to watch for the Čuđit, who were coming through the strait on a raft. When they noticed the Sámi boy, they were happy, since they would be able to rob him and take his possessions. They sang about the boy like this:

—Sámi boy, Sámi boy, hah-hah-haa!
Black spot on his backside, hah-hah-haa!

But the boy wasn't as helpless as they thought. When they came close enough to the boy, into the range of his bow, he shot his bow, whose arrows had the loon beaks. He aimed at the head of the nearest one, and he rolled into the lake. Then the other Čuđit got scared, and turned back toward the open water, where they had come from. But before they could get up the strait to the other side, the seiners were already coming back and they saw the Čuđit. They rowed up behind them, beat them, and pushed the Čuđit into the lake, where they drowned.

The Boy Who Hunted with a Bow, Version 2
Uula Morottaja (T. I. Itkonen)
ATU 968; ML 8000

There was a boy who was alone at home, and he was making a bow. The other people were out seining. Just when he got his bow finished, he noticed that two fugitives were coming up the strait, swimming. The boy shot the one first in the head with his new bow. The second turned to flee. The boy shot after him. And so he killed them both. It was the first game with his new bow.

The Death of the Čuđit
Uula Morottaja (T. I. Itkonen)
ATU 968; ML 8000

Some Čuđit came to a *goahti*. They lay down off to the side of a field, so when night fell they could go rob the people. Some old woman saw the Čuđit,

---

5. Loon beak tips were considered especially lethal, even bearing supernatural power.

when they were lazing about. She let the people of the house know that Čuđit were coming. In the evening two men went with axe in hand to guard each side of the *goahti* door. When the invaders started to come in, they struck them all with their axes and killed them. Only a few were able to escape.

Futile Fear
P. Valle (A. V. Koskimies)
ATU 968; ML 8000

In the times when Čuđit were traveling throughout Lapland, and also in Aanaar, people lived always in fear. One time, at some household, there were people leaving to go seine, and one old woman stayed home, and her name was Ajla. The seiners stayed until dark and came back in the dark and started to hang their seine on the rack to dry. But no fire was seen in the home. They thought that perhaps Čuđit had again come and killed their woman at home, since she was not seen burning a fire.

They sent a boy quietly to creep up and look to see if any of the women were still alive. The boy crept to the doorframe. He opened the door, stepped inside, and called the name of the homekeeper.

—Ajla, hey, are you here, Ajla?

And that old woman, who had fallen asleep, jumped up and started to crawl to the doorside of the *goahti*, where the wood was, and started to light a fire and grab for some wood. And in grabbing some wood, she touched the boy's outer coat. The boy became alarmed and jumped out again, ran to the shore where the people were hanging the seine, and said:

—There was someone in the dark *goahti*, and they crawled to me and started to grab at me!

Then they got scared and tossed their seine onto the lakeshore, took to the water, and rowed to the open water. There they stayed for the night, up until morning. When their person at home, that old grandmother Ajla, lit a fire and it started to glow out the smoke hole, and it illuminated the area next to the *goahti* beneath the pine canopy, they thought that some Čuđit were already burning a fire within the pine canopy, and they said:

—Some devil is burning a fire in the pine canopy.

And they became even more frightened, and they rowed into hiding as fast as they could.

When day came they went back and rowed near their home and looked at the shore and the field to see what they would find, but they didn't see anything other than that old grandmother, whom they had left at home. They rowed to

Santeri Valle next to his fish-drying rack, 1914. Photo: Toivo Itkonen. Image courtesy of the Finnish National Board of Antiquities.

the shore and came home, and there were no Čuđit who had come to destroy their home and kill their people, as they had imagined.

The Disobedient Daughter
Uula Morottaja (T. I. Itkonen)
ATU 968; ML 8000

During the time of the Great Fear[6] people didn't dare to move about outside of their homes. If they rowed on the lake to fish, they went by night through the

---

6. *Palo äjgin* (*pelon aika*) literally translates as "the time of fear," a rather ambiguous reference. Most likely this refers to a period of time of war between Russia and Sweden, probably in the eighteenth century, when three wars lasted a total of twenty-five years between the two nations, including the Great Wrath (1713–21). However, border wars were common at least since the late fifteenth century. *Palo äjgin* tends to be associated with the time of the Čuđit.

shores and islands and they wrapped their oars in leather or pieces of fabric so that they wouldn't squeak. If an oarlock would break, then it wouldn't be thrown into the water, lest Čuđit see it and think that there were people nearby. For their part, they lived in the forest and in caverns, under the ground even.

One family had dug themselves a place to live in the ground under a small pine so that they wouldn't be noticed even if someone came near. They didn't dare to light a fire even, to ensure Čuđit would not see smoke. The eldest daughter was weaving a band with a heddle and a bone cone, and she had tied the end of the string to the root of the young spruce, which was on top of their roof. The parents forbid her from weaving as such, since the tree always moved when she tightened the weft. But the daughter didn't mind them, and kept weaving anyway.

So some Čuđit happened to come right by there, and one noticed that the young spruce was moving, even though it was quite calm out. They stopped, started to look around, and found the people hiding there. They killed them all and stole their goods.

The Čuđit Fall into a Ravine
Iisakki Mannermaa (A. V. Koskimies)
ATU 968; ML 8000

Long ago there was a man who lived on an island in Aanaar, and his name was Laurukàǯ. The island, which was near Juvduu (Juutua), had the name Sädisuáloi (Säisaari).

The Russians were in those times the enemies of the Sámi. For Laurukàǯ, who could speak Russian, it was easy to recognize Russians. One time when Russians came, who in those days were called Čuđit, Laurukàǯ told everyone that he was a Čuđit chieftain. The Russians believed him and were pleased to take him as their guide.

Laurukàǯ set off walking as a Čuđit guide. They climbed to the summit of some high mountain and waited there until it got dark. Laurukàǯ told the Russians that it was steep on the other side of this mountain, and below the precipice there stood a wealthy home. But he, in fact, knew the real path to that house. He set off to walk there, but before they got to the top of the precipice, he lit a fire. And when the fire was well lit, Laurukàǯ told the Russians to take a piece of burning wood in their hands and said:

—We will depart in a single-file line. You need to be a little bit behind me, and when you see me take off quickly with my burning firebrand, you need to run as fast as you can.

After saying this, Laurukȧǯ took his torch in his hand and left to lead the Russians. When he came to the top of the high cliff, he threw the torch down and he himself jumped off to the side. The Russians fell down the cliff to their death.

The Čuđit Drown in the Rapids
Iisakki Mannermaa (A. V. Koskimies)
ATU 968; ML 8000

Once Laurukȧǯ and Russians met each other in the forest. The invaders tried to shoot Laurukȧǯ, but he yelled in Russian:
—Don't shoot me! I'm a Čuđit leader!
The Russians came to talk with Laurukȧǯ, and they were happy that they had found such a guide. Laurukȧǯ took the Čuđit to the shores of Aanaar near his home, where he had a large boat already prepared. He pushed the boat into the water, and they got into the boat and set off rowing along the great waters of Lake Aanaar, toward Pȧččvei (Paatsjoki). The Russians were very tired and they weren't able to row any longer, and Laurukȧǯ wouldn't let them row to any land to sleep. He said to the Čuđit:
—Since we are in a bit of a hurry on this trip and we can't take the time to sleep on dry land, you can all go to sleep right here in the boat. I'll wake you up.
The Čuđit thanked him for the welcome words, and they lay down to sleep. Because they were so tired, they fell into a deep sleep. Laurukȧǯ rowed along Pȧččvei fjord, where the Tebdokievŋis Falls (Teutokönǥäs) were nearby. When the boat neared the neck of the falls, one Russian lifted his head and said to Laurukȧǯ:
—I hear a strong wind.
Laurukȧǯ said:
—The wind has not yet picked up. You hear but a whisper. I'll wake you when we come near the village. Sleep now in peace.
The Čuhti again went to sleep. Tired as he was, he soon was back in a sweet slumber.
When Laurukȧǯ saw all the Russians were deep asleep, he set off quickly to row into the neck of the rapids. He jumped onto a stone and let the boat go into the great falls, where the invaders finally woke up, since water was coming into the boat. But there was no time to react: suddenly the boat capsized in the falls and broke apart. The Russians drowned, with not a one able to reach land. Laurukȧǯ gathered the Russians' bows from the shores of a still water below the rapids, as well as their clothes and other goods.

The Čuđit Die of Hunger[7]
Pietari Valle (A. V. Koskimies)
ATU 968; ML 8000

Once Laurukàʒ was ferrying Čuđit across Aanaar Lake. They came to an island on Kálbáiääpi's (Vasikkaselkä's) western half, so he urged them to go onto the shoal to eat some cloudberries, and they all hurried off to pick some berries. In the meantime, he himself pushed all the boats out into the waters. Well, he jumped into the last boat and said:

—These boats are mine!

The Čuđit called after Laurukàʒ:

—Come back! We're cooking some porridge for you!

But he repeated:

—These boats are mine!

The Čuđit remained on the island, but one of them swam behind him and grabbed onto the side of the boat. Laurukàʒ struck his fingertips with an oar, and a silver ring clinked into the boat.

After a week, he went to check on them. They didn't have the strength to do anything but turn their heads and grimace. Still this island is called Oaivipunnjâmlássá (Päänvääntämäluoto; Head-Turning Shoal).

Once Laurukàʒ set off to take some Čuđit down the Pàččvei (Paatsjoki) river. They came to the neck of a rapids. He tied the boats together, one after another, and said to the Čuđit:

—You should go under the canopies, so you don't get wet. I will steer from the last boat.

Right in the neck of the rapids there was a stone. He let the boats go, and he jumped onto that stone. The rest floated into the rapids and drowned.

Once Laurukàʒ was accompanying some Čuđit who were traveling in the dark. He tied the Čuđit together, who were traveling in a single-file line. He took a fire torch and commanded them to run after the fire, wherever it went. There was a sleep cliff, which Laurukàʒ knew about, and there they all fell. He ran and threw

---

7. These three stories are grouped together in Laitinen's edition, although only the first involves Čuđit dying of hunger.

his torch down the cliff as well as the stone, which he had tied to the end of the rope, so it pulled the invaders into the ravine. The Čuđit thought that Laurukåǯ was still traveling with them and pulling them. The invaders chased the flame, down the cliff, and found their deaths there.

The Čuđit Drown in Lake Aanaar; Hundred Pine Island
Uula Morottaja (T. I. Itkonen)
ATU 968; ML 8000

Laurukåǯ left as a guide with some Čuđit. He himself had left traveling in a small boat in the lead, and the Čuđit were in a large one behind. Laurukåǯ had carved a really large hole in the boat and stuffed paper into it. And when the paper got wet, the boat was breached, and water started to come quickly inside. They didn't have anything to bail it out with. When Laurukåǯ saw that they had become distressed, he started to row off to escape, and so the boatload of Čuđit sank into the depths of Lake Aanaar. That's the long and short of it.

Another time Laurukåǯ went with Čuđit, under the pretext that he was also a Čuhti. They came to an island in Lake Aanaar. Laurukåǯ supposed:
—There could be a lot of cloudberries on this island. Let's go eat them!
They landed their boats on the shore and ran off in different directions. Laurukåǯ hurried to get the boats into the lake, and he set off rowing. The Čuđit yelled:
—Come back, come back, Laurukåǯ! We're cooking some porridge! We have all the fixings for porridge!
One said:
—If you come back, then you'll get some hot tin in your throat.[8]

They killed the man right away who made that threat. After two weeks, Laurukåǯ went to see if they were still alive. All were already dead. Only one lifted his head and grimaced. They had eaten the bark from a hundred pines in their hunger, and from this the island got the name Čyetpecsuáloi (Satapetäjäsaari; Hundred Pine Island).

---

8. "Hot tin in the throat" is an unusual expression in English, but tin's relatively low melting point (232°C; 450°F) makes it a useful metal for casting, while still being dangerous to contact. Here it is a threat that plays with the idea that the Čuđit are cooking porridge for Laurukåǯ.

Once the same Laurukàǯ again was traveling with Čuđit. He started to entertain the notion:

—There is a house near here. You need to tie yourselves together, so that you won't be left behind when I set off running.

So they tied themselves and went to walk in the dark over the tundra.[9] Laurukàǯ walked in the front as their guide, holding a torch. When he came to an edge of a cliff, he threw his torch down and jumped off to the side. The Čuđit thought that he had set off running. So they all went running and fell down that cliff to their deaths.

Hundred Pine Island, Version 2
unknown (A. V. Koskimies)
ATU 968; ML 8000

Laurukàǯ lived on the shore of Lake Aanaar. Once fugitive robbers came to his home. He left to take them with a boat across Lake Aanaar. And as they rowed, they came to some island. Laurukàǯ said:

—On this island there are a lot of cloudberries.

So the fugitives started wanting to devour some of those cloudberries on that island. Laurukàǯ took a boat there and the robbers ran off into the forest: only one stayed to guard the boat. Laurukàǯ said:

—You too should go and eat some cloudberries! I'll stay here and watch the boat.

So he too left to gobble up some cloudberries, but since everyone had scattered, Laurukàǯ set off rowing toward the open water and stopped farther out. When the fugitives noticed him, they started to yell at him to come back:

—We're going to cook some porridge, and you can eat with us, and we'll even give you the master's spoon!

But one yelled:

—Come here, and we will cast some tin inside your throat!

But the fugitives killed him right away, and Laurukàǯ set off rowing home in his boat filled with goods.

After some time, the thought came to Laurukàǯ's mind:

---

9. In the Sámi sense of the word, "tundra" refers to a tall hill that is at least partially above the tree line, and only has low tundra vegetation on the top.

—Why don't I go check on those Russians on that island to see whether they've died yet.

So he did, he pushed his boat into the water and set off rowing there. And when he came to the island, they all were indeed dead. One was still alive, but he didn't have the strength any longer to do anything or even speak but just grimace at Laurukȧʒ and turn his head, and for that reason the island's name is Oaivipunnjâmlássá (Päänvääntämäsaari; Head-Turning Island).

Laurukȧʒ Kills Čuđit with a Sword
Uula Morottaja (T. I. Itkonen)
ATU 968; ML 8000

Once in spring-winter[10] Čuđit came skiing to Laurukȧʒ's home and demanded that he drive them with reindeer across Lake Aanaar to a village, which they planned to loot. Laurukȧʒ went to the forest to gather up some reindeer. He took the draught reindeer, but he singed the best driver's flank hair with a hot iron. Then he returned home.

The Čuđit chose the draught reindeer for themselves, but they didn't care for the best reindeer since it looked so unseemly. Then they set out to drive, Laurukȧʒ in the front as a guide, along the expanses of Lake Aanaar.

The sun shone quite warmly, and the Čuđit quickly fell asleep in their *geres*-sledges, since they were tired from skiing. Laurukȧʒ drove off the side of the trail, so that the others in the caravan drove past him. When the last Čuhti was next to him, he attacked him, killing him with a large knife so quickly that the man didn't even have time to make a noise. Then he snatched a sword from his sheath and raced his reindeer along the caravan as quickly as he was able, and every time he came to a sleeping Čuhti he struck him in the neck.

But when he started to kill the final man, the leader of the Čuđit and quite large and powerful, he woke from the noise and jumped from the *geres* with a sword in hand. They started to fight, but Laurukȧʒ was faster and was able to take his life. He threw the bodies on the snow crust, gathered up their war weapons, and returned home with his reindeer.

In the old days, people had supposedly still seen the skulls and bones of those Russians on the shore of some strait on the edge of Äijihjorŋâ (Ukonselkä).

---

10. Sámi people recognize eight seasons rather than four. Spring-winter generally occurs in March and April.

PEEIVIH-VUÅLÅPPÅƷ

The legend cycle of Peeivih-Vuålåppåʒ (Päivän Olavi) tells of Vuålåppåʒ's feats of seemingly superhuman strength and his influence in the Christianization of Sápmi. These feats include the origin of two distinctive rock formations in the region, the destruction of *sieidi* sites, and the emergence of Christianity in Sápmi from earlier religious traditions. This cycle dabbles in both heroic legend and saints legend, with certain stories simply pointing to Vuålåppåʒ's strength in fighting and others explicitly connecting his powers with miracles (e.g., changing the weather through prayer to facilitate the destruction of a *sieidi* site). Regardless, these stories serve as tools to celebrate and commemorate individuals of historical importance, as well as champion certain founding values and important founding social principles that explain why a local place exists as it does today.

Peeivih-Vuålåppåʒ bears considerable similarity to another well-known figure, Olaf II Haraldsson (St. Olaf) (995–1030 CE), known elsewhere in Nordic oral tradition for his stature and for his role in legends involving the Christianization of Norway. Peeivih-Vuålåppåʒ's name itself is Olaf: Vuålåppåʒ in Sámi and Olavi in Finnish are derived from the name Olaf. And his father's somewhat portending name, Peeivih, refers to the sun—a seemingly divine influence over his birth. Although Vuålåppåʒ's stories do not otherwise conform well to the corpus of St. Olaf legends, these stories potentially offer interesting insight into an active Sámi reinterpretation of a Nordic figure to suit their own cultural purposes and needs.

Other well-known regional legends, the Kalevanpojat, also figure into Peeivih-Vuålåppåʒ stories. Common throughout northern and eastern Finland, through Karelia and into Estonia, Kalevanpojat are physically powerful giants whose feats of strength in bygone times result in the creation of distinct landscape features (cf. "Peeivih-Vuálåppåǯ on the Sea Shore" and "The Capstone"). Peeivih-Vuálåppåǯ stories have seemingly adopted aspects of this tradition as well.

From a contemporary perspective, the narratives surrounding the destruction of sacred *sieidi* sites and the condemnations of the "ungodly" ways of Sámi ancestors are somewhat difficult to palate. Still they serve as important reminders to the social realities of late nineteenth-century Sámi communities. Older religious practices are respected as real and powerful in these stories (though ultimately inferior to Christianity). A certain anxiety also exists around the history of pre-Christian Sámi religion and perhaps even its continued presence in the community, since the physical reminders of those ways—the *sieidi* sites—remained well known to all community members.

A religious shift is seldom a simple or easy process, particularly when missionization is connected to colonization efforts. There are undertones of trauma, erasure, and lateral violence in some of these stories, with elements that intentionally overwrite earlier histories. For instance, in "Peeivih-Vuálåppåǯ on the Sea Shore," the stone that Peeivih-Vuálåppåǯ sets was a well-known ancient *sieidi* site near Unjárga (Nesseby), which today is still easily accessible in a prominent location. The heroic retelling of these exploits justifies the destruction—or at least displacement—of certain aspects of Sámi history, reflecting the legacy of colonization in the community.

About Peeivih-Vuálåppåǯ's Father, Peeivih
P. Valle (A. V. Koskimies)

There is a tundra[1] in the northern half of the Kittâl (Kittilä) parish, and beneath it was the residence of the old man Peeivih. The place is still visible, but juniper and mosses have grown up around it.

Old man Peeivih was said to be a powerful man and a good wild reindeer hunter—and a *noaidi* as well, so he was able to bring wild reindeer from one tundra to another.[2] He was a wonderful skier and great at descending hills—so good that no one could compare to him. Once, after striking up a wager, he

---

1. In the Sámi sense, a tundra is a high hill with low tundra vegetation dominating its peak.
2. The implication here is most likely that he can call reindeer to the places he will hunt by means of his *noaidi* powers.

descended from that high tundra with a burl cup filled with fat on top of his head, and it didn't spill during his descent down that slope to the fields surrounding his home.

He had two boys, the older named Uvlå[3] and the younger named Saara. The father said about them:

Uvlå Ūulson is a sluggard, but Saara can hold his own to me.

He didn't guess at all that Vuålåppåǯ (Uvlå) was to become a wonderful man in strength and manners, just as the stories of Sápmi now tell, and they—on the other hand—say nothing about Peeivih's youngest boy, Saara.

Peeivih-Vuålåppåǯ Burns a *Sieidi*
Mikko Aikio (A. V. Koskimies)

In those times when the Christian faith first arrived here in Sápmi and started to become better known, there was a man by the name of Peeivih-Vuålåppåǯ. He too had come to hear of the Christian faith and the triune God, but in those times people still worshiped at *sieiddit*. Peeivih-Vuålåppåǯ, however, suspected that the *sieidi* was no proper god. For that reason he started to despise *sieiddit* and started to destroy them. But the *sieidi* had powers so great that they made Peeivih-Vuålåppåǯ sick, so that he couldn't even go out seining. He had to stay at home while others went out seining. So he waited in sickness for the seiners and looked out from the hole in a spool and then noticed a naked child crawling along the seining rack.[4] He guessed the *sieidi* had been haunting him. Vuålåppåǯ said:

—The old woman of Muddušjävri (Muddusjärvi) Lake[5] is crawling along the rack, but don't you worry, you damned creature . . . I'll get better and once I do, you indeed will burn!

And so after he recovered, he went to the *sieidi* and gathered wood onto the *sieidi* stone. When he started to light the fire, there came rain and wind so that no flames would spark. He had to start trying to light the fire again, when once

---

3. Uvlå is a variation of the name Vuålåppåǯ.

4. Looking through the spool is likely a means to see invisible supernatural beings. When he looks through the spool he sees a spirit being (the naked child), which causes him to suspect that the origins of his sickness are supernatural in origin.

5. The reference to the old woman most likely refers to the spirit associated with that particular *sieidi* site on Muddušjävri.

again there came rain and wind, extinguishing the flames again. Then he lit it yet a third time and recited those words, which he had heard and learned:

—In the name of the Father, the Son, and the Holy Ghost!

Then the flames sparked and the *sieidi* burned.

This *sieidi* place was on the shore of Muddušjävri, on the north side of the Sieidivaarâ (Seitavaara) Mountain. And in that *sieidi*-place you can still see wild reindeer antlers and bones as a remnant of our ancestors' ungodly worship there.

Peeivih-Vuȧlȧppȧǯ Burns a *Sieidi*, Version 2
Yrjänä Sarre from Paadar (Paatari) village (A. V. Koskimies)

Peeivih-Vuȧlȧppȧǯ went off to set fire to a *sieidi*. There came a strong wind, so that he struggled to get to his destination, to the *sieidi*-site. Well, when he got to that *sieidi*, when he started to light a fire, there came a hard rain so that the fire wouldn't ignite. But finally he got it to burn, and then he went back.

Yrjänä Sarre's home in the early 1900s. Photo: Väinö Tanner. Image courtesy of the Finnish National Board of Antiquities.

The Capstone
Iisakki Mannermaa (A. V. Koskimies)

Peeivih-Vuȧlȧppȧӡ lived once on an island in Aanaar whose name was Mavra (Maura). In its clearing, there were some inhabitants, and that village's people had pagan gods.[6] One idol's name was Äijih (Ukko; Old Man); another name was Ȧkku (Akka; Old Woman). They were summits of mountains, which were near the Veskonjargâ (Veskoniemi) *siida*.

Peeivih-Vuȧlȧppȧӡ was such a strong man that there was no one in the whole world who could hold his own to him in those times. For this reason Peeivih-Vuȧlȧppȧӡ, knowing he was the strongest, dared to destroy the *sieiddit* that the people worshipped, for he thought it was terrible that people in their foolishness and madness regarded the tops of mountains and stones as their gods.[7] Peeivih-Vuȧlȧppȧӡ realized that the one and only God was in heaven. People really became angry with him after they lost their gods, which were the most unusual mountain peaks or such things that they had built in those kinds of places from stone, whether they were statues or other things of that fashion. But yet they didn't try to kill him, for they feared Peeivih-Vuȧlȧppȧӡ's great power.

When Vuȧlȧppȧӡ noticed that people feared him because of his strength, he said to the villagers:

—Let's all go row in single file to Konišnjargâ (Konesniemi) peninsula. There I will show you my power.

They rowed there and went aground. Peeivih-Vuȧlȧppȧӡ said:

—Come along with me, everyone.

They walked a while, and Peeivih-Vuȧlȧppȧӡ stood and said to his companions:

—I will take this large stone and carry it onto this great boulder.

Not a one of them believed this was possible, of all those people who were there, even though they knew he was a strong man. One of the people said:

---

6. The word most commonly used here is *ep-imelijd*, which in English is best represented as "ungod" though is often historically translated as "idols" or "demons"—words that are difficult to use in contemporary contexts. I've tried to capture the disparaging nature of the word used by the storytellers here as it is illustrative of the harsh tensions that exist around religious identity in the late nineteenth century.

7. It is perhaps more accurate to say that *sieiddit* were not worshipped themselves but rather were worshipped at. This misunderstanding is suggestive of the ways that missionaries in Sápmi chose to frame certain aspects of non-Christian religious practice as idolatry.

—This work you're planning to do is entirely impossible for a human.

Peeivih-Vuáláppáǯ suddenly snatched up the stone from the ground, carried it hurriedly next to the boulder, and threw the stone onto it, climbed it, and said to the people who were spectators there:

—Bring three small stones. I will set them as legs for that larger stone I just moved.

He set the large stone he had moved on top of three small stones, which he arranged so that they were each under a corner of the stone. Peeivih-Vuáláppáǯ said to the residents of the village, who were very afraid of his great strength:

—Here you see my strength, and this stone that I have lifted onto this boulder, let it be a reminder for you and to those who come after us.

They returned home to the clearing at Mavra, where their homes were. After that, Vuáláppáǯ lived in peace and harmony with the villagers and all the others in Aanaar. This stone of Peeivih-Vuáláppáǯ is still called today Pajalaskeđgi (Päällyskivi; the Capstone).

Peeivih-Vuáláppáǯ on the Sea Shore
Mikko Aikio (A. V. Koskimies)

Peeivih-Vuáláppáǯ, whom his father called a sluggard, was by nature a decent and well-disposed man, and he did not often show off his great strength. He went also fishing on the sea, where he came to see Russians and Norwegians. The Russians caught word of his strength and badgered him until he agreed to a

Ceavccageađgi, near Unjárga, 2004. Photo: Thomas A. DuBois.

rowing competition with them, even though he was alone and they were many. He set off rowing with one pair of oars, and the Russians with five or six pairs. His boat started to go so fast that he needed to tie his wife, or—as some say—his mother, who was along with him, tight to a rib, so that she wouldn't fall into the sea. But the Russians, who were rowing with five or six pairs of oars, were left behind and ended up losing.

Another time he was taunted by Norwegians, when they too had heard of him being strong and wanted to see his great strength. He agreed again to show his strength and took a large stone, lifted it into the air, and threw it so it stuck into the ground. That stone is still to this day visible at a place called Ceävǯui-keđgi (Ceavccageađgi) on the north shore of Värjivuona (Varanger) Fjord, near the sea.

Peeivih-Vuȧlȧppȧǯ on the Sea Shore, Version 2
Matti Sarre, Pȧččvei (Paatsjoki) (A. V. Koskimies)[8]

Once Peeivih-Vuȧlȧppȧǯ was competing on the shore with eight Russians and left Mȧk-koppe (Matokupa)[9] rowing to Čäcisuáloi (Vesisaari-Island). Peeivih-Vuȧlȧppȧǯ told the Russians to start rowing. As for himself, he remained behind to carve his oars. He took a large log, split it in two, and carved the log halves in the shape of oars. He made pommels and set off rowing. But he started to row so hard that he needed to tie up his wife. Then he caught up to the Russians. They asked:

—Are you rowing as hard as you can?

Peeivih-Vuȧlȧppȧǯ said:

—I haven't even used half of my strength yet.

He rowed by them and the Russians remained in the middle of the Värjivuona (Varanger) Fjord.

Peeivih-Vuȧlȧppȧǯ Fighting
Matti Sarre (A. V. Koskimies)

Once three strong men came to wrestle Peeivih-Vuȧlȧppȧǯ, but he wasn't home, only his mother. He himself had left to check his nets that he used to fish under the ice. And before that he had brought home a large pine for the fire.

---

8. The significance of including Pȧččvei on this identifying line is unclear. It may indicate that there are two storytellers named Matti Sarre, and this one is from Pȧččvei. It also may suggest the story is from Pȧččvei.

9. Laitinen notes this is a bay on the south side of Varanger Fjord.

The strong men came and asked his mother where her son was. The mother said:

—Fishing under the ice.

Well, they went out and noticed the giant tree that was brought near the woodpile. They started figuring out who brought that tree there, and they asked the mother about the matter. Peeivih-Vuȧlȧppȧჳ's mother said:

—Vuolliჳ.[10]

Then the strong men began to think:

—That Vuolliჳ must be sturdy. Do we even dare to wrestle with him at all?

Well, they decided to wait until he came. After he came home, he wrestled with the first, and then the second, and neither were able to hold their own. Finally, he wrestled the third, the strongest. So they tested their strength. Peeivih-Vuȧlȧppȧჳ grabbed on, and the third man grabbed back so hard that he started to lift Vuȧlȧppȧჳ up, but Peeivih-Vuȧlȧppȧჳ threw the strong man into the ground so that blood came to his mouth and nose. Then the mother said:

—Why, Vuolliჳ, did you slam him so hard?

—Because I got mad when he lifted me.

And so those three men went on their way.

Peeivih-Vuȧlȧppȧჳ Fighting, Version 2
Matti Sarre (A. V. Koskimies)

Once three strong men came to Peeivih-Vuȧlȧppȧჳ's house to wrestle. Vuȧlȧppȧჳ wasn't home. He had left to check his nets under the ice. He had got a draught reindeer for checking his nets, and he also moved his reindeer, and when he was returning he knocked over an old pine tree with roots, carried it on his shoulders, and threw it near the woodpile. He then went to fish under the ice. And meanwhile those three strong men came along.

They asked Peeivih-Vuȧlȧppȧჳ's mother:

—Where is your boy?

—Checking the ice nets, the mother answered.

When they saw that great pine in the wood-chopping area, they asked her:

—Who brought this great tree here?

The mother said:

—Vuolliჳ.

---

10. Vuolliჳ is an affectionately shortened version of Vuȧlȧppȧჳ, bearing the same effect as adding a -y to the end of a first name in English.

The men then started to wonder if it was a good idea to wrestle him after all. But they were still there when Vuȧlȧppȧჳ came home. So those three strong men started wanting to wrestle, and they set to work. The first one wrestled with Vuȧlȧppȧჳ and wasn't able to hold his own, and then the second. He also didn't win. Then the third and the strongest of them started to wrestle. He was able to start lifting him, but Peeivih-Vuȧlȧppȧჳ got mad and threw the man to the ground so hard that blood started to come from his mouth and nostrils. Peeivih-Vuȧlȧppȧჳ's mother said:

—Why, my little imp, did you throw him so hard?

Peeivih-Vuȧlȧppȧჳ said:

—I didn't realize. I got mad when he lifted me off my feet.

Peeivih-Vuȧlȧppȧჳ Hunting Wild Reindeer
unknown (A. V. Koskimies)[11]

Once Peeivih-Vuȧlȧppȧჳ was hunting autumn wild reindeer with one companion. They followed the reindeer and were stalking them. They watched the reindeer: not a single male, just females. Peeivih-Vuȧlȧppȧჳ said that they shouldn't shoot, since it was only females. His friend said:

—The meat of the female reindeer is good enough to eat, too.

Then Peeivih-Vuȧlȧppȧჳ tossed away his bow, left running behind the female reindeer and he chased them until he caught up and grabbed some doe. He wrung its neck and threw it on his shoulders. He brought it to his companion, saying:

—Here is a female reindeer for you, since you had to get one.

Peeivih-Vuȧlȧppȧჳ's Race with a Draught Reindeer
unknown (A. V. Koskimies)[12]

Once Peeivih-Vuȧlȧppȧჳ struck up a bet with some man that he could equal a draught reindeer in a race. The other man retrieved his best draught reindeer and harnessed it in front of his *geres*. Vuȧlȧppȧჳ stood next to him, wearing a heavy outer reindeer fur coat and heavy leather leggings on his legs. One of his friends stood next to them, and said:

—So you're planning to race wearing a heavy coat and leggings?

---

11. Translated into Finnish by Erkki Itkonen.
12. Translated into Finnish by Erkki Itkonen.

Peeivih-Vuáláppáž answered:

—Don't worry, brother. The feathers of a bird don't weigh it down.

When the wagerer set off into a gallop, so Peeivih-Vuáláppáž dashed with his *beaska* fur coat and leather leggings, running abreast of the reindeer driver, near the lake's other end. In the end, he ran past the reindeer driver, leaving him behind, and he reached the other end of the lake before the other, defeating him in the wager.

This thing happened at Aanaar's old church, where there used to be winter *goahti* in former times, and where Peeivih-Vuáláppáž lived in those days.

STORIES ABOUT THE SKOLT SÁMI

Aanaar Sámi have long been bordered to the east by Skolt Sámi (whom they call *nuorttâlâččat*, or easterners), whose westernmost villages were on the northeastern edge of Lake Aanaar. Skolt Sámi use a different Sámi language, which is difficult (though not fully incomprehensible) for Aanaar Sámi speakers. Skolt Sámi maintained different economic systems, keeping their traditional *siida*-system alive until World War II, whereas Aanaar Sámi had increasingly turned toward farming, permanent settlements, and Finnish-style governments in the early to mid-1800s. And, perhaps most importantly, Skolt Sámi have long been Russian Orthodox (unlike the devoutly Lutheran Aanaar Sámi), a faith that many Lutheran practitioners misunderstood and regarded as superstitious. These tensions all led to somewhat strained relations between these groups.

The following stories are humorous anecdotes poking fun at Skolt Sámi women for a supposed tendency to take fright and lapse into fits of frenzied behavior. While these stories have little to do with actual Skolt Sámi, they do speak to the perceived differences between the groups, a tendency that Aanaar Sámi had to exoticize the Skolt (for instance, some stories suppose Skolt have magical abilities that other Sámi do not), and cross-cultural misunderstandings that emerge from differing religious practice. Further, these stories all invite feminist critique, insofar as they not only present Skolt women as weak and foolish but also as, to some degree, sexually exploitable ("Scaring the Skolt Wife" [versions 1, 2, and 4]).

It is important in reading these stories to realize they're told by men about women, by Lutherans about Russian Orthodox, and by Aanaar about Skolts. People often tell these kinds of stories to shape internal social values by clarifying and laughing at the things that they are not, or at least do not want to be perceived as (foolish, rash, easily disturbed, sexually naïve). Additionally, these stories are valuable in dispelling the romanticized mythos of a perfectly harmonious Indigenous world. Conflicts with neighbors, sexisms, and religious prejudices have long histories in all societies across the globe, and people use humor as a way to both maintain and disrupt the discrepancies of power they see around them.

Scaring the Skolt Wife
Paavali and Santeri Valle (A. V. Koskimies)

One winter we came to the household at Mazažjävri (Masažjärvi), to Paauvaš-Vaaska's place. An old wife was there, and she was sensitive to frights. The boys often tried to frighten her, just for laughs. One time, her husband started bending the keel piece of a *geres*, and he wanted our help as well. We started to pull on it with a rope into the bending form by means of our manpower. That old woman hid herself in the corner of the sleeping area and started to babble:

—What if it breaks! What if it breaks!

The master of the house had secretly taken a thin piece of wood, and he bent it until it snapped. Now that old lady took fright. She rose from the bed and started to shriek, and she was jumping back and forth. She babbled:

—Oh dear, oh dear, oh dear! Now some great disaster has happened. The old man broke his tool![1] It will have to be tied up just like you do for a fractured bone, so that it can get better!

As she jumped about, she took a string, and with it she wrapped up the log between her husband's legs, and she thought:

—Well, if it straightens out, then I'll know he's been cured.

The womenfolk held her until she recovered.

When the people of the household that same night came home from fishing with nets under the ice, they hung their net line to dry on a hook on the wall. As it started to dry, it fell into the sleeping area. The wife said:

—Since you jumped, so too will I jump.

And she started to jump back and forth. Another family also was living in

---

1. In this usage, "tool" also has the loose connotation of "penis" in Sámi, as does the reference to his "log" later on.

the same *goahti*. They had cooked some fish and had put the dishes right in the middle of the floor, where people walk. The woman started to jump over the dishes. They needed to restrain the wife until she calmed down.

There was another time when they started to celebrate Epiphany (January 6), which was Russian Christmas. They started to wash the laundry, and they put their clothes and shirts on a stool. One shirt fell to the floor. The wife became frightened and said:

—Was that the ghost of my deceased father?

She started to jump about. Another wife was there, and she was on the floor bent over with her butt sticking up into the air, so that she tried to jump over her, but her leg hit the wife, and she struck her head against the wall. She knocked herself out and got a big bump on her head. For a half hour, it was like she was dead. But then she woke again and sighed:

—Hohooi!

She set off again to wash clothes and thought:

—Where did this bloody bump come from? I don't remember it before, and now suddenly there's a bump!

The widow named Pàràsk explained where it came from:

—A shirt fell from the stool to the floor, and you started to jump around because of it. And you jumped over me, but your foot stuck in my butt crack and you fell, as if you would have stepped into a ravine. We thought that you died for good, but we listened and heard you were still alive. What would you have said if we also would have started to jump around like you did, or dragged you outside and shoveled snow onto your breast?

The wife listened mouth agape and began to calm down:

—Hohooi, I don't know. I was scared and then it happened—*Hospoti Pommeloi*.[2]

Scaring the Skolt Wife, Version 2
Paavali and Santeri Valle (A. V. Koskimies)

Once a woman named Nààskà left in the autumn to peel or scrape some tree bark for bark bread, and she stepped on small willow grouse chicks. She

---

2. The Kyrie eleison is an important and oft-repeated Russian Orthodox prayer. *Hospoti Pommeloi* (*Hospody Pomyluj*) translates as "Lord, have mercy."

took fright, threw away her axe, took off all the clothes she had on, and went running back naked.

At home they noticed her coming, and they asked:

—Why are you returning like this?

The wife explained:

—Some different kinds of creatures were there, berry pickers and ball-butts.[3] I needed to give them my axe and my load rope and my dress and everything I was wearing, and then I left. Look for yourselves, and see what you think!

But after having explained the matter she no longer could remember where it happened and where she left her clothes. Then they realized that she needed to be scared again. So she set off running and the others followed behind her. When she came to that same place, she said:

—Ah, here's where everything is!

And she gathered up all her clothes.

Scaring the Skolt Wife, Version 3
Paavali Valle and Santeri Valle (A. V. Koskimies)

In the village of Mazaǯjävri (Masaǯjärvi), there was a widow suffering from a terminal illness. When my late father and some others went there, they took me along as well, when I was only a little boy. When we came to her place it was Prayer Sunday, even though the people were off fishing and others were doing work.

At midday they came in for prayer. My father was at that time our very first catechist. Matti Valle was his name. He took a hymnal from his bag. The other people of the house said:

—Do they plan to bow down in prayer?

The sick one noticed this and started to bemoan:

—Goodness, goodness! They've started to handle God's sacred books. My heart cannot bear this.[4]

And she started to rise from her bed. The guests from Aanaar needed to go out to hold their prayer in the yard. The womenfolk went into another house

---

3. This is an uncommon, cutesy gibberish term that infantilizes the chicks. I have translated it literally here from the Sámi word *pållupoođah*.

4. The woman seemingly thinks that they are about to administer last rites for her, instead of conducting a simpler worship service, which may include the wedding referred to later on.

and they tied their shawls to one woman's head.⁵ And so they went to the house, where the sick woman was. But when she noticed she sprang up to sit, and started to ask:

—Well, well, well, who is that (the one with the shawl on her head)?

Then a man named Ivvàn answered:

—She has come to retrieve the sacred books. She had already confessed, and she came now to be my wife.

Then the sick one tried to scramble herself up but wasn't able to lift herself from her place. Suddenly she jumped up onto one of her bedposts and, standing on one leg and looking over her guests, said:

—And she's beautiful too!

She stepped to stand on her other leg, and she said to the guests:

—I will jump from here. Yes, I'm going to jump from here.

The wife was taken down and put into her bed until she regained her senses. And she didn't live more than a couple of days before she died.⁶

Scaring the Skolt Wife, Version 4
Paavali Valle and Santeri Valle (A. V. Koskimies)

In one household there were many womenfolk, and some women from another household were living there as well. They were easily frightened. It was the time of Pärdipeeivi (Perttulinpäivä; August 24). The boys were entertaining themselves with the thought that it would be fun to scare everyone, since so many people were together.

In the summertime place, where they were, there was a large *goahti*. And in its center there was a place for a fire, and in the roof a smoke hole. The women went together to chat about something or other. The boys stashed away all the axes and knives, and they went into hiding. But one of them climbed a tall pine, which was near the *goahti*, and he started to growl in a horrible tone. But as was to be expected, when the womenfolk heard it, they became frightened,

---

5. Although women's headscarves were common during religious worship, the significance of tying the scarves to one woman is unclear. At that time people didn't put their shawls on their heads, only on their shoulders.

6. This story defies easy interpretation but is perhaps best understood in the context of a Lutheran catechist and his family expressing their bewilderment at not understanding the customary practices of their Orthodox neighbors. The Skolt Sámi families in this story may have been just as confused by the actions of the Valle family.

set off running outside, started to look into a pine, and howled with a single voice:

—Oh no, oh no! There's a bear in the pine! We need to cut it down.

They left running to fetch the axes from the woodpile but couldn't find any. They ran back to the base of the pine, wondering how they could cut down such a tree. In haste, they all tried to bite at the tree,[7] but when their teeth weren't able to withstand it, they thought:

—No, nothing will come of this. How can we get the bear out of this pine?

One wife remarked:

—Hey, if we lift our skirts, that should do the trick![8]

They all lifted their skirts, and one said:

—Lift them higher! It might not be able to see our places, since it's so high up. Do you all understand?

The lifted their skirts over their heads and stuck their bottoms out toward the bear.

—Well, what do you think about that, bear?

They chided further:

—For shame, bear, that you might be God's own creation![9]

The boy in the pine was about to burst into laughter. He didn't want to stay in the tree, but it wouldn't be a good idea to come down either, since they would kill him because they were in such a frenzy. When the other hiding boys started to laugh somewhat carelessly, one wife heard it and said:

—What is that? It could be another bear!

They raced off.

—Where's the bear? Where's the bear?

The boys panicked, and they didn't know what to do. One boy thought to pick up a piece of wood and throw it into the lake. The wives ran right into the lake, and everyone calmed down when they get soaked. Then the boy in the tree had time to get down from there.

---

7. Using one's teeth to try to cut down a tree is a motif that shows up in many Sámi stories (note "The Haunting of the Old Deceased *Noaidi*"). It mostly is indicative of the frenzied behavior of the women in this instance.

8. Bears were considered to be afraid of female genitalia in Sámi, Karelian, and Finnish tradition. Many scholars attribute this fear to a gynocentric magical power that women possess, although skirt-lifting does have the practical effect of making a person look larger than she is. This was a common way to chase off a bear.

9. This line is said in Skolt Sámi and not Aanaar Sámi.

Scaring the Skolt Wife, Version 5
Paavali Valle and Santeri Valle (A. V. Koskimies)

In the village of Njiävđám (Näätamö; Neiden), there was a man named Siidar whose wife was easily frightened. Travelers came through his house, and they often stayed there for the night. Once several guests came along who were traveling to Norway. On the roof there was a large board drying. One man grabbed hold of the board, put weight on it, and suddenly it fell down, making a loud noise. The wife was starting to give the sheep some water. She was just starting to pour the water from a pot into their trough. She got scared and started throwing water at each and every guest with her ladle. They all went running out. The wife ran after them, but when the water ran out, she pushed the ladle under her dress and peed into it. She tossed it at them and said:

—Here's something more than just water for you!

Scaring the Skolt Wife, Version 6
Juho Petteri Lusmaniemi, by letter (A. V. Koskimies)

Finsku (Figenskog) said once to Lerk (Lerche):[10]

—You wouldn't believe how terribly a Skolt woman gets mixed up in the head when she's scared. She might kill someone, but if she can't find a weapon, in her distress she'll attack with nothing but her bare hands.

Lerk said that he didn't believe there could be a person who took such great fright that they would attack. Finsku said:

—Well, let's put it to the test!

So they left. They came to the door of a Skolt Sámi's home. Lerk went in front, and Finsku behind. As he entered, Finsku threw his hat into the Skolt woman's lap. The woman took fright and yelled:

—A bear is coming!

And she jumped up attacking Lerk, and grabbed his hair and beard so firmly that it twisted his chin. And again:

—A bear's coming! Get the axe, get the axe!

Finsku then helped the man get free from the woman and they hurried back.

---

10. According to Laitinen, Lerk was a former Norwegian merchant at the mouth of the Pǻččvei (Paatsjoki) River, near the Skolt village of Boris-Gleb and the Rihvana (Triton) Market.

Some Skolt boy was in the forest, and he returned home and came to the door of the cottage. He took the load off his draught reindeer. When the reindeer was free, it jumped. The boy's mother got so terribly frightened that she ran out of the cottage and set off running after her boy. The boy needed to flee into the forest, and he climbed up a spruce. The mother went to get her axe and started to cut through the tree. Then the boy's sister ran to her mother and blurted out to her:

—Look, it's coming down!

The wife looked up and the daughter said:

—You missed it. It went around the spruce.

The mother, when she started to look about, finally regained her senses.

There was a Skolt wife who never ate gruel. Once her family went to seine and the wife stayed by herself. She started to cook some gruel for when the seiners returned. She set down her pot, but the sheep were tied up in the house, and just then the sheep got loose and kicked over the gruel pot. The wife took fright, grabbed a ladle, and said:

—Oh, is that some guests who are coming?

And she started to slurp up the gruel together with the sheep, as long as she was able. The seiners came home, and the wife was in a bad state. They asked:

—What's bothering you?

—Oh, some visitors showed up. Since I ate some gruel to keep good company with the guests, I got a stomachache.

A Skolt woman went to pick some berries and stepped on some willow grouse chicks, which were so small that they didn't even have tails yet. They set off trying to fly with great difficulty and were still peeping. Well, she became afraid and got confused and said:

—They're ball-butts,[11] with necks turned inside out.

---

11. This is an uncommon, cutesy gibberish term that infantilizes the chicks. I have translated it literally here from the Sámi word *pållupoođah*.

And she took off her clothes and set off running home naked and sputtered:
—They're ball-butts, upside down they rolled.
People said:
—Ball-butts ate your clothes?
The wife went back, put her clothes back on, and came home and said:
—The ball-butts have disappeared.

Scaring the Skolt Wife, Version 7
Uula Morottaja (T. I. Itkonen)

A Skolt woman was peeling birchbark when a willow grouse burst into flight. She got scared and ran behind the willow grouse, throwing all her birchbark away to waste. Then she reckoned:
—I peeled some birchbark, but the willow grouse threw it all away.

Another Skolt wife was hanging a scarecrow, dropped it, and took fright. A boy was next to her and he set off running to hide so the woman wouldn't chase him. The woman indeed started chasing him, and she chased him until she calmed down.

A Skolt girl was sewing a *beaska* fur coat; when pulling on the hide, it ripped. The girl's mother took fright. She ran from one house to another saying:
—Your sister reached the hole.[12]

A boy scared a Skolt wife, and he ran outside. The woman started to run, saying that they needed to kill a bear. The boy climbed up a spruce. The wife got an ice chisel from the ice hole at the shore, planning to stick the boy with it. But the boy had enough time to get down from the tree so the wife couldn't find him.

12. Itkonen marks this final unusual line with a question mark, suggesting that there may be a transcription problem with this phrase.

In one house there were a number of women drinking coffee and one of the women dropped her cup on the floor. Right away, everyone took fright, threw their own cups of coffee on the floor, jumped up yelling, and ran out, shrieking for the longest time, until they came to their senses in the cold.

Kååššå
Juho Petteri Lusmaniemi (A. V. Koskimies)

There was once a Skolt Sámi whose name was Kååššå. He was so crazy that once he tried to kill his wife, but he couldn't get his hands on her. Once the wife said:
—How are we going to live, when we can't even get along with each other?
The man said:
—I would need to be hanged.
The wife put a rope around his neck, and she started to pull him up a tree. But she didn't have the strength to lift him. She said to her son:
—Son, lift up his backside.[13]

---

13. This punchline refers to the impossibility of hanging Kååššå while holding him upright. It represents a numskull motif in an otherwise dark set-up for a short anecdote.

HUNTING STORIES

Hunting can lead to great discomforts and even dangers for hunters, particularly when hunters routinely traveled several days away from their homes by foot, ski, or *geres*-sledge. Unpredictability is the norm in the bush, and the ability of the hunter to not only function but thrive in the woods was a valued skill, developed over the course of a lifetime. These skills are also passed down from elders to youth, and stories play a key role in the transmission of this knowledge.

One interesting dimension of these hunting stories is what is not present. Becoming lost is not a concern, nor is a terrible turn in weather. This is likely because of Sámi proficiency in navigating large tracts of their own land and reading and predicting upcoming weather. Fishing stories, which often have much in common with hunting stories, are also underrepresented here, perhaps because net fishing does not lend itself to the unpredictability that hunting or angling does. Alternatively, this could have been a product of Koskimies's own interests, seeking out narratives that specifically speak to the dangers of hunting in a perceived wilderness environment.

Instead, we are treated to hunting stories that are either humorous or tell of the brave feats of hunters. Often, hunting tales contain cautionary dimensions when things do not go well in the woods. These stories contain messages that are fairly instructive: be careful if you're trying to kill a bear ("The Bear Hunter"); know what you're killing ("A Draught Reindeer as a Wild Reindeer"); think and don't become frightful ("The Soddy Root Ball as a Bear"); be thoughtful in your actions ("The Ermine Hunters"). These stories are often used to provide real-life examples of what not to do, and they can be used to educate young hunters when they are not in the field.

The Late Haannuʒ's Bear and Wild Reindeer Hunt
Mikko Aikio (A. V. Koskimies)

In former times, maybe a hundred years before now, there was a famous hunter whose name was Haannuʒ. He was born at the end of the Aanaar River, and he lived here and there in Aanaar and in Muddušjävri (Muddusjärvi) Village. He also hunted for autumn reindeer in Myeđhituoddar (Muotkatunturi), as did the other residents of the village. And he kept *piärtušm* (*hangas*) fence traps there and checked them.

A *piärtušm* is a kind of trap in which you construct a two-rail fence, and you leave a trap-opening of 5, 6, or 7 fathoms (30–42 feet) at the end. How it's done is that you build it, and it always ends on a lakeshore or riverbank, or the edge of a marsh or at the edge of a mountain, and usually it is a half or full Scandinavian mile (3 to 6 miles; 10 kilometers) in length.

Once Haannuʒ was again checking his *piärtušm*, and it had caught a wild reindeer, but a bear had found it and had started to eat it. And it was already getting toward evening, when Haannuʒ was checking the *piärtušm*.

As he started nearing the place where the bear was eating the reindeer, the bear started to get scared and grunt. He grabbed his rifle from his back, cocked it, and shot toward the head, but he didn't hit his mark. It only went through the chin bone. Then the bear got angry and charged near Haannuʒ, to the other side of a fallen tree in the water that he was behind, and started to growl out a bloody gurgle at him. Haannuʒ snarled:

—Don't you come at me!

And he grabbed his axe and intended to swing it at the bear, but he couldn't reach him. So for a long while, they were on opposite sides of that fallen tree in the water. In the end, however, the bear left and went to the reindeer carcass and reached it. Haannuʒ went to the place he left his draught reindeer, and he remained there until the next day. In the morning, he checked to see where the bear had gone off to. When he got to the place where the bear was, it no longer had any strength, so it wasn't able to fight Haannuʒ. It was already so terribly wounded. Haannuʒ shot it again, and that's how he killed the bear.

Another time Haannuʒ was again hunting for a bear, which had been circled.[1] He had two companions with him. They didn't know for sure where the bear's den was. They started looking in such a manner so they would be able to see

---

1. In hunting denned-up bears, hunters looked for tracks and walked ever-narrowing circles without crossing the bear tracks in order to pinpoint the location of the den.

and hear their companions, if someone should yell or speak up, after finding the bear's den.

They were looking when Haannuǯ yelled:

—I found it!

The others ordered:

—Don't touch it!

Haannuǯ said:

—I won't touch it. I won't even disturb anything nearby!

Even though he had in fact already struck the bear dead with his axe.

The companions came and saw the bear was already dead. They asked:

—How did you kill it?

—I had a small hatchet under my arm. I grabbed it and knocked it on the head.

This happened on the north side of Muddušjávri, north of the Eedlihjävri (Edlihjärvi) Peninsula.

A Draught Reindeer as a Wild Reindeer[2]
Mikko Aikio (A. V. Koskimies)

My late father and the late Jukkuu-Vuolli were hunting wild reindeer one spring on the same tundra, but they weren't together. My father was already heading back and had walked for a day, and he stopped for the night on some riverbank. In the morning, it was pretty damp weather. He woke from his sleep and stayed inside his sleeping place, thinking he should fetch his draught reindeer to move onward.

Then a rifle shot fired, and he jumped up quickly and said:

—Who is out there shooting my draught reindeer?

The other said:

—Just a person, I am.

He asked:

—And who would that be, that person?

---

2. Sámi languages contain dozens upon dozens of words for reindeer, indicating their sex, age, coloration, and degree of tameness. A draught reindeer (*ergi*) takes considerable time and energy to tame and develop trust with. Wild reindeer (*kodde*), on the other hand, are considerably larger and stronger than the semi-domesticated reindeer that Sámi people herded. Wild reindeer hunts occurred in this region until the late eighteenth or early nineteenth century. In North American standards, mistaking an *ergi* for a *kodde* would be as egregious as mistaking a wapiti elk for a whitetail deer.

Then he saw who it was along with his tethered reindeer, which that man had shot, fallen on the ground. My father asked:

—What do you think you're doing?

He said:

—I thought it was a wild reindeer, since there was a fog. I couldn't make out the tether on it. And I didn't think there was anyone else here. I am sorry, my godfather. I didn't do it on purpose.

My father said:

—The damage is to be your own.

And so Vuolli needed to collect the remains of the draught reindeer he shot and give my father a living one.

The Bear Hunter
Mikko Aikio, by letter (A. V. Koskimies)

An Aanaar Sámi man had found a bear, and he left to kill it, taking with him a friend. To this friend he promised half of the bear, should they kill it. So they left to hunt that denned-up bear, and when they got there, they came to the bear's home and killed it.

The man circling the bear said:

—Too bad I didn't know how to kill a bear by myself. Instead, I had to bring along a partner and needlessly give him half. If another bear should come along to hunt, I surely would go and try to kill it myself.

When another autumn came and the reindeer were already caught,[3] a bear came along and ate some reindeer from that same man, who was circling the bear the previous fall, and who regretted that he had taken along a companion and given him a share.

So he went alone to hunt the bear, and when he left he even said:

—You'll be getting your own hide this time, won't you?[4]

And so he went alone to hunt the bear that had eaten his reindeer. And when he started to get close to the place where the bear had denned up, the bear started to get angry and came at him. The man had a rifle and an axe as a weapon. He shot but didn't hit his mark. He only wounded the bear's eye, and the bear got even angrier and attacked him. The bear clawed him so badly that

---

3. This seemingly refers to reindeer roundup, where reindeer are sorted, gelded, marked, and slaughtered.

4. This refers to him getting to keep the entirety of the bear.

in a panic he could barely get to his draught reindeer and *geres*. He set off driving home, but after a couple of days the man died.

Other people went to look for the bear, following its tracks. They killed it and saw that that deceased man had done more damage to the bear than just its eye.

For that reason, there are sayings about the bear:

"Don't sell a bear's hide before you have killed it."[5] And "The bear has the strength of nine men, but one man's mind."[6]

The Soddy Root Ball as a Bear
Mikko Aikio, by letter (A. V. Koskimies)

A man went to hunt some birds. He took his rifle on his shoulder and went walking up the river. It was spring, just when the ice was breaking up. Ice was moving down the river. The flooded river and ice was naturally ripping loose sod-covered root balls and taking them along with it. The man didn't notice that the ice was moving or that there were root clusters floating in the current. He was such a timid person that in seeing something black he became frightened and thought it was a bear. He ran off to hide, and he went to some pond where it had melted only around shore. A large tree was leaning over the melted shoreline. He climbed into the tree and stayed there so long that the people at home started to get worried. They went to look for him and figure out what had happened to him, since he had been gone for so long. They left and saw from his tracks that he had been running. They guessed he was scared, wherever he might be. They started to follow his tracks to see where he had gone to. They followed them to the shores of a pond, where a tree was leaning over the melted shoreline. They found him in the tree, which he climbed up into. They asked him why he went up that tree. He said:

—What would you do if a bear came clawing at you?

The others asked:

—Where's the bear?

—It ran along the riverbank, with great speed.

—Well, why didn't you shoot it?

---

5. In Finnish, there is a similar expression: *Älä nylje karhua ennen kuin se on kaadettu* (Don't skin the bear before it's felled). In English, the closest approximation is the expression "Don't count your chickens before they hatch."

6. This is a commonly used expression (present in, for instance, Johan Turi's writings), and pairs with a wolf having the strength of one man and the mind of nine men.

—A bear like that isn't going to die from such a small rifle.
The others asked:
—Why didn't you come home?
—I didn't dare!
The others said:
—Well then, why don't you stay up there in that tree your whole life?

And they went back. And so the old man hastily came down from the tree and ran home with the others, before they left him behind.

That soddy root ball, which scared the old bird hunter, was seen by those people, who were downstream from it, and they figured that's what frightened the old bird hunter.

Meniš-Antti's Bear-Hunting Stories
Antti Kitti (A. V. Koskimies)

I was fifteen years old at the time, when I set off to walk into the forest, so I could maybe see something while hunting. When I had walked a long while, I saw a bear's den. I guessed there was a creature inside. I left it there and went back. After the snows came, I brought Kiro-Aadam and Meniš-Irjàn[7] along with me, and we set off to hunt that bear. After we came to the den, we cut some wood for spears, but since the opening to the den was wide, the bear came out under the spear and grabbed my leg. I had an axe, and I tried to hit the bear on the head with it. But since there was a crooked birch in front of me I couldn't hit him, since the axe-head would hit the birch. The bear got free.

Kiro-Aadam yelled:
—Take the axe, Irjàn, and hit it!

Irjàn swung, but he didn't hit it. The bear went on its way, when I loaded my rifle. We went to see where the bear went off to. It had crawled under a large spruce. I said to Aadam:
—You shoot. You have the big rifle.

Aadam said:
—Go, go. We're coming too.

Well, I set off skiing, and I saw the bear come into view in a clearing. When the bear got into the clearing, it noticed me and came after me. I then shot it in the chest. In the clearing, there was a small spruce. It attacked the spruce, thinking it was surely the spruce that shot him. It wrestled with it until it fell.

We got into position, and my leg started to limit me greatly. Aadam and Irjàn

---

7. Note that Meniš-Irjàn's *joik* can be found in appendix A.

went to get the bear and skin it. I had heard that bear bile was good to treat a bear bite. I took some bile and drank it. The bile came out of the bear's tooth marks.[8] After that I got better, and we split up the meat and went home. We had no worries, since we had killed a bear.

Then another fall, I went out again looking for a bear. I saw tracks where the bear had walked. I went to follow it. And I noticed that the bear was eating berries. I crept really close to it and shot. There wasn't much space at all between us, only 3 fathoms (5.5 m; 18 feet). So the bear took the bullet in the side and went under a large spruce. But before I knew it, the bear charged me. I set off running to escape. I left my gun case behind, at the place where I shot. The bear went to my gun case and circled back, so I couldn't see him anymore, and went again under the large spruce tree. I crept to another place and shot a second time, and that's how I killed the bear.

A third autumn I again went hunting for bear. I circled the same place of the bear, where I had killed the other bear with Aadam and Meniš-Irjàn. I took Junnaz and the churchwarden Irjàn along with me. And we went there, where the bear was, and we killed it. And that was the third bear that I killed in my life.

A Bear Story
H. Kitti (A. V. Koskimies)

I went out once with Antti to bring some reindeer to a *siida*, when a bear met us. Neither of us had a rifle. We circled back to get a rifle. Then we followed its tracks and we came upon the bear at the bottom of a gorge. Well, the bear noticed, and, well, it went climbing up the gorge's walls. Well, it came into view, and when it started to get into our sights, we shot it. The bear growled and set off bounding toward us. I jumped behind a pine tree and glanced at my friend. He ran to escape, already about a hundred fathoms ahead. The bear died there at the bottom of the ravine. I yelled:

—Come on back! It's already dead!

---

8. The language here is a bit unclear. Although the source of the bile literally comes from the "tooth marks," or bite marks, in the context of the story it seems most likely the bile is extracted from the recently felled bear's gallbladder, and perhaps some secretion related to the drinking of the bile emerges from Kitti's wounds. Seemingly, Kitti suggests that after one drinks bear bile, the bile itself comes out of the wounds. This latter interpretation is more consistent with other traditional healing practices. DuBois and Lang (2013) note that Johan Turi recommends drinking bear gall for internal ailments, and open wounds can be treated with bear gall and bear fat. Bear gall has been shown to alleviate inflammation. Bear teeth also can be used to reduce pain—for instance, in toothaches.

The Bear Hunters
Juho Petteri Lusmaniemi (A. V. Koskimies)

Two men were in the forest hunting for wild reindeer. They found a bear den, tied up their draught reindeer, and got their rifles ready. They went to see if there was a bear in there. They dragged some pieces of rotting wood, and chucked them at the mouth of the bear's den: nothing stirred. Well, they figured there wasn't a bear in there after all, and one went to peek into the mouth of the den. Then a bear jumped out, nearly grabbed his face, and set off running. It ran through a bush, when one hunter shot. The bear fell, but again it jumped up. The other shot, and the bear fell again. It again lunged up, and it left slowly with blood flowing from it. The men followed behind it, and they let their dog loose so the bear would come after it, but it didn't come. They followed its tracks, and the bear went into a dense thicket. The dog went to the thicket and came back. One man went to examine the thicket. In the middle of the grove there was a big birch. He climbed up the birch, noticed that the bear was in the middle of the thicket, and told his companion to bring the rifle to the birch. There was a branch outstretched from the birch right in the direction of the bear. He grabbed the branch with three fingers and held the rifle with two, so he wouldn't drop the rifle as it fired. He shot. The bear started to jump and growl. The men said:

—Now its stomach is wounded, and things will now go well.

The Girls and the Bear
Heikki Mattus, by letter (A. V. Koskimies)

One time two girls went to move some reindeer, and when they got near the reindeer, they came across a bear, for it had taken the place of the herdsman, and had killed one reindeer and was eating on it.

Those poor girls, who were Heeihi Máárjá and Heendi Iggá, tried to run back, but the bear then caught them, jumped onto two feet, and started to snort so that its spittle blew onto their faces. It kept running closer and closer. And again it came, and it snorted and jumped so that it almost grabbed them with its paws. But when the bear went a little bit behind some trees, Heendi Iggá took off her dress quickly, and she hung it on the branch of an old pine, so the bear thought it was a person. And then they left running home. But Heeihi Máárjá, who had a limp, could barely keep going, but she was so scared at the time that even she escaped as well. No one even knew how she made it over the fence. And so they got home.

The Bear and the Women
an elderly woman from Juvduu (Juutua) (A. V. Koskimies)

We were rowing along an island and we called our sheep:
—Tava, tava!
Then a bear stood up, looked at us, and set off running. It went into the lake and started to swim. We rowed out there, so that it came toward us and growled. Well, the farm matron stuck it with a spear, but the bear took it into its mouth and flung it aside. And I had an oar in my hand, and it took it and threw it away as well. And the woman stabbed with her spear, but the bear took it too and threw it. I started to think that it would get into the boat, and I turned the boat sideways. And so the boat turned sideways, and the bear lost its grip. The matron stabbed with her spear and hit its heart. The bear went swimming away and went to the island, and it was there until the men came.

The Squirrel Hunters
Juho Petteri Lusmaniemi (A. V. Koskimies)

Once there were some hunters who had gathered at some house to hunt wild reindeer. There was a pine tree growing in the doorframe. When the men woke in the morning they noticed that there was a squirrel in that pine. That group of men raced after the squirrel to catch it without having to shoot. One of them climbed the pine, and others went to the yard to stand guard. One older girl watched them to see how they would kill it. The squirrel jumped from the pine, and since there wasn't anyone guarding there, it ran right up that girl's leg and inside her fur coat. The poor girl became distressed, since she had a squirrel running about in there and clawing at her everywhere. Everyone exploded in laughter and the fur coat was stripped away: there was no other recourse.

The Wild Reindeer Skiers
Uula Morottaja (T. I. Itkonen)

Once, in ancient times, there were some Sámi who were off skiing after wild reindeer. The talk had been that those who managed to first kill the game would get to keep the whole of the catch for themselves. They stopped at some place to cook some porridge. Some of them got to eat before others, since the second group's porridge was hot. The second group became hurried! They mixed some snow into it, but the porridge started to freeze up, but only on the surface. And in a hurry, they guzzled the hot porridge and burned their insides, and they all got sick and some even died.

The Moose Hunters
Uula Morottaja (T. I. Itkonen)

Some head of a household was seining with his two sons when he noticed that there was something that must have been an animal swimming across the lake. He mentioned it to his sons. The older son, when he heard, threw his rope of twisted roots[9] into the lake and started to row. The oar broke. He yelled to his father:

—Bring me your oars! Quickly!

And so they went, the three of them, to row after the moose, and they caught up to it. They didn't have a rifle, but the older boy grabbed the moose by the ear and started to stab it with his knife, and he killed it. It was so large that these three men could barely drag it up onto the shore to skin it.

Irján-Ánná and -Antti on a Fishing Excursion to Lággujävri (Lankojärvi)
unknown (A. V. Koskimies)

Irján-Antti and Ánná started to argue when they were gutting fish. Irján-Ánná scooped a birchbark basket filled with water from the lake and started to throw it at Antti. Antti countered, taking the birchbark basket into his hand, and the water ended up splashing on Ánná herself. Ánná went to get another basket full of water, and started again to throw it, but Antti pushed at her with his hand and again water splashed all over Ánná. Ánná went again to get water. Antti rolled a piece of charred turf toward Ánná. It rolled toward Ánná. Ánná tripped on it and went toppling into the lake. Since the bank was low, she only got thoroughly soaked. After this, they both burst into laughter.

The Ermine Hunters
unknown (A. V. Koskimies)

Once there were some people on Säđisuáloi (Säisaari) Island, and they noticed an ermine running. All of the men there went chasing after it. And one

---

9. *Kieuđas* here refers to the rope used for pulling a seine, commonly made from twisted roots. Here he is seemingly abandoning his seine to pursue the moose.

old woman who had a limp was also there too. The ermine ran onto one of the poles of the fishing lean-to. And the old woman grabbed a skewer stick, and she too went next to the pole to stand guard. The ermine ran along the pole, and the old woman threw the spit and it hit the ermine directly. The poor ermine curled up there. The men all fell to the ground laughing, since it was the slowest of them all who killed it.

PERSONAL EXPERIENCE NARRATIVES

Personal experience narratives are perhaps the most common form of oral tradition, although for most early story collectors, they took a back seat to the study of myth, fairy tales, and legends. Although their value has been neglected until recent times, these types of stories can communicate many crucial details that other genres do not about everyday life, customary practice, and social relationships. Itkonen separated these life stories and general descriptions of Aanaar folklife from other nonfictional stories in the collection (for instance, Hunting Stories). These stories are meant to represent how life used to be in general rather than give a specific recollection of any single course of events.

The following stories span a wide range of topics, detailing the poverty of Heikki Mattus, the courtship of Pekka Aikio, and a tragedy in Åkšujävri, and giving accounts of hunting, trapping, and fishing techniques. Although some practices, like *juoŋâstim* ice-net fishing, are still practiced today in similar fashion, other practices have disappeared. For example, the collapse of the wild reindeer populations in the late eighteenth and early nineteenth centuries signified a major economic and cultural shift for all hunting Sámi peoples. The reasons for this collapse are still debated. Older scholarship tended to target excessive hunting and improvements in hunting technologies as the cause for the decline of wild reindeer populations. However, such claims tend to reflect ethnocentric prejudices of erroneous theories of human evolution that suggest hunting economies need to transform to herding economies. More recent thought has suggested the culpability of the increase in semidomesticated reindeer herds that absorb wild reindeer populations, the stress of border closings in the far north on Aanaar Sámi traditional economies, and the encroachment of settler agriculturalists from the south who burned forest lands to transform them into pastures. Losing the wild reindeer hunt had major impacts on the Aanaar Sámi economy, culture, and social organization, which faced a period of rapid transition in the nineteenth century. Some of these changes were responsible for the decimation of the Kemi Sámi culture in the later half of the eighteenth century.

Above all, these personal narratives are tales of transition, growth and change, and the overcoming of hardship that define our own lives: from hunting to herding, from poverty to prosperity, from bachelorhood to family.

The Life of One Aanaar Sámi
Heikki Mattus, by letter (A. V. Koskimies)

I was born the tenth day of September in the year 1838, from poor parents, in the Pààđàr (Paadar) *siida*, and in the house of Jormo (Jurmu). My parents didn't have food or clothes. And we were seven children. They had a lot of work to do and trouble supporting us. And from time to time they didn't have anything to eat other than a pine-water concoction, whose name was *peciliema*, pine-bark broth. That's how we survived the winters until my father started hunting birds in the spring, and when the lakes melted we would also get a little fish. So we always were able to survive. But in between the summers there wasn't anything to eat besides pine-bark broth and crowberries, and we were lucky to even have those.

But in the evening when we were eating such foods, my late mother always recited to us children our evening prayers, and the Our Father and Priestly Blessing. We needed to each say with hands crossed: "Jesus bless our bedtime." And the youngest daughter she still lulled to sleep, and she sang:

> Don't you my little Aila cry, cry
> Mother lulls you, mother lulls you
> Father surely will come from hunting birds
> He'll bring his daughter a bird's eye.

But then a priest came along, whose name was E. W. Borg, and I think I was about eighteen years old and still hadn't been confirmed. He took me to his place, where he held catechism. I would get through, and he would even feed me during catechism, since I didn't have anything to eat.

Then the following summer he took me to his place and taught me to read and write Finnish better and to recognize numbers. He kept me at his house until I learned so much that in 1865 he eventually made me another catechist in Aanaar to teach children. The same pastor was for me like a foster parent as long as I was here in Sápmi. And I didn't forget him for my entire life. He would have taken me along to Láádàn (Lanta; Finland), but since I got married a little before his departure to Láádàn, I stayed here in Aanaar.

I lived a good life with my wife. God gave us seven children, of whom four died and three are alive. But one of them is deaf. And I started to get pay as a catechist. We had success with our reindeer, and cows and sheep were born, and we started to get fish, and still in addition to this I got a regular catechist's position and became a sacristan.

And now there's little to worry about. I am satisfied. Here it can be seen again, as they say in the hymn, that God, the miracle worker, can both lift us up and lower us down.

An Aanaar Marriage and Life Story
Pekka Matinpoika Aikio (A. V. Koskimies)

My fiancée's home was on the other side of Aanaar. I had sent my engagement gifts with someone over there. Well, around Christmas I got word that I could come. So I went there. Two matchmakers came along with me. Another suitor from a different place also came, and he was saying that the girl didn't need to go with me. The girl's stepfather told him:

—You need to go on your way.

He still didn't go. He said a second time:

—You need to leave.

Still he didn't leave. He said a third time:

—You need to leave.

And the man left. So we got to talk to the girl. We had our engagement party, and we went back. And I went to the church to have the announcements read out loud.[1] In Aanaar, the winter was thought to be the best time for weddings. That's when I was married, too.

We married at the time of court, and the same day we had our party, which we Aanaar Sámi usually hold in the church. Well, cakes were made, butter was bought, reindeer cheese was prepared, and two or three jugs of liquor were

---

1. At the time there was a custom of having the engagement announced in the church on three consecutive Sundays before a couple could be married. In English, this was referred to as "the banns of marriage."

procured. We cooked the best meats and coffee, we set the table, and we set drinks and foods upon it. It had all the makings of a customary Aanaar Sámi wedding. When we finished dining, a goblet was passed clockwise around the table to everyone. Each said before drinking from it:

—Good fortunes to all the invited guests, and in remembrance of the young couple!

Then we thanked God, and the guests wished the young couple good fortunes. After that they started to give gifts: some gave a reindeer; some five or six marks; some gave cloths; some seining equipment; or a retrieval net; some gave a ring and whatnot. We thanked the gift givers.

So the wedding ended, and we left driving back to our home and we started up our household. I worked as a driver,[2] and our reindeer grew in numbers. We lived happily and prosperously, and we had seven children, who are still alive.

Some Misfortune
from Ákšujävri (A. V. Koskimies)

In one house a great misfortune happened. A man was off rowing somewhere, and his wife was alone with their three children. At night, the mother woke when she started to hear a noise in the entryway. And when she opened the door, there was a fire in front of her and her clothes caught fire. In distress, she barely saved herself by throwing herself out the window. How did the children manage? The oldest boy, who had woken taking fright and who also jumped out of the window, heard the yelling of his two sisters and he tried to save them from the burning cottage. The effort was in vain. He was badly burned. The boy and mother were in the doctor's care. Those two children remained in the fire. There was no certain information about what started the fire, but we think it was the work of an enemy.

The Old Man of Soađigil's (Sodankylä's) Forest Memories
unknown (A. V. Koskimies)

In my youth, some old man from Soađigil (Sodankylä) said there was so much game everywhere that you wouldn't believe it, but now the game has run out, so that a poor old man can't even get by anymore. When we used to hunt

---

2. In this context he is most likely hired to drive other people or their property by reindeer.

Lààutàǯ (*njollâ*) storehouse near Gárasavvon (Karesuvanto), 2018. Photo: Jostein Henriksen.

birds with *liestiij*-traps[3] or *kàskàstuuvaj*-traps,[4] there usually would be so many birds that we couldn't even carry them home. Instead, we had to build a cache for our meat in the woods, where the game could be stored until the coming of winter, when the meat could be brought by reindeer to its destination. And such a cache, which was called a *puorna* (Finnish: *purnu*), was made like this: you cut through a thickish old pine tree and you leave the stump to be about one fathom's (1.8 m; 6 feet) length. At the end of the stump, you build a small four-cornered frame in the style of a storehouse. It was called a *lààutàǯ* (Finnish: *lauttanen*), a cubit or two in height (45–90 cm; 1.5–3 feet), you put walls on it and the rafters, and fashion some kind of roof from something, and finally you make a small four-cornered door. And you put the game in there and hang it from bars. This kind of food box is made so high off the ground that no wolverines or other forest animals will get to eat the food in it.

3. A style of deadfall trap, called *sadin* in Finnish.
4. A three-walled trap with pole and bait, called *rita* in Finnish.

In the fall, when it snows, we always went to hunt squirrels, and often we got two *kittalas* (Finnish: *kiihtelys*; bundles of forty squirrels). But when we were out squirrel hunting, we got larger creatures as well, and sometimes it went so badly that there happened to be a reindeer in front of a bullet and it too was killed. In those dark forests one can't always discern what's what. Foxes we killed with poison we bought in Norway, for you could get it there from an apothecary even without a doctor's permission. Otters too we hunted, though only with iron traps, but the most productive hunting for us was for wild reindeer, and it was our best means of livelihood. We left home, two men toward the front waiting for wild game and the other men setting off behind, and if the latter ones noticed any wild reindeer, they would make camp and set up their positions. If people thought the game was close by, close enough that they thought they could get it the next day, then they enjoyed a good dinner, with chopped reindeer tallow.

In the spring-winter,[5] around Märji's Day (The Feast of the Annunciation; March 25), we went to Suáloi-čielgi (Saariselkä) hunting wild reindeer, for those tundras were the best for the wild reindeer to lounge about on. When we started to get near the tundras that we thought the wild reindeer were on, we made a fire, where we lodged the whole hunting trip. When we noticed a herd of reindeer, we tried to near it always from downwind, for otherwise we wouldn't be able to get even a shot off. Wild reindeer smell people in the wind.

On the excursion we would stay usually two or three weeks, but then we had usually about sixty pelts to bring home.

Now this too has come to an end, so we don't really go there that often anymore.

The Autumnal Wild Reindeer Hunt in Aanaar
Heikki Mattus (A. V. Koskimies)

On the first day of September there would always be a two- or three-men party setting off for the tundras where they knew the wild reindeer would be residing. And they each took three pack reindeer and each their best wild reindeer dog. But as they came alongside the herd of reindeer, circling downwind of them, the dogs started to pull the men so they had to run behind with all their might, until they came to the reindeer. Then they muzzled their dogs and tied

---

5. Sámi people traditionally recognized eight seasons. Spring-winter has plenty of snow, but the weather is warmer than winter and the daylight is considerably longer.

them to a stone or branch. They took off the packs from their reindeers' backs, tied the draught reindeer up someplace, and went to stalk. They walked, the most skillful one in front, until they got within shooting range. Well, I wonder what happened next . . .

Pow! The leader shot, and a large wild reindeer died. Bam! Another shot through the leg of a female reindeer. Pow! The third also shot, and a two-year-old male reindeer's tail was broken. The best dog was released after the female, which was shot through the leg, and it too was killed. But the two-year-old male reindeer wasn't killed, since it only had its tail broken. The wild reindeer were skinned and put into a food cache, and they stayed there the night. In the camp they set up a *lávvu*, or *goahti*, from the canvas that they brought with them. And they cooked venison and gave their dogs the blood and the lungs. And they slept until morning. And again they went out in the same fashion, and they kept moving the entire autumn until it was All Saints Day (November 1) and the snows came. And everything killed in the fall was put in the same fashion into *puorna* and *lààutàǯ* food caches and submerged into springs. But the pelts and leg pieces[6] they hung on a stretching rack to dry.

That fall the men got twenty wild reindeer and five bears, and so they returned home. But when Feast of Christ the King (November 20–27) came, they left with their reindeer and sledges to drive and retrieve their reindeer and bear meats, along with the furs and legs, and everything they had gotten, when the lakes froze and the snows came. They took then their rifles along, so if they saw a wild reindeer's tracks they could go follow it and get it. And then those geezers killed another thirty wild reindeer, in addition to the many things they had trapped. And so they returned on the Feast of Christ the King, with their sledges filled with meats, and even then not bringing back everything that they caught.

This is, in short, a story of autumnal wild reindeer hunting, or also called *ordostallam-* (Finnish: *uurto*) and *kesijaš-šammaainas* (Finnish: *kiesioiminen*).

This was written in 1887 by an Aanaar sacristan by the name of Henrik Mattus.

Vuàvnum (Vuongunta), or Hunting Wild Reindeer in the Spring
Heikki Mattus, by letter (A. V. Koskimies)

In the spring, people from Aanaar would go on springtime wild reindeer hunts around May Day with reindeer and *geres*, or at the time when the snows

---

6. The leg pieces were cut from below the reindeer's ankle joint and used to make a shoe.

ended with pack reindeer. And they went where they knew there were large bogs or swamps, and if there was a tundra on the edge of those clearings, they went onto it during the day to watch for wild reindeer, or went along some grassy brook to wait until some wild reindeer would come along. If no wild reindeer came, they would move to other places, where they knew reindeer would reside. The wild reindeer were so many, and they would hunt in this way so long, that each of their pack reindeer along with them was carrying a load. And when each reindeer had a full pack, they went back with their packed meat. Upon their return, they put the meat out to dry so that it wouldn't spoil or rot. Or if they killed so many that they couldn't carry it all back, then they would make a structure in the forest and put the meat in there to dry, and they would come back to get it with a draught reindeer.

But now people no longer do the spring hunt, since it's no longer permitted. And since the time since it's been banned, people stopped hunting wild reindeer, and all the wild reindeer also disappeared. And during these years, nobody has heard anything about a reindeer being killed anywhere in these parts, neither in the spring nor fall. These times weren't like they were before, the old people now say.

Juoŋâstim (Juomustus) and Netting under the Ice
Antti Sarre (A. V. Koskimies)

An opening is made in the ice, and a person pushes a float-pole, which is 4–5 fathoms in length (7–9 m; 24–30 feet), into the hole as far as it reaches. Then you chop another opening into the ice, where the other end of the pole is, in such a way that the pole can be pushed forward. At one end of the pole, you tie a rope that is as long as the pole extends. When the line runs out, stop pushing and put a net into the hole and tie the rope to the end of the net. And in this fashion, you pull the net through the section closer to the shore that is one and a half nets under the ice. And you start to chop another hole. When it is chopped, you again pull the net into the outer hole interval in the same fashion as the inner section. In this way, you can use nets under the ice. When it's finished, three nets will be there.

When you're ready to check the nets, chop open the middle hole, which in the meantime has frozen up, and then open the hole closest to shore, and the rope is tied to the end of the net from the hole closest to shore. Then pull the net to the middle hole, so you can see if it's gotten any fish, and again pull the net with the rope to the hole closest to shore, and in the same fashion do this with the outermost hole.

If you want to pull ice nets,[7] you bring the nets to the *geres*, and you set off to bring it to where the catch is. And when you come to the place where you will lift the nets, chop a large ice hole, push two float poles with rope on their ends into it. And then you start maneuvering the poles, guiding them under the ice, making holes in the ice and pushing as long as you want, until they go around the catch and you can lift them up through the hole. Then start to pull the seine under the ice with the rope and chop around the catch until it can be brought to the lifting place. Pull the rope and nets until they're up. Make sure in the end that the fish don't swim away and are caught in the bottom net and are pulled into the base of the seine. From there fish will be found in the bottom of the seine, just like in a bag.

7. Whereas the first two paragraphs detail stationary netting, the following description details how one pulls nets to seine beneath the ice.

PROVERBS AND FIGURES OF SPEECH

Proverbs are best characterized as short, pithy sayings that are used to convey wisdom through a metaphor based generally in the guise of experiential knowledge. Although they are associated with a sort of timeless wisdom, proverbs are not simply a repository and expression of a community's shared knowledge. Rather, they often contradict each other ("you can't judge a book by its cover," but "the clothes make the man"), they are used in context to help understand meanings and shape interpretation of events, and they are interesting tools that help guide how communities negotiate knowledge and action. If you can apply a proverb to a difficult situation, you can begin to make sense of it and understand what course of action should be taken.

Proverbs are notoriously difficult to interpret, as their metaphorical nature can be understood in different ways by different people. For instance, the famous "a rolling stone gathers no moss" has been interpreted in different contexts to both praise and criticize restlessness, migrancy, and the refusal to settle down. The interpretation depends on whether one recognizes moss as a symbol for comfort or stagnation, and whether it's more desirable to settle down or keep on trucking.

These Sámi proverbs share much in common with wider traditions of Nordic and European proverbial wisdom. Some of the proverbs have a Sámi color to them, with references to fishing or reindeer, but many of these have variants found cross-culturally. Despite the probability of at least some misinterpretation, I have attempted here to clarify a meaning for each proverb in italicized parentheticals following the proverb. Any notes from the original text are included in unitalicized parentheticals.

Figures of speech, on the other hand, are seldom interpreted as containing much deep wisdom, though they still draw analogies between different situations and reflect the attitudes and beliefs of the people using the expressions. Koskimies and Itkonen annotated most of these sayings to explain their use, and they are accordingly translated here in unitalicized parentheticals.

Proverbs

Never look at a gifted horse's teeth. (*Don't look a gift horse in the mouth.*)

Give to your dog and you will hear bad words. (Don't be selfish or have your priorities wrong, or you'll hear about it later.)

Time changes and people age. (*Changes in life are inevitable.*)

There are always fish in the water, even if there isn't always a catch. (*The world isn't rotten, even if you've had some bad luck; or, there are other fish in the sea.*)

Every pine needle will stick the lone boy. (*Life kicks you when you're down; or, said sarcastically, your outlook on life shapes your experience.*)

The start of work brings beauty, in the end thankfulness stands tall. (*Work is its own reward.*)

From the word a man, from an antler a draught reindeer. (*A person's word is everything.*)

In Lake Aanaar there are just as many islands as days in a year. (*Every day is different, just as every island is different.*)

By its talents, even a mouse squeaks. (*Every person has their own talents.*)

Being timid doesn't make you live longer. (*Be bold.*)

Do not wrestle with people, but with the tasks you have. (*Don't focus on fighting, be productive.*)

Beardless boys should not challenge me to fight, says the bear. (*Don't send a boy to do a man's job.*)

Days are not set atop each other, but rather lie next to each other. (*You walk a mile by putting one foot in front of the other.*)

Proverbs and Figures of Speech

Not everyone is lulled by the same mother. (*People aren't all the same.*)

In a country, by the country's customs. (*When in Rome, do as the Romans do.*)

A horse isn't alone when it kicks in the barn. (*It takes two to fight.*)

There's no greater haste than in a flea hunt. (*The smallest things often seem the most pressing.*)

Morning is wiser than evening. (*A good night's sleep brings wisdom.*)

No man lives on a name. (*Actions and not reputation are what matters in one's character.*)

The eye does not participate. (*If you're watching, you're not helping with work.*)

Harm won't announce its arrival. (*Be vigilant for danger.*)

Shame won't tear your forehead apart. (*Shame won't physically kill you; or, you need to learn to live with your shame.*)

Haste does not help. (*Haste makes waste.*)

You don't get fish in the bottom of your nets from just any old place. (*Knowledge means productivity; or, don't plant your seed in infertile ground.*)

A juniper branch cannot touch a flame, for it immediately flares up into the flame. (*Some things just cannot mix.*)

A stray dog's hair is nothing to look at. (*Don't judge a book by its cover.*)

An empty sack isn't able to stand upright. (*Poor people need help.*)

There is no harm from the anger of a powerless one, nor in the bark of a toothless one. (*For some, the bark is bigger than the bite.*)

A year is not a brother of another year. (*No two years are alike.*)

It's dire when the bread runs out, but it's truly a catastrophe when the tobacco is gone. (*Keep your priorities straight.*)

It isn't good that tracks leave a scent. (*In reference to predators; don't leave a mark on the world.*)

Learning won't make you fall into a ditch. (*A little bit of learning won't hurt you.*)

You're never so poor that you cannot help your companions, and never so rich that you don't need help. (*Always give and accept help.*)

The night is never so long that it's not the remnants of the day. (*When things are bad, they'll eventually become good.*)

The day is never so long that it's not the remnants of the night. (*When things are good, they'll eventually become bad.*)

A mark doesn't come while asleep, nor big money to your reindeer-fur bedding. (*Laziness won't bring you money.*)

No one is born with an axe in hand. (*You need to learn to work.*)

One harsh word won't kill you. (*Sticks and stones may break my bones, but words will never hurt me.*)

No human lives only by power, but also by sense. (*Think before you act.*)

No day is so long that the night will not come. (*All good things end.*)

No dog knows if it can swim before it is submerged. (*Try new things.*)

Shit won't always fall on the exact spot you're aiming for. (*Things don't always go as planned.*)

A hat won't come from birchbark. (*You can't squeeze blood from a stone.*)

You don't need to sow or plow to get crazy people. (*There will always be fools around, independent of your own actions.*)

He who has not seen distress does not know distress. (*Don't judge the ill fates of others.*)

He who will not get his feet wet will not get fish. (*You can't make an omelet without breaking some eggs.*)

Emptiness does not burn. (*Nothing will come of nothing.*)

Misfortune does not arrive with a bell around its neck. (*Misfortune will sneak up on you.*)

Help is also to be had from children: eat a fish, gut two. (*A child is not completely useless, even if somewhat inefficient.*)

Your own shit doesn't stink, but another's does even from afar. (*Don't think your own shit doesn't stink.*)

I have not taken on a dog's labors: I won't bite the string, said the bear in the trap. (*Don't think too highly of yourself.*)

The eye already knows the food. (*Desire is powerful.*)

The old women won't forget to keep their net shuttle[1] safe. (*Small chores can be of great importance.*)

A raven will carry fat alright. (*Some people will profit from the hard work of others.*)

A man comes from a snot-nosed kid as well. (*Even a great man was a boy once.*)

He who has five jobs has six hungers. (*Some people have an insatiable desire for more.*)

A stone will never stay on the surface, but will sink every time. (*You can't change your nature.*)

A bird sings with its tongue, it can't hear the powerful. (*Might is not connected to beauty.*)

---

1. A net shuttle is used to repair fishing nets.

The poor have time to cook but no time to cool it. (*When you're poor, you do as you must; or, don't romanticize poverty.*)

Poverty isn't able to hide. (*People in poverty do not have the luxury of being able to hide their problems.*)

He who only fishes in the summer will be killed by hunger in the winter. (*Prepare carefully for the future.*)

Who would buy a pig in a sack? (*Don't buy a pig in a poke; know what you're buying.*)

A cold man is not the right person to make a fire. He would burn up the whole goahti. (*Don't let someone who is emotionally involved respond to a situation.*)

Overturned water will never return to the dish. (*What's done is done.*)

He who tries to mimic his father or mother usually ends up falling into his shit. (*Be your own person.*)

He who won't look forward looks backward. (*Don't dwell on the past.*)

He who can't stand the heat can't stand the cold either. (*People who can't handle one extreme can't handle another.*)

He who throws stones up high receives them on his own head. (*Don't show off.*)

That which suddenly charges will have its tail flip against all kinds of things. (*Move forward thoughtfully to avoid unintended consequences.*)

He who has rowed only a little has weak arms. (*He who does, achieves.*)

A king, the highest of gentlemen; a minister, the best of guests. (*Perhaps said sarcastically about people thinking too highly of themselves.*)

A bear has the strength of nine men and the mind of one man. (*More of a saying than a proverb, it contrasts with the wolf that has the strength of one man and the mind of nine men.*)

Proverbs and Figures of Speech

Santeri Valle demonstrating pine-bark peeling in 1914. Photo: Toivo Itkonen. Image courtesy of the Finnish National Board of Antiquities.

As many rivers flow into one, a great river is born. (*A great man stands on the shoulders of many.*)

When a sacristan starts a hymn, the congregation is sure to sing along. (*People will follow a leader.*)

A decent person hides his pine-bark chisel[2] in a corner of the *goahti*, but a wreck will throw it to the ground or wherever it lands. (*Take care of your belongings.*)

When someone disputes something without talking, they dispute profusely. (*Silence speaks volumes.*)

---

2. Aanaar Sámi routinely harvested the inner bark of pines as a staple food. The bark has nutrients and can be ground into a flour.

A wolf's "enough" is never. (*Greed can never get enough.*)

Two big ones won't fit into the same sack. (*Two big personalities will clash.*)

What's on another's plate looks like more than what's on your own. (*The grass is always greener on the other side of the fence.*)

Never take a knife suddenly from another's hands. (*Don't make quick decisions that will have unintended consequences.*)

The lazy man counts his steps. (*Instead of doing work, lazy people will pay attention to how much work is to be done.*)

A lazy person does not care about real work but only about useless things. (*Lazy people will busy themselves with not working.*)

A sacristan is a pastor's pocket. (*Perhaps, a sacristan is a pastor's right-hand man.*)

There are no sides on a sacristan's purse. (*Sacristans don't accumulate wealth, and it's the parishioners who keep the church running.*)

"Almost" is not ever true. (*"Almost done" is not done.*)

An escaped squirrel is out of reach. (*A bird in the hand is better than two in the bush.*)

A famished person isn't suitable to prepare food. (*Don't let someone who is emotionally involved respond to a situation.*)

An indecent woman wanders with her leggings down. (*Clothes make the man.*)

A burbot doesn't die even from a whipping. (*Don't beat a dead horse.*)

Not even water is given to one without a mouth. (*One who cannot be helped will not be helped.*)

A bird cannot fly high with weak wings. (*Work hard to achieve great things.*)

Proverbs and Figures of Speech 191

A gust is always followed by a gust. (*Like breeds like.*)

A reindeer always come from the southwest and to the southwest it must return. (*You return to what you know.*)

One cannot strike good fortune. (*One cannot always control what happens to them.*)

A stranger's eye is exact, when a person looks. (*Outside perspectives can sometimes provide clarity.*)

Previous misfortune is not on the lookout for the next one. (*Just because you've already had hardship doesn't mean you won't face it again.*)

Tell a bad person to do something, and run after it yourself. (*Tell someone incapable to do something, and get ready to do it yourself.*)

When the bad spirit parted ways with God, it *joiked*. (*Joiking is connected to evil behavior.*)

A pastor's sack is bottomless. (*Pastors cannot keep anything for themselves; or, pastors will never be satisfied.*)

A bad wife doesn't stop harping before crying nor the east wind's blowing before the rain. (*Difficult wives will never stop nagging.*)

The speechless one squeaks. (One becomes wise from being injured.) (*Once bitten twice shy.*)

The days come one after another. (*Take things one day at a time.*)

With reprimands a fire burns, with eating the fire extinguishes. (*A full belly fixes crabbiness.*)

Fat doesn't stay on a dog's nose: it licks it right away. (*Don't offer temptation to others.*)

An older dog bites through a thicker string. (With age comes wisdom.)

Better to have a songbird in the hand than a moose in the forest. (*A bird in the hand is better than two in the bush.*)

Better late than never.

Better to have a bite in the mouth than a wound in the head. (*Small problems are better than big ones.*)

It's better to leave good food than to have a badly bursting stomach. (*Don't glut yourself.*)

It's better to live carefree with no lice in your clothes than to let lice keep about in them. (*It's best to take care of small problems that keep bothering you.*)

Good is to give from what little you have, and bad is to not from your plentitude. (*Be generous, even if you're poor.*)

Good always gives, and bad never does. (*Be generous.*)

The cat too would eat fish, but it wouldn't wet its claws. (*One needs to do unpleasant work sometimes for the results.*)

The bold hold their food, the shy die of hunger. (*Don't be too shy.*)

A Sámi made everything from branches, but couldn't make a person. (*Sámi are clever, but only God creates life.*)

Many trod about on their tail. (*Many step on their own foot.*)

A sack doesn't plead itself full. (Be happy with less.) (*Wanting more won't bring happiness.*)

Diligence will defeat even the difficult. (*Diligence is a virtue.*)

He who quarrels with the womenfolk won't have his tongue burned by the porridge. (*There's no end in sight if you start quarreling with women, and you'll argue so long the porridge will get cold; or, you won't be served hot food by the women you depend on if you start such quarrels.*)

Proverbs and Figures of Speech

It seems like the mute one is commanding. (You learn from mistakes.) (*It is a mistake to let a mute person give commands.*)

You need to shoot when you are at shooting distance. (*Seize the day.*)

Fresh wood will dry as much as dry wood. (*Give things the time they need to mature.*)

You know an indecent person when she is hanging around tugging at her dress-strings. (*Avoid flirting with temptation.*)

As goes experience, so goes the mind. (*Experience brings wisdom.*)

A bud-hat[3] walks during the fall hunt, a white collar drives with a white reindeer. (About hunters and show-offs.) (*Don't be a show-off; value the simple, practical, and industrious.*)

Empty doesn't burn even in a pipe. (*Nothing will come of nothing.*)

Work thanks the doer. (*Work is its own reward.*)

A shy man does not get a beautiful wife. (*Take risks to get what you want.*)

Mistakes make wisdom. (*You learn from mistakes.*)

Try catching a mouse when it has already slipped into its hole. (*Be aware of your surroundings and use them to your advantage.*)

Caution does not overturn a boat. (*Being cautious never hurt anything.*)

Blood is thicker than water. (*Family is more important than friendship.*)

Even descaling a perch requires know-how. (*Even the simplest tasks require skill.*)

---

3. An ambiguous reference, a bud-hat seemingly refers to the simple workwear of a hunter. It is likely meant to contrast with someone wearing an easily dirtied white collar.

An unlucky man has things pulled from his mouth, an unlucky man has things shoved up his backside. (*Unlucky people have things they need taken from them, and things they do not want forced on them.*)

Figures of Speech

Ahaa, the talk turns there! (Is something bugging you?)

The heel of the moon-tarring man has already worn. (Said when the moon turns to its later phases.)[4]

The boogeyman is coming and you are without shoes. (Said to children who don't want to wear shoes.)

Weren't you a good old man to follow those tracks! (Said to a good dog.)

Black flies from the eye. (Said about someone getting angry.)

It too perhaps is the dark-man's (devil's) own. (Said in confusion—i.e., What the devil?)

Clear as a tear. (Said about, e.g., fish.)

Stump-pisser. (Said about carelessness and wanderers.)

The sun shines so swelteringly, it looks like rain might come. (Said about young love.)

My father knows. My grandma knows. My grandpa knows. (Said about matters where the speaker doesn't know.)

Hui, hui, the boy child! Thanks to God for the girl child! If only the boys would all die and only the girls would stay alive! (A Sámi boy's first test of manhood is to kill a squirrel.)

He isn't strong, as his backside is low to the ground. (Said about children.)

4. Note the related story "Aaččan, Who Tarred the Moon," in the chapter "Belief Legends."

He hasn't pulled his hat over his eyes. (Said to the bold or presumptuous.)

He hasn't the lungs of a hare in him. (Said about the bold.)

He hasn't left his name. (Said about thieves.)

Good, handsome bridegroom; good, beautiful bride.

I don't care at all about it!

They clamor like they're from the underworld.

There was usefulness with the trip. (Said when a trip is productive.)

She is really like a female reindeer with a bell. (Said about a woman striving to lead.)

Carcass of an old man; poor creature of an old woman; scamp of a boy (about fifteen years old); sweetheart of a girl, a half-grown girl.

Beggar's food, now wasn't that ideal for the beggar? (Said about a sudden catch of fish or game that happens when you're quitting.)

Who might have driven him here? (Said about someone whose customs are unfamiliar.)

Now was it worth mentioning a dog's age, since it's already dead? (Said when a pet unexpectedly dies.)

You have the reputation of the late, great Raassaӡ. (Said about wily people.)[5]

You are like the girl in that story. (Said about lazy people who people think are hardworking.)[6]

It is like the skin of a burbot. (Slippery.)

---

    5. Note the stories about Raassaӡ in the chapter "Historical and Regional Legends."
    6. This refers to the girl in "The Story of the Girl's Spinning Rack" in the chapter "Humorous Stories and Anecdotes."

What was it that brought you here? (Said to an undesirable visitor.)

Famous frozen burbot. (Said about a cold and stiff tool.)

Lazy rag. (Said about people.)

There's magic in it.

What need was there to talk loudly about the *goahti* with holes in it? (Said about being noisy.)

Beautiful as a reed.

It's at least blacker than snow. (Said about, e.g., insufficient and meager food.)

Now isn't it a sprout! (Said about a poorly behaved child.)

Well, isn't there a whole lot of reindeer in that thing? (Said about a very large reindeer.)

I've already slid downhill too much. (Said about driving with reindeer or skiing.)

Oh, now then! And this is just a piece! (Said about sweet or good food.)

Oh dear, button-nose. (Said in puzzlement.)

Oh dear, you wisp of a cloud. (Said about thick hair, a forest, or dense reindeer antlers.) (*The connotation is that cloud wisps appear tangled.*)

Oh scrap, oh rifle rattletrap! (Drat!)

Oh you little fire. (As a flame extinguishes or shines dimly.)

I'd rather take than give.

The sun wades in water. (Said when the sun is seen through the fog.)

Bounces like tinder. (Said about a proud reindeer.)

Proverbs and Figures of Speech   197

It was like honeycomb: the poor rag. (Said about broken or bad kitchen tools.)

The fox hangs his leg pieces.[7] (Said when the birch starts to yellow.)

It looks like you got your book wet. (Your lies have come to light; you've spoken yourself into a corner.)

It seems like he went to hear Paul preaching. (Misfortunes make one wiser.)

Now there's such air like a dog's backside: still festering.

This won't withstand oxen. (Said about weak or bad things, e.g., a knife.)

It looks like this one is not going to hear the cuckoo. (Said about someone who is believed will die before summer.)

This knife will not see wars. (Said about bad knives.)

A one-winter-old ram.[8] (Said about a bad *joiker* or hymn singer.)

No daughter-in-law will disappear in his speck. (Said about a large-sized daughter-in-law.)

He has big-head thoughts.

There's a pine cone in there. (Said about anger.)

There's length there, wow, what a heel!

He has a grayling's tongue. (Said about a well-spoken person.)

A fat-mouth, there. (Said about one who is suspected of being a participant in a matter, e.g., in courting a nice girl.)

---

7. The leg piece refers to the skin beneath a reindeer's ankle joint, which was used for a style of shoes. The expression may refer to the yellow birch leaves resembling these small pieces of pelt, suitable for a fox.

8. Alternatively, this can be read as "winter's old ram."

Oh, how did I curse!

It's a lamb's head. (Said about something empty.)

He is a real ram. (Said about someone persistent or fierce.)

It came like a whale onto the shore. (Said about misfortune.)

Wait until the raven carries fat. (Said to children who play with or are unwilling to eat their food.)

There are word-changers over there. (Said about quarrelers.)

There is an endless quarrel over there.

There are squeaks and noises over there. (Said about fighting.)

They sure seem to want to pull their hides off. (Said about angry people.)

A grayling runs aground; you, grayling, cannot be without making noises. (Said about noise that wouldn't be tolerated.)

There's no distress in his pants. (*Said about impatience.*)

He will surely get a wife. (Said when a bachelor does good work.)

Just like a quarrelsome lamb.

Just like a perch on the opposite shore.

It is long as a spring of famine.

Then he still dozed off. (Said when someone is a real sleepyhead.)

He is the whole of Vuolappi (Peeivih-Vuáláppáǯ).[9] (Said about bold and strong men.)

---

9. Note the chapter "Peeivih-Vuáláppáǯ."

Neither of them had fed only on the remains of the dead. (Said about robust fighters.)

The mother-in-law digs a nook. (Said about someone whose mixing tool takes food from the pot to lick or wash.)

Oh čáhálig![10] (Said about nudity.)

Oh pin! What kind of pin are you? (Said about a short person.)

You are really a ram head.

---

10. Note the stories in "Belief Legends" about these naked treasure keepers.

RIDDLES

Riddles are used largely as an interactive and playful game, most commonly among young people. Riddles can be used in a playful competition of wits, to tease people who don't know the proper solution, or even for flirtation—although riddles that tease out erotic content are not represented in the below collection. Telling riddles encourages constant creativity and invention, since the game depends on at least one participant not knowing the answer. After someone knows the answer to a riddle, it's no longer terribly interesting until a person comes along who doesn't know that riddle. Much of the artistry in a good riddle comes in the creative and metaphorical setup, which should not be applicable to everything nor so specific and obscure that the answer would be impossible to guess. Poorly crafted riddles can prove quickly frustrating and undermine the fun of the challenge.

The best riddles often have solutions that are in plain sight, and for these reasons they reflect concerns with everyday life and work. The preponderance of riddle solutions being "a fishing net," for example, is closely tied to the reliance on net fishing in the Aanaar community. The following serve as a snapshot of everyday life in Aanaar, with questions and answers often tapping into different kinds of everyday metaphors and associations. Therein lies the challenge.

Always walks with a burden on the back, and never tires. (A spinning wheel.)

A storehouse underneath, mill on top, misty thicket on the mill. (Stomach, mouth, and hair.)

An old woman sits in a nook with red berries in her lap. (A fireplace.)

Higher than all mountains, lower than all twigs. (A path.)

Riddles

A man goes into the forest, tossing woodchips behind him. (A skier.)

Black as a priest, small as a pin, jumps like a Sámi. (A flea.)

Black horse jogs night and day and doesn't ever move its pole. (A river.)

Black horse goes into the shed, red horses come out. (When you take coals from an oven.)

Seven siblings peek out of one hole. (A *lávvu*.)

Through it you can see and keep warm. (A window.)

Widow in autumn, suffers winter, in spring a new bride. (A birch.)

A hundred-year-old man and on his head a one-night-old hat. (A stump of a tree that has fresh snow on it.)

Stands in the water, sleeps on the land, eye an arrow. (A net.)

Stands in the water, but not on dry land. (A net.)

Horse in the barn, tail outside. (A fireplace.)

The horse stands, shoulder moves. (The door of a cottage.)

Beats nights, beats days, and never gets enough. (A clock.)

Walks through the forest and leaves its tail in the forest. (A needle.)

Feet in stone, ankles in yarn, and head in pine. (A net.)

Dead out of the living and pulls out of the forest. (A comb.)

Eats summer, never gets enough; in winter sleeps in the storehouse. (A net.)

Who is the wisest in the world? (A balance.)

Flies and sings, and doesn't have head or neck. (A fart.)

In a hook upward, and in a hook downward, and curving from the middle. (A kitchen hook.)

When is a person closest to death, so close that there is seemingly just one inch between life and death? (When he is in a boat on the water.)

When does a person have the most fun thing of all? (When the draught reindeer runs with all its might.)

When does a person use all his power and his means? (When he poles up through a rapids.)

When does a person measure their mind and hold open their eye? (Shooting a rapids.)

When does a person have their greatest agony? (When they lose their only beloved.)

Which is richer, a river or lake? (A river is richer because there are rapids in it.)

When it is on his back, it is empty, when it is upside down, it is full. (A hat.)

Two pieces of gold fight on two sides of a perch. (Eyes.)

A bird flies across open water, and water drips from the wings. (A person rows in a boat.)

Lidless and bottomless, however full of fresh meat and bone. (A ring.)

What does a Sámi love most of all? (A coffee pot.)

Goes inside from one hole, but comes suddenly out of three. (A person dressing in a *beaska*.)

What animal is closest to people? (A louse.)

What is a Sámi's most faithful servant? (A dog.)

Riddles

What is a lake's scythe handle? (An island.)

What is it that goes above all? (The sun.)

What is in a *beaska* in the summer and in the winter without one? (A birch.)

What stands in the lake and sleeps on the land? (A net.)

What is quiet on dry land, and with water it spits in your face and then leaves? (A stone.)

What starts to fight with innocent people, and when jealous people lie in wait, they aren't given any regard? They would rather only fight with innocent people and get killed. (Mosquitoes, gnats, and bugs.)

What has a rifle on its back half a fathom to the end, and without aiming shoots forward, and from this gets the soup? (Lasso.)

What loafs about lazily and doesn't move itself anywhere, it has a tart, and all the other lazy and hardworking people it pulls toward itself? (A pipe and tobacco pouch.)

What walks only along smooth surfaces but on uneven surfaces can't get anywhere? (A pen.)

The length of a tree, the width of a string, all the branches it fishes with. (A tree's heart.)[1]

Wooden head, thread ribs, stone feet. (A net.)

A maiden sits alongside a spring with a hat on her head. (A yellow water lily.)

Eats with the mouth and vomits from the neck. (A wood plane.)

Eats with the mouth, food comes down the chin from the shoulders to the hands, along the hands moves only to the stomach. (A spinning wheel.)

---

1. The tree's heart refers to its innermost heartwood.

You see it, but can't grab it. (A shadow.)

One barrel, two kinds of beer inside. (An egg.)

One little mountain ash extending over the sea. (A kettle's handle.)

The front half like a loaf, the middle part like a barrel, and the back like a broom. (A horse.)

Before father is half done, there is a boy already in the forest. (Smoke.)

On one leg stands, a hat on the head. (A mushroom.)

Upward turned empty, downward full. (A hat.)

Walks for days, walks for nights, but never finds the door. (A clock.)

By day fastened, and at night loose. (Toes.)

By day on the ground, at night nowhere. (A shadow.)

By day in prison, by night loose. (Toes.)

In the wood rushes a heap tumbles, a rumble is heard here. (Thunder.)

Without roads it moves in the forest, it brings a road as it comes, all its things are pulled together. (A stick.)

A sea capercaillie flies over the open water, and blood drips from its wings. (A boat being rowed.)

A wood chip in a pond, will never rot. (A tongue.)

Aims at the heel, hits in the head. (A person farting.)

Sleeps winter, awake at summer. (A bear.)

Stands on its top, roots upward. (A cow tail.)

Barely thicker than a salmon net's string, but it never sees the light of day. (A tree's heart.)[2]

Small as an egg, but impossible to see its bottom. (A person's heart.)

Five men in front, one baldheaded old man in back who can't be caught or left behind. (Toes and heel.)

Goes through the woods, its tail disappearing in the forest. (A needle.)

---

2. The tree's heart refers to its innermost heartwood.

OMENS AND SIGNS

Although the word "omen" remains haunting and portending, people everywhere use signs to predict the weather, develop mnemonic sayings to help recall natural cycles, and watch for signs of coming good or bad luck. March comes in like a lion and goes out like a lamb; step on a crack, and break your mother's back; or, in seeing crows, knowing that one's bad, two's luck, three's health, four's wealth, five's sickness, six is death. Even today, many people knock on wood, throw salt over their shoulder upon spilling it, and avoid walking under ladders.

While the dependency on natural cycles has diminished over the past century, as has the need for individuals to accurately predict the weather, many farmers and others skilled in the outdoors still recognize these kinds of patterns in nature: birds fly low before a storm because of the low air pressure storms bring; bark is best peeled before late July; and the timing of unseasonably warm or cold spells will often suggest what sort of weather will follow. Though certainly not absolute rules, these sayings provide a framework to understand important patterns in weather and nature.

Though weather and natural-cycle omens figure large here, Koskimies and Itkonen also include other sayings and signs that can be useful to tell what will become of young people, when unruly guests might arrive, or what reckless behaviors might injure your relatives. Some of these are likely based in the same close observation that characterizes the weather lore, although others were likely taken far less literally in the community. After all, do we really expect our mother's back to break if we step on a sidewalk crack? Or, more importantly, do we still take good care to avoid the cracks, just in case?

Around Eiruh-peivi (Erkinpäivä; May 1) the calves bleat, the cuckoo sings, the sap runs, the birchbark is peeled, and the grayling spawns.

Omens and Signs

On Jååkkup-peivi (Jaakonpäivä; July 25) harsh weather.

Jonssåh (Juhannus; June 24) weather is harsh.

It's said that Candle Day (February 2) is freezing cold.

Around Maati-peivi (Matinpäivä; September 21) there is bad weather.

Loads of inner pine-bark and birchbark baskets for cloudberries are to be made before Jååhu-peivi (Jaakonpäivä; July 25).[1]

On Pärdi-peivi (Pertunpaiva; Aug. 25) harsh weather.

On All Saints Day (November 1) there is an unexpected summer.

On Simman-Juud-okko (Simon-Judas Week; the last week of October) it is mild.

If it is summery before Nomma-peivi (Maaria day; May 20), spring will be harsh; if it is summery afterward, spring will be short.

If a goose is seen before May Day, winter will not last long.

If there is bad weather on a Sunday, then the week will be dry, excluding Thursday, when usually there will be bad weather. If the week has bad weather, then the Sunday and Thursday will be beautiful.

The third week of September's winter is the devil's winter.

The woodpecker gets diarrhea, and knows it will snow.

If there is sleet and the clear water freezes into slush and snow falls on top, then there will be bad ice.

If reindeer walks with the wind, then the wind will blow from that direction the following day (generally reindeer walk against the wind).

---

1. Inner pine bark was an important food source in Aanaar. Toward the end of summer, it is harder to peel pine and birchbark.

If a reindeer shivers in the cold, it will become mild.

If a reindeer bounds about, bad weather is coming.

The cuckoo retches: it sees rain then.

The sun's "front glove" represents the weather now and its "back glove" the weather already passed.[2]

The sun falls into darkness: bad weather will come.

The chimney is like a skewer: a snowfall comes (when the fire shines from the chimney upward like long, narrow rays of light).

Now a long rain will come, when it rains like a diving bird (on the surface of water you see raindrops similar to the rings you see when a bird is diving).

When fall is very mild, spring is very cold.

If autumn is snowless and it starts to snow nearing New Year's Day, a snowy winter will follow.

When a pike's liver is wider in the direction of the head, it means there will be spring floods. When the tail-side of a pike's liver is wider, it means autumn floods.

When willow ptarmigans sit in the branches of a tree, a snowstorm is coming.

If a black woodpecker starts to linger near a place of inhabitance, it's not a good sign: then a person will die in the house or someone will supposedly get married.[3]

---

2. The "front glove" and "back glove" are part of the sun's halo. The front glove refers to the part in the direction of where the sun is going, and the back glove refers to the direction the sun came from.

3. Historically, in many Finno-Ugric cultures, marriage and death were related practices, and marriage was seen as a time of mourning. Both signified that someone would leave the house. Note the woodpecker omen in the story "The Dead Constable" in this volume.

If a crane starts to linger about near a house, it's not a good sign.

A cuckoo can't sing after the cloudberries have ripened; they stick in its throat.

The cuckoo dried its tears: the dipper has killed the cuckoo's brother.

When the cuckoo sings, the dipper hides in a thicket.[4]

When lemmings appear as if they're everywhere, great wars are coming.

In a crane's gizzard is a precious stone or piece of gold.

Where a reindeer buck or bull directs its spray, from that direction comes a vulgar guest on that day.

A snow bunting comes under the wing of a swan, and a wagtail comes under the wing of a goose.

Don't eat last year's berries; the cuckoo has dirtied them.

Don't go into a lake or a *čáhceháldi* will snatch you up.

Don't crush weeds so fine or your mother will go blind.

If a woman is pregnant, don't let her hear people talking about children born with birth defects, so her own child isn't born that way (when she hears it, then starts to think of it).

If two people meet each other in a doorway, then they'll become godparents.

If a girl or boy cooks a ladle (leaves the ladle in the pot), then they will cook themselves a bad wife or bad husband.

Don't eat while wearing only one shoe or your mother will die.

---

4. Note the disappearance of the dipper as explained in the story "The Wagtail and the Dipper."

Don't drink from an overturned wood cup or your father-in-law will hurt his head.

You ate my leftovers, so you will end up following in my tracks.

Hiccup, go from my birth-source to fetch some water, and I will cook the lungs of the hare for you. (Said after a hiccup.)[5]

About the Dipper Giving Luck

In ancient times in Sápmi, people thought—and still today some think—that the dippers bring good luck. For that reason, when people need to get something they believe is largely unattainable but yet still need, they hunt a dipper and take it and put it into a chest, which they believe will bring better luck. And when they start to litigate, they take only the claws from the dipper and put them in the corner of their breast-cloth,[6] so that they can win their trial. And the dipper is believed to bring the best luck of all, whether you're hunting in the forest or caring for cattle, or in all kinds of activities.

---

5. Though the language is a bit ambiguous, the idea here is seemingly to persuade the hiccup to leave the person, and go fetch some water, so that it can enjoy hare lungs when it returns. Hiccups are apparently desirous of lungs. The saying also reminds people to drink water for hiccups.

6. According to Laitinen, this refers to a thin bag worn around the neck and contains an assortment of small things, which rests on the breast under a jacket.

Appendix A

This appendix of supplementary texts mostly consists of selections from the 1917 edition that were omitted from the 1978 edition. These include several North Sámi *joik*s, a short story ("The Lazy One"), and a Skolt Sámi–language variant of a story already in the collection ("The Haunting of the Old Deceased *Noaidi*"). Also included in the 1917 edition were Aanaar Sámi–language translations of Psalms 103, 137, and 146, along with Matthew 5:1, although they are not included in this appendix since English-language versions are readily available. Finally, two letters from Mikko Aikio, included here, represented the final chapter in the 1978 edition.

The exclusion of these materials in the 1978 edition is predicated at least in part on the idea that language groups neatly correspond with culture groups. The reality is, of course, much more complex. Good stories and songs get around, and Sámi people have a long history of multilingualism and cultural and social interchange with their many neighbors. These few selections reflect the problematic academic legacy of assuming that "uncorrupted" texts are somehow more valuable than ones with clear cross-cultural dimensions. Though not numerous, their reinclusion is important to understand Aanaar Sámi life in the 1880s.

NORTH SÁMI *JOIKS*

Juhan Vesta's *Joik*
unknown

The big one was rich joj-joj-joj-joj
silver and gold . . .
two gold belts . . .
five silver purses . . .
one gold purse . . .
silver cups . . .

silver spoons . . .
silver pipes . . .

Meniš-Irjan
unknown

Meniš-Irjan jaj-ja-de-jaj-ja-de-jaj-jā
sits on the neck of his large draught reindeer . . .
a pipe in his mouth, he sits and sits . . .
a bear-fur cloak still on his neck . . .

Mihkkus-Āslak
unknown

Here's a boy jā-ja-ja-jā
a hundred pounds of money . . .
fifty untrained reindeer . . .
five brothers . . .
new power . . .

Let Us Leave
unknown

Let us leave, my Lassi, to the lake, to the lake joj-ju-de-joj-ju
we feel the pangs of hunger here jo joj-ju-de-joj-ju.

Pulju
unknown

Old man Pulju surr-urr-urr-urr-jē-de-nū-jē-de
productive old man tik-tak-tik-tak-jē-de-nū-jē-de
pih-puh-pih-puh smoking a pipe
nun-nun-nun-nun-jē-de-nū-jē-de.

Ninka-Ūla Kāre
unknown

A handsome girl of Russian Lapland jaj-jaj-jā-i

was Ninka-Ūla Kāre . . .
with the boys of the west competed . . .
three days drove . . .
her beautiful shoe lost . . .
they wed in Aanaar . . .
she certainly had adorned herself . . .
snow really swishing . . .
four people carried her hem . . .
to the wedding-church jaj-jaj-jaj-jaj-jaj-jaj-jā-i.

Pike
unknown

Pike-heel te-juj-juj-juj-jū-ju
mouth like a whale . . .
jaw like a rapids . . .
teeth like a wolf . . .
chin like a prow of a boat . . .
nose like a board . . .
eyes like stars . . .
the back is black . . .
the side is brown . . .

Burbot
unknown

The burbot is plain and slithers jē-de-je-jē-de
head like a frog . . .
skin like slime . . .

Perch
unknown

A sausage of a fish te-juj-juj-juj
Sausage fish, needle . . .
head like a mouse . . .
needle-backed . . .
skin like a file . . .

Kaapi, Kaapi
Mikko Aikio (A. V. Koskimies)[1]

Kaapi, Kaapi, la lal lal lā
Thank god, hat in hand, la lal lal lā
The pastor rejoices in the fear of the night, la lal lal lā
Up the Lord went la lal lal lā . . .

STORIES

The Lazy One
unknown

There was once, not so long ago, some lazy person who didn't trouble to ever undress himself. Whether he was in the forest in the winter or seining in the summer, he didn't ever bother to take off his seining or his cold-weather clothes. He slept just as he was when he had woken up. And he didn't ever bother to even eat sitting upright either, but rather he leaned on his elbow. For this reason people called him lazy. This lazy person still has children who are alive. We too have seen them, heard them, and spoken to them. He had two boys and two girls, and the former are deceased but the latter are still alive. One is a wife in Aanaar, the other in Värjivuona (Varanger Fjord), on the shore of the sea.

Skolt Sámi Story
P. Valle, who could speak Skolt Sámi

There was once an old man *noaidi* who got sick and died. There was a poor old-timer who was asked to take the body to the graveyard, and he thought: "Why shouldn't I set off to take him there, since they will give me ten rubles as pay? I can't get my hands on this much money in any other way." So he set off driving and came to the first village and started to think: "Why did I leave to transport this old *noaidi*? I would like to keep my life." After eating, he said to the farm master: "Wouldn't you, my friend, set off to take this deceased old man? I would give you as pay ten rubles." Well the second old man thought: "Why shouldn't I leave, since I can get so much money as pay?"

---

1. This song was not present in the 1917 edition but was found in Koskimies's original notes and published by Marko Jouste (2011).

So he left, and the day was getting darker, and he didn't come to notice this before it started to really get dark. Then he quickly thought: "Why did I leave before sunrise and where will I stay until night's end? This deceased old man was even a *noaidi* in his life, and who in his right mind would spend the night with him? If I had someone with me, I'd keep a campfire the whole night." But when he looked behind him, the old *noaidi* was sitting upright in place.

Then he tied up his draught reindeer's strap to a big spruce, ran to the base of another spruce, and climbed into the tree. The old *noaidi* wasn't visible, but the glow went out, and then he heard him coming and starting to bite the base of the tree. The man grabbed the rubles from his purse and took his knife in his other hand and clinked the rubles against its edge. The old man ceased his biting, remained still for a while, up until the biting was heard again.

The man clanked again the ruble on the edge, and the old man stopped his biting again. He was away for a little while, but then started to gnaw away again. The man dropped some rubles. They started to run out, but he searched for new ones. Many rubles he lost, but the night was not coming to its end. You see, it was Christmastime. The man thought: "Why did I take on this task? I'm not even poor. Ten rubles is not enough for this, and they too are already at their end, and the night isn't even over." The spruce was already starting to yield.

The man yelled: "Now I can see the dawn!" The old man stopped his biting again and was quiet for a long time, but once again started to gnaw. The man yelled again: "Now I can see the dawn!" The old man now stayed away so long that dawn started to be seen. Then he went into his coffin and didn't appear anymore.

The man climbed down, got his draught reindeer from its tether, and set off driving. There was a large root mass next to the road. He flung the deceased *noaidi* to the side of the road, ran to the root cluster, threw the body of the old man on it, and lit it on fire. He himself ran home, as fast as he could. The poor man asked him: "How'd it go?" "All right." He didn't say anything to anyone at the time about what happened. Only afterward he once told what he had done.

LETTERS

Aanaar, March 20, 1887

Dear Mr. W. Forsman [Koskimies]!

I have been so long without writing you that I myself am feeling bad about it too. But please forgive me! I thank you for your goodness, when we were together in Inari; I still am alive, even though you have probably already thought me to be dead, since so long I have been without writing you. I still am alive but it's a poor and lowly life—I am so bound to my ten fingers that I don't have time to even look anywhere. I have made 17 sledges this winter and it is my only means to support myself. I can't manage much more onto this paper. I'll say, farewell.

M. Aikio

Aanaar, April 17, 1887

Master W. Forsman [Koskimies] in Helsinki!

Now I write you still another word, as I intended when I last wrote you. Might you have received it in your hands? I don't know.

Now we have already seen flying swans and snow buntings, which come under the wings of the swan. It is now the 17th of April, but the weather is cold, colder than in December and January, and so it really is that "when fall is very mild, then spring is very cold." So it is now as well.

I wanted to know, did you get my writings in your hand, and how you are faring? Have you been well and do you plan to still visit Aanaar? Be so kind and write me a word. I wish you well.

M. Aikio

Appendix B

The following pages serve as the full introductory content to the 1978 edition. These translations from Finnish include an introduction by Lea Laitinen detailing changes made between the 1917 and 1978 edition and the introduction from the 1917 edition. They help us understand the evolution of this anthology as well as Koskimies's fieldwork process. His travels alone are a fascinating historical document detailing the difficulties of travel in Lapland in the nineteenth century. One can even today use maps to follow his route, even if some legs now lie beneath giant hydroelectric reservoirs. I have tried to mimic Koskimies's writing conventions, including the occasional capitalization of proper names and systems of abbreviation, particularly as the work delves into bibliographical content toward the end.

Introduction to the 1978 Edition by Lea Laitinen

A. V. Koskimies's 1886 collection of Inari [Aanaar] Sámi oral tradition, which T. I. Itkonen translated into Finnish, finalized from transcriptions and supplemented with his own notes, was published as part of the Suomalais-Ugrilaisen Seuran Toimitusten XL [Finno-Ugric Society Publications Vol. 40] as *Inarinlappalaista kansantietoutta* [*Inari Sámi Folklore*] in 1917. Sixty years later, when the work started to reach its end and there was a great need for printed Inari Sámi language material, the Finno-Ugric Society commissioned a new printing.

The collection's new vision deviates a little from the first. The spelling follows contemporary Inari Sámi orthography. In practice, this orthography is generally more precise, and for that reason alone it seems a functional change. Through this orthographic modernization, even a hundred years later, a picture takes shape of spoken Inari Sámi language for the reader. Additionally, the accuracy makes it easier for language study and for the work of researchers.

A. V. Koskimies's original notes are used as the basis of these texts. These notes were preserved by Suomalaisen Kirjallisuuden Seura [Finnish Literature Society] in their manuscript archives. For this reason, there are some details that deviate from the previous text. Also, the organization of the contents has changed. The texts are grouped roughly by traditional genre. The purpose is to only further make the collection easier to use. It is not really possible to group these works by genre. The table of contents lists the pagination of the former versions. Also included is A. V. Koskimies's original foreword and travelogues. T. I. Itkonen's orthographic appendix, however, has been omitted.

I have omitted mountain Sámi *joik*s, a story presented in Skolt Sámi, plus other religions translation texts, which do not belong in the scope of this collection. Added to the contents are some selections from Koskimies's notes: some story variants, proverbs, and a couple of poem translations. Two letters written in customary Inari Sámi from the 1880s from the previous edition are also included here in their original form. As a matter of fact, Koskimies received many stories and proverbs for the collection by letter only after his travels were completed. Mikko Aikio, Juho Petteri Lusmaniemi, and Heikki Mattus were all skilled writers.

The scholar Erkki Itkonen was so kind as to examine the manuscript for this new edition of the collection. Matti Morottaja, Elsa Valle, and Samuel Kuuva assisted in the translation of headings. Textual errors are naturally my own. Hopefully, any errors notwithstanding, the book will be both useful and bring joy to Inari Sámi themselves and people interested in their language and culture.

Introduction to the 1917 Edition by A. V. Koskimies (Reprinted in the 1978 Edition)

In the spring of 1886 the Finno-Ugric Society chair, O. Donner, recommended me to go to research the Inari Sámi dialect the following summer, and he got me the necessary travel stipend for it. I want to present the trip's prehistory and early stages with the following letters, which I wrote him then and now dare to present here [below]:

Hämeenlinna, December 21, 1885

Respected Professor!

You have recommended me, through Master A. O. Heikeli, to go to Finnish Lapland to research the local Sámi dialect on behalf of the Ugric society. From this confidence, which you, Mister Professor, then have honored me with, I am greatly thankful. But at the same time, it is my obligation to straightly confess that I cannot guarantee my ability is fully trustworthy. I have many years read about the Sámi, but my prior knowledge is little and I have already forgotten much. With hard work, I think I would be able to supply the necessary food for thought for myself so that I will be well equipped for my departure on this research trip, but these days I feel I have little time and opportunity. I would need to apply myself to this special purpose for at least a couple of months in the coming year, or perhaps an entire semester as well, before I can even begin to serve the Society.

Otherwise what is offered serves me well. Then I might really consider "quid ferre recusent, quid valiant humeri."[1]

After I spend Christmas in Pohjanmaa [Ostrobothnia], I will go to Helsinki after Epiphany [January 6]. Before any decision is made, or another fellow is asked, I would therefore ask to get to present myself to the professor. When I have arrived in the capital, I will without delay visit Mister Professor to speak about the matter in question.

Inari, July 25, 1886

Dear Professor,

As I now have been in the field for some time, I am glad to fulfill my obligation to you by offering some words about my trip, in addition to the outcomes of my findings up to this point.

I arrived in Inari on June 29. The trip happened just as, as you may recall, was planned in Helsinki, via Sweden and Norway. I had luck getting company for my excursion to Lapland in two companions, [the first] named Master K. CANNELIN, who had taken to researching the dialect that Finns use in Inari, Sodankylä, and Kittilä, the so-called Lapland Finnish. The second companion was the student G. STENVIK (now KIVISTÖ) who planned to research Inari and Utsjoki parishes' ancient monuments on behalf of Muinaismuistoyhdistys [the Ancient Monument Association].

On the evening of June 11, we stepped onto a boat in Vaasa, and we arrived on the Swedish coast as quickly as the following morning. The trip went forth

---

1. "What my strength can bear, and what it cannot."

through Sundsvall and Österstund to Trondheim, where on the 15th we got onto a large steamboat, which plowed through the waves of the Atlantic toward Ultima Thule.

It's some 210 Scandinavian miles [2100 km; 1300 miles] between Norway's ancient capital, Nidaros [Trondheim], and north Norway's main city, Vesisaari [Vadsø]—though the trip went relatively quickly, while watching our ship diverge from countless merchant and fishing places along the Norwegian shore. On Juhannus, the 26th of June, we came to the Sámi world to admire "Čacce-suolo" [Vesisaari; Vadsø]. En route the boat also went to Tromsø, where I had hoped to meet the seminar leader, QVIGSTAD, but we came to the city at night and spent only a couple of hours there, which made it impossible to try to seek Qvigstad out, even though I would have been very pleased to complete the honorable undertaking I received from you in my sources, that I would go to the aforementioned researcher of Sámi language to convey greetings on behalf of the Finno-Ugric Society. On my trip I did not meet other people who would have been worthy of being led into the Society's sphere of influence.

On June 26 again there came an occasion to continue my trip. Through Varanger Fjord we went to Pukeija [Bugøynes] and from there to Näytämö [Näätämö], and in both of these places there were blossoming Finnish immigrant spaces in the Norwegian areas. In the latter, about eight families of Skolt Sámi, Russian Orthodox Sámi, were still living there. I did not even begin to inquire about their dialect, even though they have likely been thus far overlooked by researchers. In Näytämö we only had time to rush to our destination. Through fields and swamp, we took our path from Näytämö to the end of Suolisjärvi, on the Finnish side. The walk was hot and in swarms of mosquitoes that bit us, although this was only 5 Scandinavian miles [50 km; 30 miles]. Fortunately, at the end of Suolisjärvi there were boats, which were waiting there for Finnish fishermen returning from Finnmark. You see, they normally return home at Juhannus from their fishing. So it was not now. These fishermen, about fifty people, had accompanied us from Näytämö to Suolisjärvi, and together we continued our trip, which still was 8 Scandinavian miles [80 km; 50 miles] of travel by water before we would get to Inari parish. Finally, "post varios casus"[2] my two companions and I, we were well indeed, even though very tired.

In the parsonage, at pastor Virkkula's place, was my place of lodging. There weren't any Sámi people living in the immediate vicinity, but it wasn't really a

---

2. "After various adventures."

long trip to the church, which as it is served as the congregation's effective center, where it was perhaps best to meet Sámi people. The Inari residents were indeed the greatest part of this population, about 650 people, who spoke Inari Sámi and their main life way was to fish. In addition to this, there were 69 more people who were reindeer herders, who had more recently moved here from Utsjoki [Ohcejohka] and who used the Utsjoki language. In the beginning of July I began my work in the region's effective center, after I had finally gotten a suitable teacher. With him I first went through the most important points in morphology, but he needed to depart from his work, and in his place I got another, who was not as talented at explaining linguistics. I started with my new teacher to fill in the gaps, which ANDELIN left in his Finnish-Sámi lexicon, whose beginning and end are missing. I have now just now gotten my hands in this work. I have taken language samples as well as a dozen or so different stories, gotten about fifty Sámi proverbs and some little songs. They don't have songs here, it's just like a lone child's song of whimsy, some playful rhymes, plus some so-called *joik*s. I haven't gotten to hear riddles despite my best efforts.

The Inari Sámi are not deep-minded but joyful by nature and socially minded, who like to talk about all kinds of things. Stories about the old days of this region could perhaps be abundantly collected. I have gotten some delightful knowledge that is found in Utsjoki's parsonage; there are plenty of manuscripts intended for a fairly vast Finnish-Sámi dictionary, beginning with A and ending with the start of T-words. Utsjoki Sámi is the dominant Sámi dialect presented, and alongside it are Kven, Skolt, and Inari Sámi translations in their different columns. This work is left behind by ANDELIN, but since Utsjoki today is without a pastor, I can't say who the mentioned property—perhaps even a treasure—belongs to. Probably A. has left it in the church archives for his successors to advise them about the Sámi language. If I succeed in getting the aforementioned work to the Society, I feel that it would be better preserved and put to use in the care of the Society than in its current location.[3]

There is one issue in which I am little satisfied with my work, especially with sorting out the phonetics of the Inari dialect. In part, different people pronounce this dialect in very different fashions; in part, it's the vocal sounds themselves

---

3. Koskimies includes the following note: The information I received about this manuscript by word of mouth was not precise. In reality it is an early draft of a Finnish-Sámi dictionary, of which there is already a copy in Helsinki. The search words are in Finnish and the translations in Utsjoki and Aanaar Sámi. The manuscript might further be in the Utsjoki church archives.

that are so faint an echo that it is difficult to notice the actual sound. Additionally, I have too little familiarized myself with this branch of linguistics. For that reason I would humbly ask how soon you could send me QVIGSTAD and SANDBERG's Inari Sámi language book, if they are already printed, for it is my memory last spring that you mentioned they were at that time in press. At the same time you send the aforementioned texts, I would ask that you then let me know what else you would afford me in my work on behalf of the Society.

In the beginning of October I hope again to be in Helsinki...

Before I continue, I mentioned that Cannelin was at the start of July already traveling on the Ivalo River to the Finnish regions, and Stenvik moved to live with a family of a civil servant 20 kilometers [12 miles] from the parsonage where I was living.

The pastor of Inari at the time, Onnela—such an auspicious name for my enterprise![4]—is located near Inari's old church about 3–4 km from greater Inari, from the bay called Pielppa Fjord, in a grassy valley, which pleasantly slopes down to the banks of Pielppa Lake. The region is among Finnish Lapland's oldest settlements, the great ancient location of the great Sámi village and market, where Danish money from the 1600s can still regularly be found. Particularly at the summertime religious gathering, business is—or at one time was—very lively there. Now all this has come to an end, and the place is empty and barren, as the church and parsonage are located elsewhere, about ¾ of a Scandinavian mile [7.5 km; 4.7 miles] southwards on the shore of Inari, or more precisely on the shore of Juutua or Iutua [Juvvadak] Fjord. But still, as I've been told, there is, in addition to the church built in 1760, the assemblage of languishing church cabins and other buildings reminding of the place's former meaning from the times when the court was held here and the bailiffs presided, when markets were held and church and shops were visited. The view was beautiful, with tallish mountains and small but steep mountain peaks: Otsamo, Luosma, etc.

Excesses of neighbors are not a problem, for the nearest house is perhaps still 5 km [3 miles] away. But it's better to work here, especially when I have at my disposal the parsonage's "little-half," or the building that had been the Utsjoki

---

4. Though not an uncommon name, Onnela literally translates to "a place of good fortune."

church official's quarters before the proper chaplain's house was built, for use of official business. I now live in this building and, with my language masters, I have busied myself for nearly three months—surrounded by great shadows,[5] including Castrén and Lönnrot as well, grinding away to sort out problems with the Sámi language. Now it's said that this small pleasant building—the same as the chaplain's house—is to be ripped to the ground and moved elsewhere, since after Inari came to be its own church district, a new church and parsonage were built in Juutua. Only once this whole summer, in the end of July, I set off from this castle of mine, when I accompanied my master on some work trip to the villages of Kultala and Kyrö.

Under the direction of Lönnrot and Andelin's Inari Sámi research, I aspired to expand and supplement the previous knowledge of the Inari Sámi language, to compile dictionary materials and language samples. At the time, my intention was the creation of a more complete and accurate picture of the Inari Sámi language. I worked diligently toward this purpose as my goal to receive, in the relatively short time that was available to me, the utmost benefit of my travels. Time was, however, too short, so my goal was incompletely realized. Of my outcomes I make further explanation below.

On September 21 I started my return trip with the student Stenvik in my company, who had lived in Inari the entire summer, plus the Oulu resident and builder ALBERT GRÖNHOLM, who had been building a new parsonage in Inari on request of the state, and now with summer having ended was returning to his home tracts. The trip went along Inari and Ivalo to Kyrö's "upper village," Törmänen, where we arrived the following day. From this point we proceeded by foot, covering about 6–8 Scandinavian miles [60–80 km; 36–48 miles] through heaths, swamps, and high tundras (Kaunispää, Utupää, Palopää, Ahopää, etc.) to the north shore of Sompiojärvi on the Sodankylä side of the border, where a Sámi village of the same name was located. The trip was very difficult, for pretty much the entire time it was snowing, which cloaked everything from being seen, and otherwise made paths and trails unclear, which in that open tundra wilderness should have been walkable, and it displaced overflowing rivers and streams from their descent, so that there was no help other than to wade to the other shore. This region, which is commonly the scene of Inari Sámi stories about bear and wild reindeer hunting adventures of former times, is desolate, almost without life, yet is a magnificently rugged wilderness.

---

5. The great shadows here allude to the legacies of other well-known ethnographers who had worked in Aanaar.

Since the autumn reindeer roundup still hadn't happened, one could see these beautiful animals gathering in a grazing herd, whose presence refreshed the eye and spirit. Some solitary forest bird too at times would burst into flight and break the silence of the wilderness. Not even a single oncoming person could be seen. It was pleasant to be on the heath lands looking how in the young snow the wanderer's tracks, kilometer by kilometer, pressed rose-red into Lapland's luscious crowberries, which by the millions squashed under foot. There was not a single human dwelling place the entire leg. At least there was one backcountry hut, which the state had commissioned as a shelter for the Arctic Ocean fishermen who walked this road, which offered us a second night with a roof over our heads, the first spent under the open sky, in very wet snow, but in the friendly glow of the warming *rakovalkea*-fire.[6] The most difficult to overcome was Saariselkä, which separates Lapland and Finland proper from each other, or better said its immense final ledge, the high pass at Nattastunturi. The mountain is bad stone and boulder fields, whose now snow-covered holes and nooks one needed to be most cautious of, and even then many times we fell waist deep into them. At last after a third day of walking in the evening dark, we arrived on the base of the tundra's southern slopes, at the Sámi *goahti*-village where we received a favorable reception. The following night was the first and only where I stayed in a Sámi *goahti*.

The Sámi in Sompio are newcomers moved from Kautokeino and Enontekiö, who at that time primarily supported themselves by fishing for the rich whitefish of Sompiojärvi [Sompio Lake], and they also kept reindeer as well, moving as genuine nomads their *goahti* whenever and wherever they want, as the fishing and reindeer herding demand. Their numbers, as I recall it, might be about twenty or thirty people, all adults reasonably able to speak Finnish. The most representative man among them was worthy of respect, the fine elder JOUNI HETTA, who had moved from Karasjok to Kautokeino and around the turn of the 1870–80s to here in Sompio. When he lived in Karasjok—at that time of course he was still quite a young man—he had been a helper to Stockfleth in the work to translate the New Testament. The old devout man, whose dictation I used to write some language samples, made a very pleasant impression. Of the other men, I remember a Guttorm Magga, or "Kutturan" (Kuhturan), as he was normally called. He was said to be a wealthy man. Somewhere further lived

---

6. A type of traditional Finnish campfire that consists of two logs, laid horizontally with one stacked atop the other, held in place by stakes. Between the logs tinder and kindling is placed. The type of fire emits a good heat and will burn for an entire night.

some other residents who were said to be migrants, among others a much-lauded-as-rich man named Ponku-Matti. Those newcomers really had known how to choose good living places for themselves: fishing small lake and river environments, plus an open lichen-rich[7] forested area between two rivers, where there was opportunity to sustain even extensive reindeer herds. These kinds of advantages later enticed more new migrants from the same regions where the previous ones came from, and all were said to have fared well. Now it's said that they already have permanent log houses in different places around the river's headwaters. Beside the previously mentioned families there now, there are said to be Hirvasvuopio, Orponen, Lensmann, and others.

In regard to their languages, which according to Dr. Itkonen, differ somewhat from the Kautokeino dialect, let the following specimens serve as examples:[8]

1. There were two men walking in the forest, and they became hungry, and they wondered to themselves if it was time for them to promise a sacrifice to a false god,[9] so that they would get a wild reindeer, since they were hungry. They set off walking, and they walked a little on their trip, and they came across two wild reindeer bucks with locked antlers. They promised their false god the antlers, but one then said: we won't give them. Then the wild reindeer got loose from each other and went on their way. They got very upset, and the second blamed his companion for the game getting away, but the first said to him: It's nothing more than a false god. The one started to cry, and said: Why did you do it? The other said: Well, what if I apologize. Well, the other promised: if indeed, I will forgive. So they went back and God gave them, in all truth, a barren female reindeer. Well, they thanked God for it, since he gave it to them. Their hearts rejoiced from that gift. When they got home, they said that God must have done this for them, since he wanted to extinguish their hunger. And they rejoiced greatly because of it among themselves, and they devoutly thanked God

---

7. Lichen is an important food source for reindeer.
8. The following three stories are printed first in Finnish, then in North Sámi.
9. The word used is the pejorative *æhpi-ibmīl* (*epäjumala*), revealing the storyteller's relationship with the Christian faith. A reading of this text from the perspective of its characters, however, would better translate this concept as "spirit." I have chosen "false god" because it reflects some of the tensions that occur during religious shift and the honest voice of the story's narrator.

and honored him for the great gift of mercy. This happened so long ago that I think it's been maybe twenty years, when this event happened.

2. Some youth had started to court some pretty girl. They would have gotten married, but their parents didn't permit it. They became very upset, since their parents didn't allow them to get together. The girl became very distraught from the matter, and became crazy. The parents saw her grief and promised that they could get married, and she got better. Then they got together. The parents were very sorry that they had forbidden the two lovers from each other, and so the mother and father made a promise, that they would never separate people as such, and they thanked God devoutly, since he gave their child back the same mental capacities that God had previously given her.

3. I was walking with my father. There was some stone, which people thought to be a god,[10] and we had a file of reindeer and packs on the backs of the draught reindeer. He said: I do not serve you. And at the same time, our reindeer file set off running, and one of the draught reindeer broke its leg. He then said: Even then, I do not serve you. He glanced at me and said: Now my child, you also may not serve this, for it is nothing more than a stone. Even though the people of the world regard it as a god, I don't even care.

It was Saturday evening when we finally arrived in Sompio- or Muteniajärvi. The sky had gradually started to clear up and promised good fortune to us and our progressing travels. And so it went. The weather was no longer worth great complaint. On Sunday morning the Sámi ferried us across the swampy-shored lake (which because of its grassy outlet was extraordinary rich in fish, but shallow and muddy—a real "Mutenia"[11] it might be!) and from there continued still from the swampy bank along Mutenia river to the Finnish village of Mutenia, whose residents might be of mixed Finnish-Sámi descent and perhaps the descendants of the region's first Sámi. In ancient times, it was Kemi Lapland's most famous and strongest village, and even now it doesn't look weak, if not even quite pleasant. After a bit of rest, we left from there, again on our travels, toward Kemijärvi, but the nearest travel-goals were Riesto's cottages, which

---

10. The stone is a *sieidi*, and more a place of offering to the spirits than a "god," as suggested by the narrator.

11. *Mutenia* sounds like the word *mutainen*, or "muddy." These words are possibly etymologically related, or at least good enough fodder for a pun.

were located a couple of Scandinavian miles [20 km; 12 miles] to the south. From there we were supposed to be able to get to our desired end point. First of all, one had to travel the almost 2 Scandinavian-mile-long river, along a very peculiar journey: the numerous striations and bends of river branches and shores, in other words, out of the channel-widening bays penetrate far to the south into small ponds that form complex island and peninsula mazes. Such formations in a soft river channel I had, however, already seen in the mouth of the Ivalo River in Inari. After leaving Mutenia, it was still some Scandinavian miles to travel to its mother river Riesto, before we arrived at the so-named houses. From this village or group of houses, located at the confluence of the Riesto and Luiro Rivers, we managed to get what we wanted. Certainly our escorts were not old and experienced rivermen, in whose care we would have felt safe to shoot those many boisterous rapids in our 25 or 30 Scandinavian-mile [250–300 km; 155–186 miles] river trip, which still separated us from the Kemijärvi village, and from there on the route leading to Kemi: they were two mostly young, boy-aged beginnings of men, but they were strong and energetic lads who were unconcerned that they only knew in part the rapids along our route—one had descended some in the beginning leg of the trip, the other the drops at the end—who dared to offer skill and their powers to the task in question. We were ourselves a bit afraid to depend on them for the long river trip, but fortunately it was entirely unfounded. Vilppu and Aatu were in their work certain and trustworthy. The proverb, he who lives on the shore of a rapids knows its behavior, showed their relationship to hold true, through and through. There was not even talk of injury. One hardly can make such a pleasant trip outside a three-day excursion, which we carried out in their company, descending perhaps thirty rapids, some of them particularly robust. The weather was clear and crisp but sunlit, the land and trees were bright blossoms of silver, the fast pace carried us along, and the boys, who strangely here in the North Country were the most beautiful youth that one could ever behold, brisk and exacting in their doings. Their only fault was that, because of their youthfulness and inexperience, they weren't able to say much about transport from the region. Since the long trips to Mutenia and then Riesto had already passed, which is almost as peaceful journey as its upper river, on that day there was no more time than to get to Lokka, a couple of Scandinavian miles [20 km; 12 miles] beyond Riesto. We had to stay the night there with the coming of dark, the greatest reason being that the next house was not for another 9 Scandinavian miles [90 km; 56 miles]. These parts haven't changed much since the times when Castrén, some fifty years before, traveled through here on his return trip from Lapland and portrayed their desolation and uninhabited nature. The economic situation has, however, improved slightly, I think. At least the spacious riverbanks show possibilities for development for animal husbandry. On the riverbanks, where the surrounding swamps seemed on a glance to be drier, were what was most lush for grass growth, though rough species, but cultivation perhaps would yield a more fine vegetation. I was then daydreaming if only there were the power and means to move men and millions, and to bring the great impoverished people of Finland and its thousands of criminals here and force them to labor to earn for themselves land and soil, game and wealth. A thousand times better for the state too than providing for these people and hardening them further in prisons, who because of poverty and the lack of independent and productive work—these being the most typical reasons—have been led to a life of crime.

The houses of Lokka[12] are probably the old settlement, at least in part. Little is known about the earlier times. The young boatmen only could say, as they recalled, that Lokka's first inhabitant had been some Sámi person named Kulsina. For my part, I thought that this name didn't sound very Sámi, which was perhaps born in the mouths of new Finnish settlers who used as a man's name the word *koalsse*, or *goalsse*, which is the name of a waterfowl (*Mergus serrator* [red-breasted merganser]; cf. Finnish *kolsa*, a water bird). Additionally, a small and erroneous translation has been made in the Finnish name for it; cf. also *kulnas*, or *kulnasaȝ* = *pilkkasiipi* (*Oidemia fusca*) [velvet scoter].

Right at the crack of dawn we departed Lokka, moving once again. The speed was now more than twice as good as that of the previous date: all the way to Tanhua. The river formed an extraordinary bend a couple of Scandinavian miles to the south of Lokka. Here, the visitors to the Arctic Ocean normally land and walk the roadless forest route some 3–4 Scandinavian miles [30–40 km; 19–25 miles] to Tanhua, at which point they again take a new boat ride, thereby avoiding the 7 Scandinavian-mile [70 km; 43 miles] loop that the riverbend serves up. This span additionally has the most rapids of any stretch of the river route. Castrén once did the same. We did not care to try it. We would have certainly regretted it, if we had stopped our joyful trek and good company so that we could set off to slog through the wet autumn forest. This day, same as the

---

12. The village Riesto and most of Mutenia were submerged by the Lokka Reservoir in the 1960s, created from the erection of a hydroelectric dam. The people living in the villages were displaced elsewhere in the region, which proved to be an extremely disruptive and destructive force in their lives and communities. The reservoir was named after the village now by the shore of it.

following, made our travelings most pleasant. The youth promised to let us know when the worst rapids were coming, so that we wouldn't need to fear or be mindful of our clothing getting soaked, but when we were in a still water, only then did they say: Well, now we are through it. And so we descended through rapids, one after another. In examining the river stem in some places, we noticed the remnants of former human habitation. The place's name was Tingisaho, 4 Scandinavian miles [40 km; 25 miles] downstream of Lokka. About a hundred years earlier there lived a Sámi man at that place named Tingis-Antti, whose wife is remembered by the name Maak(k)a-rukka (Magga-rokke). It's customary to give to those who die accidental deaths the moniker *rukka*, "poor," so too to Maakka, who had drowned in some of those rapids in those parts. In one of those rapids, Laurukainen, the folk hero of the Kemi Sámi, caused the demise of an entire boatload of Karelians, whom he promised to guide down the rapids. In the most dangerous spot, he himself had used his pole to first jump to the shore, but the Karelians whom he had entranced to sleep earlier using charms, all drowned. Because of this, the rapid's name is Karjalais-marvima-koski (*mavrrat* = *kuorsata*) [Karelian-Snoring-Rapids].[13]

A night in Tanhua; the next day again onto a leg still along the widening Luiro River, and in the evening we arrived at its twin brother, the Kitinen, which conjoins it from the west, and the river continues with that name, until it reaches its mother-river, the Kemi River, and from this point it swells from the strength of its tributaries' waters, if even into a calm but wide and powerful river. We didn't have time on this day to get to this confluence point but only to the village of Alaperä at the mouth of the Luiro, where we spent the night at a house by the name of Karkko. The master, Karkon Simppa, was an especially enlightened man: in addition to being relatively well read was also able to write. He knew how to give a full account of my travels to my intended destination.

The following evening, on September 29, we were at the end of our boat travels, three days and at least still as many tens of Scandinavian miles, and just as many tens of rapids we shot through along those celebrated rivers from Mutenia's gloomy wilderness up to this point in Kemijärvi in the middle of the civilized world or at least up to its threshold—so at least it felt to us Lapland sojourners. Thankful and yearning—at least I for my part—we took leave from our brave "boys," who had with honor escorted us through those long legs without complications or misfortune.

---

13. See the chapter "Stories about Čuđit" for similar stories.

I have perhaps been needlessly broad in portraying the details of my travel, but I have done it for the reason that the road I traveled might these days not be widely known, since one can already get to Lapland with an automobile.

It would have been nice to have stayed in this region a bit, which still in its autumnal finest tantalizes the eye with its beauty. It indeed makes a rather great impact: in every direction, on the borders of one's sight loom vast and huge hills and beneath them great lake basins with hundreds of islands and straits—not deserted and unoccupied water of the wilderness, but rather on the shores there can be decent houses and old cultivation. But one must hurry, for there was still an interruption of 10 Scandinavian miles [100 km; 60 miles] to be measured on the on-land leg to the shores of the Gulf of Bothnia. The road, in addition, was poor, filled with many holes from overuse, and the fall rain caused the road to become muddy. We endured three days on this trip, resting a little in Rovaniemi, and at that time there was no railroad there to bring in the business and magnificence of the greater world, whether from the city or from the natural beauty of the parish. The greater hospitality was welcome, whereby one of the merchants patronized us, even though we had been entirely unknown to him before—at least me. I barely had tasted champagne before this—would I say in the Paris of Lapland? But the trip was on my mind, having to depart these good delicacies. From the long drive, we finally arrived, broken down, in Kemi on the 2nd of October. "*Thálatta, thálatta!*"[14] I could have yelled, if with glum spirits I would have thought about these long and arduous *parasangs*,[15] which on my Lapland travels I carried out, but in good spirits I indeed state that my most difficult legs were behind me and in front of me only perhaps light travel based on modern transport. I remember longing for the many novelties and interesting things I had experienced during the last few months, and when I now speak of them, they are memories in my mind that shine more beautifully than they perhaps ever actually were.

About these stages of my Lapland travels I need to add to this story only that on a coastal ship we continued our journey to Oulu and arrived on the 4th of October. Since my companions Stenvik and Grönholm stayed there, which was their home city, I carried out my final journey alone, and it hadn't been as

---

14. *Thálatta, thálatta!* (The sea, the sea!) refers to the joyful shouts of the mercenary army upon seeing the Black Sea, following Cyrus the Younger's unsuccessful attack on the Persian Empire in 401 BCE.

15. *Parasang* refers to a historical unit of distance used in the Western Mediterranean and Middle East: the distance one travels in one hour by foot.

pleasant as I had expected. The Oulu rails were already finished but still not put into use. I had, however, presumed that one could travel on it in the meantime, but such was not the case. In part by ship, in part by horse, I got to Vaasa and from there to Isokyrö, where my home was located at that time. I arrived there on the 8th of October. After a couple days among my closest relatives, I traveled onward to Helsinki and arrived there the 11th of October, or exactly four months from the day when I started my Lapland travels from Vaasa.

As an outcome of the travel, I brought along with me approximately one hundred fairy tales, ancient legends, and stories; about two hundred proverbs and sayings; about seventy-five riddles (a type of folklore that at first I hadn't had come to know at all); twenty or thirty charms and omens; plus twenty-some shortish or entirely short poems and songs. In addition to this, there is also an abundant amount of grammatical material (about inflection, conjugation, and derivation) plus a vocabulary. I might mention as well that I partially examined ANDELIN's *Enarelappska språkprof med ordregister* (Acta. Soc. Scient. VI), whose collection of language samples (about fifty large pages), does not seem to be very pure and reliable Inari Sámi at times.

All this language material here listed, plus that which was recorded before my visit, I planned in the near future to arrange for use as basic materials in a new and more complete presentation of Inari Sámi language. This, however, did not come to pass. My chosen career in life, plus many other tasks, prevented me from surrendering myself to this work and—if I had been given the opportunity—renew my visitation to those distant destinations, which after all would have been absolutely necessary for the revision and augmentation of my linguistic content. I could perhaps have still published the language samples, but the Finno-Ugric languages phonetic research and semantics was formed and developed at that time toward the goal of scientific precision, and in my mind I wasn't able to satisfy these demands, since my notes were mainly based on the writing customs used by Stockfleth and Friis. The same lack of time and courage still further prevented me from this work, now more than a thirty-year span since it passed from my hands. It was essential to me though to get my collected texts to publication. But only two years ago a happy occurrence offered for my use Dr. TOIVO ITKONEN's skilled hand, a man who had been familiar with the Inari language since his growing years, by which this publication was made possible and is now coming to fruition. He has cleared up the writing in the texts and changed it to contemporary orthography, and he also has translated it to Finnish and made corrections to the entire publication.

I wish to express my most sincere thanks for this help as well as for these numerous additions (seventeen selections) that he has added to my story collection. Similarly, to Provost VIRKKULA and his family, in whose pleasant care I had good and undisturbed opportunity to make my notes, plus to those enlightened men of Lapland, who agreed to serve as a language instructor for me—and some have still remembered me even afterward here in Helsinki by sending me greetings by letters, even language samples as well. Of those, let me mention first and foremost the five men with whom I mostly worked. Inari's cantor, HEIKKI MATTUS, the schoolmaster IISAKKI MANNERMAA (d. 1908), the farmowners MIKKO AIKIO and JUHO PETTERI LUSMANIEMI, plus the former merchant, senior lay judge, and church master PAAVALI VALLE (d. 1906), who to the people of northern Finland at one time was well known as a diligent correspondent to Oulu's Finnish-language newspapers and in his parts as a talented spinning-wheel turner. Other of my helpers that I also am indebted in thanks to are ANTTI JUHANPOIKA KITTI (Menes-Antti), ANTTI and MATTI SARRE, and the lay judge PIETARI VALLE.

Since my language instructor primarily used western Inari, the language samples best portray this principal form of Inari Sámi, and toward that style Dr. ITKONEN has slightly smoothed the phonological structure, also in the language samples that represent the language form spoken elsewhere in the region. All things considered, these texts' primary value is in their contents and in the interest that they might offer for the researcher of folklore, the followed procedure may sooner purpose this work for use than serve as a drawback. Naturally, however, different regional lexicons always to some extent deviate from each other, even in the same parishes. To illuminate the matter it might be worth mentioning that AIKIO, MANNERMAA, MATTUS, and KITTI represent western Inari; PAAVALI VALLE, regardless of the fact that he lived in western Inari, used southern Inari, where he was born and lived his childhood and youth; LUSMANIEMI (even though living in western Inari) and PIETARI VALLE primarily the eastern dialect; and both SARREs primarily the northern dialect. UULA MOROTTAJA, whose name was added to the language specimens by Dr. Itkonen, is from Paatsjoki.

The value of my collection of language specimens from these men is naturally quite varied—in the eye of a literary critic. As language samples, these however might have their significance, especially for those who want to get familiar with the language usage of these Sámi people of ours using easy-to-read texts. In the appendix for this reason I included some translations and some forgotten selections from the primary texts, as well as some North Sámi language samples from Inari, despite the fact that they deviate from the region's normal dialect.

Appendix B

I think my collection of texts will interest a researcher not only as language specimens but for another reason that might be even more primary than the one just mentioned. I think that through it material could have been saved to benefit the ethnological understanding, material that no longer might be the same or of the same quality, languishing in the memory's storehouse of the Inari Sámi. At least they complement the relatively scarce matters that to my knowledge have already been published about Inari. For the benefit of younger enthusiasts, I would like to list the publications I know in this area:

E. LÖNNROT, *Ueber den Enare-lappischen Dialekt* (Acta Soc. Scient. Fenn.,[16] Tom. IV, 1856). As language samples, Sámi translations of Finnish proverbs, some of which might be authentic Inari or adaptations of Finnish variants into Inari, for example #72.

A. ANDELIN, *Enare-Lappska Språkprof med Ordregister* (Acta Soc. Scient. Fenn., Tom. VI, 1861). Five first-language samples—a dozen proverbs and expressions plus a fairy tale—which according to the publisher's note are Inari writings (presumably the fairy tale is from Andelin's language instructor P. VALLE's writing, as I recall hearing from M. AIKIO).

E. V. BORG, 3 fairy tales as an appendix to the aforementioned publication (probably dictated from I. MANNERMAA).

J. QVIGSTAD and G. SANDBERG, *Lappische Sprachproben* (Suom.-ugr. Seur.[17] III, 1888). Two ancient legends.

F. ÄIMÄ, "Matkakertomus Inarin Lapista" (*Suom.-ugr. Seur. Aikakausk.*[18] III, 1888). Two songs (of these one translated into Swedish in K. B. VIKLUND's written "Lapparnes sång och poesi," in the series "Småskrifter utgifna af Norrländska Studenters Folkbildningsförening," I: 2. 1906).

A. LAUNIS, *Lappische Juoigos-melodien* (Mémoires de la Societé Finnoougrienne XXVI, 1908). Large collection (311) of Inari collected *joik*s and *joik*-melodies; at least in part mountain Sámi.

The collection of unpublished folk poetry from Inari is rich and of great value, and Dr. ÄIMÄ has had the additional outcome along with his Inari language research: thirty-six fairy tales and stories, fifteen songs, plus about fifty proverbs and charms. The contents are, however, in part the same and with the same narrators as well dictated in my own collection.

---

16. Acta Societatis Scientiarun Fennica.
17. Suomalais-Ugrilainen Seura (Finno-Ugric Society).
18. *Suomalais-Ugrilaisen Seuran Aikakauskirja*, journal of the Finno-Ugric Society.

Additionally, Dr. QVIGSTAD has given for his use the collection of Sámi fairy tales, which Uuniemi's [Unjargga's; Nesseby's] pastor G. SANDBERG (d.) had collected in Inari or from Inari Sámi and in which two pieces are published just recently in the aforementioned publication (*Lappische Sprachproben*), but eight are still unpublished in the original language. In these the subject sometimes seems to be the same as in my own collection.

The same fairy tales are, I presume, all in the Norwegian language in QVIGSTAD and SANDBERG's pleasant publication *Lappiske eventyr og folkesagn*, Kristiania 1887. In the work are additional Inari Sámi-themed legends obtained from elsewhere.

These include also M. A. CASTRÉN's travelogue *Resa till Lappland*, 1838 (Nord. resor o. forskn. 1, pp. 14–24, 28–29) J. FELLMAN's work *Anteckningar under min vistelse i Lappmarken*, in some places, for example v. I, pg. 223 (Čuđit), pp. 244–45 (Laurukainen), v. II, pg. 78 (Akimeelik), 114– (Laurukainen), 127– (shape-shifting), 135– (Päiviö), 187– (Vuolappi); K. Cannelin's research with the Kemi language dialect, 1888, and his portrayal "Lapissa" *Joukahainen* X, 1881; J. A. FRIIS's *En Sommar i Finmarken*, Russ. Lapl. o. Nordkarelen, p. 66 (about Vuolappi). The above list might be the most important sources of essentially Inari Sámi folk legends and other poetry. But additionally, one can encounter the same or similar stories in many places elsewhere as well, particularly Laurukainen (in Savo Laurikainen, Karelia Larikainen, or Larikka, Lari), who is handled as a folk hero. I mention only for example the following publications: J. TORNÆUS, *Beskrifning öfver Torneå o. Kemi Lappmarker*, 1671 (Peder Päiviö and Vuolappi), cf. JOANNES SCHEFFERUS, *Lapponia* (1673), pp. 84–85 (about the same, according to Tornæus); I. FELLMAN, *Finska Lappmarken o. Lapparne* I, p. 107 (JOH. BARTH. ERVAST's writing *Descriptio Lapponiæ Kiemiensis*, ~1727—cf. Peldan's correspondence, *Mmy. Aik.*[19] VI, pp. 153–55—some Laurukainen exploits are told as happening at Oulujärvi ~1611); P. LÆSTADIUS, *Journal öfver mina missionsresor i Lappmarken* II, pp. 482–, 1833 (Laurukainen), ELIAS LÖNNROT, *in matkat* I, p. 368 (Laurikainen), p. 370 (Ikimieli = Akimeelik); *Suometar* 1858, nos. 10, 13; J. V. CALAMNIUS, *Suomi* II, 7, p. 206; J. F. THAUVÓN, *Kirj. Kuukausl.*[20] 1869, no. 3 (Laurukainen), no. 7 (Ikämieli and more); J. A. FRIIS, *Lappiske Eventyr og Folkesagn* (1871), pp. 110–31 (Čuđit and Laurukainen stories); J. MAUKONEN, *Mmy. Aik.* IV, pp. 144–45 (Lari or

---

19. *Muinaismuistoyhdistyksen Aikakauskirja*, journal of the Finnish Ancient Monument Association.

20. *Kirjallinen Kuukauslehti*, which ran from 1866 to 1880.

Larikainen); Hj. APPELGREN(-KIVALO), *Mmy. Aik.* V, pp. 55– (Ikämieli and more), p. 80 (Laurukainen); R. TIRRONEN, *Mmy. Aik.* VII, pp. 33, 37, 39 (L);[21] A. H. SNELLMAN (VIRKKUNEN), *Mmy. Aik.* IX, pp. 190–91 (L); J. W. JUVELIUS, *Mmy. Aik.* X, pp. 62, 65, 87 (L); J. PAASONEN, *Mmy. Aik.* X, pp. 135, 141 (of Laurukainen story-type); Z. CASTRÉN, *Mmy. Aik.* XIV, pp. 269–90 (L); etc. A similar story from Neitsytsaari in Äänisjärvi (Lake Onega): some girl has revenge on the Lithuanians (ПАМЯТНАЯ КНИЖКА ОЛОНЕЦКОЙ ГУБЕРНИИ 1867, pp. 117–18).

---

21. Hereafter, Koskimies begins abbreviating Laurukainen as "L."

Bibliography

Akujärvi, Anja. 1998. *Morottajan Suku.* 2nd ed. Tornio: Tornion Kirjapaino Ky.
Bogdanova, Sandra. 2016. "Bark Food: The Continuity and Change of Scots Pine Inner Bark Use for Food by Sámi People in Northern Fennoscandia." Master's thesis, the Arctic University of Norway.
Cambrey, Leonne de. 1926. *Lapland Legends: Tales of an Ancient Race and Its Great Gods.* New Haven, CT: Yale University Press.
Christiansen, Reidar Th. 1958. *The Migratory Legends: A Proposed List of Types with a Systematic Catalogue of the Norwegian Variants.* FF Communications 175. Helsinki: Suomalainen Tiedeakatemia.
Cocq, Coppélie. 2008. *Revoicing Sámi Narratives: North Sámi Storytelling at the Turn of the Twentieth Century.* Umeå: Sámi Studies, Umeå University.
Demant Hatt, Emilie. 2013. *With the Lapps in the High Mountains: A Woman among the Sami, 1907–1908.* Translated by Barbara Sjoholm. Madison: University of Wisconsin Press.
DuBois, Thomas A. 1995. "Insider and Outsider: An Inari Sami Case." *Scandinavian Studies* 67(1): 63–76.
DuBois, Thomas A., and Jonathan F. Lang. 2013. "Johan Turi's Animal, Mineral, Vegetable Cures and Healing Practices: An In-Depth Analysis of Sami (Saami) Folk Healing One Hundred Years Ago." *Journal of Ethnobiology and Ethnomedicine* 9:57. https://ethnobiomed.biomedcentral.com/articles/10.1186/1746-4269-9-57.
Fjellner, Anders. 2003. *Biejjien Baernie (Sámi Son of the Sun).* Edited by Harald Gaski. Translated by John Weinstock. Kárášjohka: Davvi Girji.
Frandy, Tim. 2017. "Fishing for Meaning on the Deatnu River: Sámi Salmon Harvesters, Tourist Anglers, and the Discourse of Place." In *Nordic Literature: A Comparative History*, vol. 1, *Spatial Nodes*, edited by Thomas A. DuBois and Dan Ringgaard, 662–71. Philadelphia: John Benjamins.
Gaski, Harald, ed. 2006. *Time Is a Ship That Never Casts Anchor: Sami Proverbs.* Kárášjohka: ČálliidLágádus.
Gaski, Harald, John T. Solbakk, and Aage Solbakk, eds. 2004. *Min Njálmmálaš Árbevierru: Máidnasat, Myhtat ja Muitalusat.* Kárášjohka: Davvi.
Halonen, U. V. 1969. *Rätthostorisk Återblick på Samernas Status i Finland.* Nordisk Utredningsserie 6. Stockholm: Almqvist och Wiksell.
Helander-Renvall, Elina. 2005. *Silde: Sami Mythic Texts and Stories.* Oulu: Kalevaprint.

Honko, Lauri, Keith Bosley, Michael Branch, and Senni Timonen, eds. 1994. *The Great Bear: A Thematic Anthology of Oral Poetry in the Finno-Ugric Languages*. Helsinki: Finnish Literature Society.

Inarin Seurakunta. n.d. "Pielpajärven Erämaakirkko." Accessed June 8, 2018. https://inarinseurakunta.fi/index.php/sivu/pielpajarvenkirkko.

Inari Saariselkä. n.d. "Kaapin Jouni Farm." Accessed June 8, 2018. http://www.inarisaariselka.fi/en/attractions/kaapin-jounin-farm/.

Jouste, Marko. 2011. *Tullâčalmaaš Kirdâččij "Tulisilmillä lenteli": Inarinsaamelainen 1900-luvun Alun Musiikkikulttuuri Paikallisen Perinteen ja Ympäröivien Kulttuurien Vuorovaikutuksessa*. Tampere: Tampere University Press.

Kent, Neil. 2014. *The Sámi Peoples of the North: A Social and Cultural History*. London: Hurst.

Kitti, Jouni. n.d. "Kunnioitetut Sotiemme Veteraanit, Hyvät Läsnäolijat." Accessed June 8, 2018. http://jounikitti.fi/suomi/maaoikeudet/avaskarinpuhe.html.

Koskimies, A. V., and T. I. Itkonen. 1917. *Inarinlappalaista Kansantietoutta*. Suomalais-Ugrilaisen Seuran Toimituksia 40. Helsinki: Suomalais-Ugrilainen Seura.

———. 1978. *Inarinlappalaista Kansantietoutta*. 2nd ed. Edited by Lea Laitinen. Suomalais-Ugrilaisen Seuran Toimituksia 167. Helsinki: Suomalais-Ugrilainen Seura.

Læstadius, Lars Levi. 2002. *Fragments of Lappish Mythology*. Edited by Juha Pentikäinen. Translated by Börje Vähämäki. Beaverton, Ontario: Aspasia Books.

Lehtola, Veli-Pekka. 2002. *The Sámi People: Traditions in Transition*. Trans. Linna Weber Muller-Wille. Inari: Kustannus-Puntsi.

Mattus, Ilmari. 2010. "Itä-Inarin Paikanniemistö." Metsähallituksen Luonnonsuojelujulkaisuja Sarja A. 53. Helsinki: Edita Prima. https://julkaisut.metsa.fi/assets/pdf/lp/Asarja/a186.pdf.

Nahkiaisoja, Tarja. 2016. "Saamelaisten Maat ja Vedet Kruunun Uudistiloiksi: Asutus ja Maaankäyttö Inarissa ja Utsjoella Vuosina, 1749–1925." Acta Universitatis Ouluensis B Humaniora 134. Tampere: Juvenes Print. http://jultika.oulu.fi/files/isbn9789526210506.pdf.

Nickul, Karl. 1977. *The Lappish Nation: Citizens of Four Countries*. Bloomington, Ind.: Research Center for Language and Semiotic Studies.

Paulaharju, Samuli. 1927. *Taka-Lappia*. Helsinki: Kustannusosakeyhtiö.

Qvigstad, J., and G. Sandberg. 1887. *Lappiske Eventyr og Folkesagn*. Kristiania: A. Cammermeyer.

Sarmela, Matti. 2009. *Finnish Folklore Atlas*. 4th ed. Translated by Annira Silver. Helsinki: Suomen Kirjallisuuden Seura.

Siida Museum. n.d. "Culture." Accessed June 8, 2018. http://www.samimuseum.fi/anaras/english/kulttuuri/kulttuuri.html.

———. n.d. "Koskimies." Accessed June 8, 2018. http://www.samimuseum.fi/anaras/english/tutkimus/koskimies.html.

———. n.d. "Lauri Itkonen." Accessed June 8, 2018. http://www.samimuseum.fi/anaras/english/tutkimus/litkonen.html.

———. n.d. "Mattus." Accessed June 8, 2018. http://www.samimuseum.fi/anaras/english/tutkimus/mattus.html.

———. n.d. "Occupations." Accessed June 8, 2018. http://www.samimuseum.fi/anaras/english/elinkeinot/elinkeinot.html.

Turi, Johan. 2011. *An Account of the Sámi*. Translated by Thomas A. DuBois. Chicago: Nordic Studies Press.

Turi, Johan, and Per Turi. 1988. *Sámi Deavsttat, Duoddaris*. Edited by Nils Erik Hansegård. Jokkmokk: Sámi Girjjit.

Uther, Hans-Jörg. 2004. *The Types of International Folktales: A Classification and Bibliography*. Helsinki: Suomalainen Tiedeakatemia.

Index

Note: Page numbers in italics indicate illustrations.

Aanaar history, xxvii–xxxi
Aanaarjävri (Lake Aanaar), xxviii, xliii, xlvi, 119–20; Čuđit and, 138–42; in proverbs, 184; *sieidi* at, 102–3; Skolt Sámi and, 153
Aanaar municipal government, xxvi, xxxi, xlii, xlvi, 153
Aanaar Sámi language, xxviii, xxxi, xxxv; *Inari Sámi Folklore* and, xxxiii, 211, 217–18; Koskimies and, xxvii, 220–23, 231–34; in linguistic research, xxv–xxvi; orthography, xx, xxvii, xxxiii, 217–18, 231; reindeer and 165n2; Skolt Sámi and, 153; in translation, xix–xx
Aanaar village, xxxvn2, xxxix, xlviii, 11n14, 103–4, 122
Aarne-Thompson-Uther tale type index, xviii, xxxiii, 17
adultery, 56, 63–65
Aikio, Mikko, xxxi, xxxiv, xxxvii–xxxix, xliv, 4–13, 15, 15n21, 72, 81–82, 86, 88, 97, 104, 115, 120, 123–24, 133, 145, 148, 164–67, 211, 214, 218, 232
Aikio, Pekka Matinpoika, xxxix, 174, 176
Aikio, Petter Mattsinpoika (Kaapin Pekka), xxxix, 21, 28n6
Äjjih (Ukko) island, 102–4
alcohol, 37, 40, 51–52, 64, 70, 128, 177; beer, 204; brandy, 5, 77–78, 101, 107, 126, 126n9; in songs, 14; wine, 15, 68, 127
Andelin, Anders, 221, 223, 231, 233
Andersen, Hans Christian, 31
animals, general, 17, 105, 110–11, 178
angelica flute, 3
angels, 13

anthologies, Sámi oral tradition, xxxiv–xxxv, 233–35
archery, 20, 25, 119–20, 124; Čuđit and, 132–34, 139; hunting and, 151; in riddles, 201; in songs, 6; *stállu* and, 96
axes, 53, 82, 121, 125, 135; executioner and, 122; hunting, 164–66, 168; *noaidi* and, 72–73; in proverbs, 186; Skolt Sámi wives and, 156–60

bailiffs, 95–96, 222
baptisms, xxvi, xxxvii, 103
bawdy tales, xxxi, 18, 56
beavers, 123–24
bears, xxxi, xl, xlviii, 17–20, 23–25, 27, 29–30, 33, 71, 85, 125, 223; Čuđit and, 74; hunting, 163–71, 180; in *joik*, 212; in proverbs, 184, 187–88; in riddles, 204; shape-shifters and, 110, 112–14; Skolt Sámi wives and, 158–59, 161; in songs, 5, 5n1
beheading, 68, 122–23
berries, 156, 160, 169, 200, 209; arctic raspberries, 61–63, 65; cloudberries, 139–41, 207, 209; crowberries, 175, 224
bets. *See* wagers
Bible, xviii, xxxiii 29n7, 94, 117, 211
birds, 32–33, 38–39, 41–42, 45–46, 55, 77, 152, 224, 228; capercaillies, 73–76, 204; cranes, 209; crows, 15, 206; cuckoos, 197, 206, 208–9; dippers, xviii, 17, 28–29, 209–10; geese, 15, 207, 209; hunting, 132, 134, 167–68, 175, 178; loons, 134; in omens, 206, 208; owls, 7; in proverbs, 187, 190, 192; ravens, 6, 26–27, 187, 198; red-breasted

birds (*continued*)
  mergansers, 228; in riddles, 202; scaups, 15; *sieidi* and, 104; snow buntings, 209, 216; in songs, 5–6, 14; tits, 7; velvet scoters, 228; wagtail, xviii, 17, 28–29, 209; willow grouse (ptarmigan), 11n16, 15, 155, 160–61, 208; woodpeckers, 19, 124, 207–8
boats, xxv, 40, 82, 119–20, 171–72, 188, 219–20, 228–30; Čuđit and, 131, 134–42; fishing, 75, 111–12; in *joik*, 213; merchant, 62–64; Peeivih-Vuáláppá3 and, 149; in proverbs, 193; in riddles, 202, 204; *sieidi* and, 104–5; *stállu* and, 95–96
bogs. *See* swamps
border closings, xxix, 174
Borg, Edvard Wilhelm (E. V.), xlii–xliii, 175, 233

čáhálig, 98–100, 199
čáhcëháldi, 32, 38, 209
Cannelin, Knut, 219, 222, 234
cannibalism, 118, 120–21
Castrén, Matthias Alexander, xxvi, 227–28, 234–35
catechism and catechists, xxxviii, xlii, 156, 157n6, 175–76
cats, 7n5, 9, 25–26, 192
cattle, 41, 49, 54, 129, 176; *gufihtar* and, 98; in omens, 210; in riddles, 204; in songs, 9, 12
changelings, 97–98
childbirth, 58, 65–66, 122, 209
children, 65–67, 92, 100, 103, 131, 133, 145, 175–77, 214, 226; *gufihtar* and, 97–98; illegitimate, 56, 58, 69; infanticide, 120–22; lullabies, 5, 12, 175, 185; in omens, 209; play, 6; in proverbs, 187, 194, 196, 198; rearing, 31; songs, 3, 221; *stállu* and, 92
Christiansen's Migratory Legends, xviii
Christmas, 11n16, 87, 116, 155, 176, 215, 219
churches, xxvi, xxx, xxxi, xxxiv, 55, 97–98, 102, 106, 108, 117, 176n1, 190, 213, 221, 221n3; Aanaar (Piälppáájävri) church, xxv–xxvii, xxxi, xxxiii, xxxvn2, xliii, xlvi–xlvii, 106, 127, 127n10, 152, 176, 221–23; cantors, xliii, 232; clerics, xlvi; *joik* and, 3–4; masters, 232; pastors, xxv, xxxi, 50, 117, 124, 176, 190–91, 214, 220–22, 234; records, xviii, xxxvii, xxxix, xlii, xlvi; rector, xxxiii; sextons, xliii, 117; wardens, xlvii, 169
Cinderella, 31, 54n8
clothing, 45, 65, 78, 95, 99, 139, 155, 175, 177, 183, 190, 192, 214, 229; *beaska*, 152, 161, 202–3; beautiful, 35–36, 47, 55, 61, 66, 69, 122; coat, 27, 121, 125, 135, 151–52, 161, 171; dresses, 122, 156, 159, 170, 193; hats, 26, 43–44, 107, 126, 159, 186, 193, 195, 201–4, 214; leggings, 121, 151–52, 190; pants, 26, 198; poor, 35–36, 46, 48, 55, 59, 64, 68, 77, 126; shoes, 9, 55, 59, 99, 107, 180n6, 194, 197n7, 209, 213; skirts, 158; undressing, 36, 93, 121, 156, 161, 170
colonization, xxi, xxviii, 88, 131, 144
confirmation, 127
constable, 118, 122–24, 208n3
context and interpretation, xviii–xx, 4, 5n1, 13n19, 18, 32–33, 57, 86, 90n7
courtship, xxxi, xxxiv, 36–39, 55, 63, 80–81, 119–20, 126, 127–29, 174–76, 226; in omens, 212–13; in proverbs, 197; in riddles, 200; in songs, 3, 11–12, 14–16; *stállu* and, 87–88
crime and justice, xxvi, xlii, 52–53, 64–65, 222, 228; execution, 120–24, 162; in songs, 4, 9–10; theft, 59–61, 125–26
Čuđit, 17, 20, 25, 71–74, 81–82, 130–42, 229n13, 234; and *Ofelaš* (*Pathfinder*), 131

death, xxxvii, xliii, 34, 64, 155–57, 167, 172, 214, 229; of children, 176; of Čuđit, 82, 130–42; by execution, 121–22; giants and, 101–2; murder, 121–24; *noaidi* and, 105, 107–8, 114–17; in omens, 206, 208; of parents, 67, 70; in riddles, 202; in songs, 5, 9n9; of *stállu*, 87, 89–97; suitors and, 119–20. *See also* fishing; hunting
Demant Hatt, Emilie, xxxiv
devils, xviii, 50–51, 103; Čuđit and, 135; in omens, 207; in proverbs, 194; *stállu* and, 88, 94
disabilities, 170, 173; blindness, 18, 22, 209; deafness, xliii, 176
Disney adaptations, 31
dogs, 77, 107, 131; hunting and, 83–84, 170,

179-80; in proverbs, 184-87, 191, 194-95, 197; in riddles, 202; in songs, 9; *stállu* and, 89, 93, 96
drums, 3

education, xxxiv, xli-xliii, 58, 61; schoolmasters, 232
elders, xlii, xlvii, 119, 163; idols and, 147; in *joik*; 212; men and, 4, 8, 10, 14, 30, 34, 54-55, 73, 103, 113, 168, 194, 201, 205, 224; *noaidi* and, 106-9, 116-18, 215; women and, 6, 42-43, 75, 82, 89, 112, 134-35, 154, 171, 173, 187, 200
ermine, 17, 21, 25, 83, 163; hunting, 172-73
Ervast, Johan Bartholdi, xxx, 234
etiological stories, 17, 85-87
exoticism, 4, 32, 153

fainting, 37, 67, 101
fairy tales, xxvii, xxxii, xxxiv, 17, 31-33, 174, 231, 233-34; giants and, 100
farming, xlviii, 23, 58, 65, 67, 79, 83, 126, 206, 232; in proverbs, 186; reindeer and, 106n20; shift to, xxix, 153
fat, 21-22; eating, 25; *noaidi* and, 145; in proverbs, 187, 191, 197-98; *sieidi* and, 102; used in healing, 169n8
fears. *See* frights
feces, 69-70, 134, 186-88, 198, 207
Fellner, Jakob, xxx, 120n1
Fellman, Isaak, 234
Fellman, Jakob, xlii, 7n5, 234
feminist readings, xx, 31-33, 58, 71-72, 104n17, 153-54
fighting. *See* wrestling
Finland, xxix, 11n15, 68n3, 130-31, 143, 176, 224, 228, 232; Finnish language, xvii, xix-xx, xxi, xxiii, xxviii, xxxiii, xxxvii, xliii, xlvi, li, 3, 7, 13n19, 29n7, 32, 53n6, 106n18, 108n22, 114n30, 122, 143, 151nn11-12, 167n5, 175, 217, 219, 221, 224, 225n8, 228, 231-33
fire: campfire, 25, 179, 215, 224; cooking, 22, 131; Čuđit and, 133, 135, 137-38, 139-40; fireplace, 69-70, 82, 200-201; fishing and, 111-12; 116; in omens, 208; in proverbs,

188, 191, 196; *sieidi* and, 145-46; in songs, 10, 13; *stállu* and, 92-93; tragedy and, 177
firearms, 24, 30, 44, 78, 89, 123; hunting and, 164-70, 172, 179-80; in proverbs, 196; in riddles, 203
firewood, xxvi, 19, 21, 82; Čuđit and, 135, 137; Peeivih-Vuálappáǯ and, 149-50; in proverbs, 193; *sieidi* and, 145; *stállu* and, 87
fish, 21-22, 32, 132, 136, 155, 176, 226; arctic char, 22, 37; burbot, 22, 190, 195-96, 213; grayling, xxviii, 22, 197-98, 206; *noaidi* and, 105; perch, xxviii, 22, 193, 198, 213; pike, xxviii, 22, 37-39, 41, 75-76, 132, 208, 213; in proverbs, 184-85, 187, 192, 194-95; salmon, xxviii, 18, 22, 205; shape-shifters and, 111-12; *sieidi* and, 102; in songs, 5, 11n16, 13; trout, 8, 22; whitefish, xxviii, 8, 22, 33, 111-12, 224
fishing, xxviii-xxix, xxxi, xxxix, xlii-xliii, xlv, 21, 32, 37, 75-76, 88, 120, 163, 172-76, 220-21, 224-25; Čuđit and, 131-32, 136; ice-fishing and *juoŋâstim*, xliv, 149-50, 154, 174, 181-82; nets, 6, 75-76, 185, 187n1, 200; Peeivih-Vuálappáǯ and, 148; in proverbs, 183, 188; in riddles, 203; seines, 6, 8, 90, 111-12, 131, 133-35, 145, 160, 172n9; shape-shifters and, 111-12; *sieidi* and, 102; Skolt Sámi and, 108, 156; *stállu* and, 90
flatulence, 18, 24, 197, 201, 204
fleas, 58, 185, 201
flint, 26, 98
food, xxviii-xxix, 63-65, 214, 219; animals and, 20-22, 25-26; Čuđit and, 73-74, 131-32, 139-41; *gufihtar* and, 97-98; horses and, 34-35; hunting and, 164, 166, 169-72; marriage and, 40-41, 69-70, 176-77; *noaidi* and, 109-10; in omens, 207n1, 209-10; Peeivih-Vuálappáǯ and, 151; poverty and, 46, 65, 175; in proverbs, 187-88, 189n2, 190-92, 195-96, 198-99; reindeer and, 106; in riddles, 201-3; *sieidi* and, 104; shape-shifters and, 112; Skolt Sámi and, 155, 160; in songs, 4-5, 8, 11, 15; sources, 86; *stállu* and, 87, 93-94; storage, 110, 178, 180-81. *See also* cannibalism

foolishness, xix, 40, 71–72, 73–84, 106, 147; Čuđit and, 131n1; in proverbs, 186; Skolt Sámi wives and, 153–54; wives and, 65, 75–79
forgiveness, xxxiv, 56, 64, 122n4, 215, 225
fortune, 48, 53–54, 175, 194, 219, 222n4, 226, 229; bad luck, 62, 184, 187, 191; marriage and, 69–70, 127–29, 177; in omens, 206, 210; in proverbs, 191, 197–98; *sieidi* and, 102, 104; treasure and, 77, 99
foxes, 17–28, 44, 179; in proverbs, 197
frights, xix, 45, 48, 50–53, 59, 61, 67, 71, 76, 86, 118–19, 177, 229; animals and, 20, 22, 25, 28, 30; Čuđit and, 134–35; hunting and, 163–64, 167–68, 170; in *joik*, 214; *noaidi* and, 107, 109, 116; Peeivih-Vuáláppáʒ and, 147; reindeer and, 94; Skolt Sámi and, 153–62
Friis, Jens Andreas, 231, 234
frogs, 20, 24–25, 213

Garen-Ovla (Kaarin-Uvla, Karen Ovlla), xx, 106–8
genitals, 13, 18, 91–93, 154n1, 158; castration and, 23–24
geres-sledge, 17–18, 21, 88, 154, 180–88; Čuđit and, 142; hunting and, 163, 167; Peeivih-Vuáláppáʒ and, 151; in songs, 6, 9
ghosts. *See* spirits
giants, xxxiv, 86, 100–102, 143
gifts, 47; marriage and, 40, 64, 176–77; in proverbs, 184; *sieidi* and, 104n15
goahti, xx, 22, 112, 114–15, 124, 152, 180, 224; Čuđit and, 131–32, 134–35; in proverbs, 188–89, 196; Skolt Sámi and, 155, 157; *stállu* and, 90–91, 93, 96
goats, 12
gold: axe, 73; birds, 41; in *joik*, 211; mountains, 34–37; in omens 209; in riddles, 202; rooms, 47. *See also* money; rings; treasure
graves and graveyards, 19, 114–18, 214
Great Fear, 81, 136
Grimm, Jacob and Wilhelm, xxv
gufihtar, xix, 86, 97–99

hares, 24, 28; in omens, 210; in proverbs, 195
healing, xxxii, 3, 24, 28, 49–50, 72–73, 168–69, 177; *noaidi* and, 105, 109
heaven, 122, 147
hell, 14
Helsinki, xxv, 216, 219, 221n3, 222, 231–32
Historic-Geographic Method, 31
horses, 17, 23, 27–28, 30, 34–37, 43–44, 47, 231; draught, 57, 59; in proverbs, 184–85, 190; in riddles, 201, 204
humor, xix, xxxii, xl, 32, 50n4, 56–57, 71–84, 119, 126, 129n11, 195n6; animals and, 17–18; hunting and, 163; Skolt Sámi women and, 153–62
hunger: Christianity and, 225; Čuđit and, 139, 141; in *joik*, 212; in proverbs, 187–88, 192; wolves and, 27, 112
hunting, xxix, 58, 89–91, 102, 114, 163, 174, 193; bear, xxxi, xl, 5n1, 71, 113–14, 164–71, 223; beaver, 123–24; birds, 14, 132, 167–68, 175, 177–78, 210; ermine, 172–73; moose, 109, 172; squirrel, 171, 179; wild reindeer, xxix, xxxii, 17, 24–25, 72, 83–84, 102–3, 110, 115, 125, 144, 151, 164–66, 171–72, 174–75, 179–81, 223

Ij-jävri (Iijärvi), xxxii, 104–6, 118, 120–21
illness, 62, 72–72, 105, 156–57, 172; *noaidi* and, 102, 105, 108–9, 145, 214; in omens, 206, 208–10; Peeivih-Vuáláppáʒ and, 145; *sieidi* and, 102, 145; in songs, 7
Inari Sámi Folklore (Inarinlappalaista kansantietoutta) (earlier editions), xvii–xviii, xxxiii, 4, 211, 217
infanticide, 56, 66, 122
injuries, xl, 155, 177; animals and, 22–23, 27–28, 30; giants and, 102; hunting and, 164, 166–67, 168–70; in omens, 206; Peeivih-Vuáláppáʒ and, 150–51; in proverbs, 191
insanity, 162, 186, 226; faking, 125–26
insider/outsider dynamics, xxxi–xxxii, 3, 72, 88, 108–17, 153–62
iron, 16, 72, 142, 179
Itkonen, Lauri Arvid, xxxiii, xli
Itkonen, Toivo Immanuel, xvii–xix, xxiii–xxiv,

xxx, xxxiii–xxxiv, xxxvii, xli, xliii–xliv, xlvii, 10n11, 13n17, 27, 50n4, 53n6, 73n2, 86, 136, 161n12, 174, 184, 189, 206, 217–18, 225, 231–32
Ivalo (Aaveel), xx, 123, 222–23, 227

joik. *See* music
Juhannus, xxv, 207, 220
Juvduu (Juutua), xliii, xlvi, xlviii, 137, 222–23

Kaapin Pekka. *See* Aikio, Petter Mattsinpoika
Kalevala, 13nn17–18, 114; Joukkavainen, 13; Väinämöinen, 3, 12–13, 114
Kalevanpojat, 143
Karelia/Karelians, xxviii, 13n17, 130–31, 143, 158n8, 229, 234
Kemi Sámi, 175, 226–27, 229, 234; language, xxviii, 110n26, 115n31; *noaidi* and, 114; songs and, 15n21
kings, 31, 35–37, 41–42, 47–48, 52, 54, 56–61, 67, 86, 125; giants and, 100–102; in proverbs, 188
Kitti, Antti (Meniš-Antti), xxxiv, xxxix–xl, 57, 67, 83, 95, 168, 169n8, 232
Kitti, H., xl, 169
Kittilä (Kittâl), 123, 144, 219
knives, xlviii, 121, 157, 215; castration and, 23, 75; Čuđit and, 142; *Gufihtar* and, 98; hunting and, 172; *noaidi* and, 73, 108; in proverbs, 190, 197; *stállu* and, 94; treasure and, 45, 78
Koskimies, August Valdemar, xvii–xviii, xx, xxiii, xxv–xxviii, xxxi–xxxiv, xxxvn1, xxxvii–xlviii, 3–4, 6n3, 10n11, 15n21, 71, 106, 108n22, 114n30, 163, 184, 206, 214n1, 215–18, 221n3, 235n21

lààutâǯ (*lauttanen; njollâ*), 178
Læstadius, Lars Levi, xxxiv, 234
Laitinen, Lea, xvii, xx, xxxiii, 14n20, 15n21, 44n3, 50n4, 56, 86, 106n18, 108n22, 114n30, 120n1, 139n7, 149n9, 159n10, 210n6, 217
lambs. *See* sheep
lassos, 6, 9, 131, 203

Laurukàǯ (Laurukainen), xx, 130, 137–42, 229, 234–35
lávvu, xx, 123, 180, 201
laziness, 29, 71, 80, 81n4, 82, 106, 214; bears and, 5n1; Čuđit and, 135; in proverbs, 186, 190, 195–96; in riddles, 203
legends, xviii, xxvii, xxxii, xxxiv, li, 4, 11n14, 17, 71, 74n2, 174, 231, 233–34; belief, 85–117; contemporary, 86; historical, 118–52; saints', 85, 143
lemmings, 209
lice, 54, 56, 68; in proverbs, 192; in riddles, 202
linguistics, xix, xxv–xxvi, xxvii, 221–24, 231–33
literacy, xxx, xxxiv, 94, 175, 218, 229, 232
livđe, xxxviii, 3–6, 8
logging, 28–29
Lönnrot, Elias, xxv–xxvi, 12n17, 13n18, 223, 233–34. See also *Kalevala*
lords, 37–40, 48, 51–53, 59, 61, 68–69
luck. *See* fortune
Lusmaniemi, Juho Petteri, xxxi, xxxv, xl, 32–34, 41, 48, 50, 72, 80, 83, 108, 111–12, 125–26, 159, 162, 170–71, 218, 232

magistrates, 122–23
Mannermaa, Iisakki, xxxi, xxxiv, xli, 24, 37, 44, 46, 54, 56–57, 59, 61, 65, 69, 71, 74, 77, 100, 121, 137–38, 147, 232–33
Mannermaa, J., xlii, xlvii, 103
markets, 11–12, 14, 77, 159n10, 222
marriage, xxvi, 32–33, 39, 42, 63–65, 69–70, 74, 77, 120, 127–29, 156n4, 176, 208; and divorce, 78; records, xxxvii; to *stállu*, 87–88
marshes. *See* swamps
Marxism and economic class, 31–32, 57
Mattus, Heikki, xxxi, xxxvii, xlii–xliii, 26, 27, 170, 174–75, 179–80, 218, 232
medicine. *See* healing
merchants, 10n11, 31, 47, 56, 61–65, 77–78, 159n10, 220, 230, 232
mice, 7, 20, 24–26; in *joik*, 213; in proverbs, 184, 193
midnight, 34–35, 114, 117
missionization, 4, 105, 144, 147n7, 234; and religious shift, 102, 110, 144, 225n9

money, 34–35, 50–52, 59–61, 65, 99, 107, 214, 222; coins, 63, 99, 102, 116; dollars, 11, 68, 127; gold, 45–46, 63, 68; in *joik*, 212; in proverbs, 186; rubles, 115–16, 214–15; silver, 19–20, 45, 63, 127–28; in songs, 12, 14; *stállu* and, 92–95. *See also* treasure, hidden

moon, 85–87, 119; in proverbs, 194

moose, 29–30; hunting, 109–10, 172; in proverbs, 192

morality, xxxi, xxxiv, 17, 31, 56–57

Morottaja, Heikki, xliii, 28

Morottaja, Uula, xxxi, xliii, 23, 73, 83, 93, 109, 112, 116–17, 120, 134, 136, 140, 142, 161, 171–72, 232

mountains, xxx, xxxiv, 34–37, 95, 115, 222, 224; Čuđit and, 132–33, 137; *gufihtarat* and, 97–99; hunting and, 164; in riddles, 200, 204; *sieidi* and, 103, 146–47; in songs, 13; *stállu* and, 90

Muinaismuistoyhdistys (Ancient Monument Association), 219, 234–35

music, 3–16, 67, 211–14; *joik*, xvii, xxxiii–xxxiv, xxxviii, xliv, 3–11, 97, 168n7, 191, 211–14, 218, 221, 233; singers and, xxxviii, xliii, 197; singing and song, 3–4, 97, 221, 231, 233

myths, xxxiv, 13n19, 17, 86, 100, 130, 174

Neiden (Njiävđám; Näätämö), xxv, 108–9, 159

noaidi, xix, xxix, xxxi–xxxii, 72, 105–10, 114–17, 124, 144, 158n7, 211; gnawing on wood, 116–17, 214–15

nobility. *See* lords

North Sámi (Mountain Sámi), xvii, xix–xx, xxviii–xxix, xxxiii–xxxiv, 3–4, 10n13, 95, 99, 211–14, 218, 225n8, 232–33

Norway, xxv, xxix, 11n15, 68n3, 106, 108, 143, 159, 179, 219–20; Norwegian language, xx, xxviii, xxxiv, 234

numskull tales, xxxii, 71, 74, 162

omens, xxvii, xxxvii, 124, 132, 206–10, 231

otter, 179; in songs, 7

Oulu, 230–31

Paatsjoki (Pááčvei), xliii, xlv, xlviii, 109–10, 138–39, 149, 159, 232

parables, 17

Paulaharju, Samuli, xxxviii

Peeivih-Vuáláppáǯ (Päivän Olavi), 85, 100, 143–44, 144–52; in proverbs, 198

Perrault, Charles, xxv

personal experience narratives, xxxii–xxxiii, 174–75

Piälppáájävri church, xxv–xxvi, *xxvii*, xxxi, xxxvn2, xlvii

piärtušm, 164

pigs, 188

Peeivih-Vuáláppáǯ, 149–50; in riddles, 201; in songs, 7, 13

postman, 125

potatoes, xxix, xlviii

poverty, xxviii, 4, 8n8, 31, 34, 37–41, 53–56, 59, 65, 69–70, 77, 128–29, 174–75, 228; in proverbs, 185–86, 188, 192; as punishment, 46–48, 214–16; in songs, 10

prayer, xlii, 101, 103, 155n2, 156, 175; Peeivih-Vuáláppáǯ and, 143

pre-Christian religion, xxx, 105, 144; forest matron and, 13. *See also noaidi; sieidi*

pregnancy, 38, 65, 69, 121; miscarriage and, 66; in omens, 209; stillborn and, xli

Propp, Vladimir, 31

prosperity, 9, 32, 44–48, 61–65, 74–77, 97, 106, 127, 186, 211–12, 190, 228; rewards and, 34–37, 48–49, 53–54, 68–70, 177. *See also* gold; money; silver; treasure, hidden

proverbs, 183–94, 218, 221, 227, 231, 233

Psalms, xviii, 211

queens, 47–48

Qvigstad, Just, xxvi, xxxii, xxxiv, 97, 106, 220, 222, 233–34

rafts, 130, 134

railroads, 230–31

rain, 46, 145–46, 230; in omens, 208; in proverbs, 191, 194

rams, 104–5; in proverbs, 197–99

rape, xxxii, 8n8, 32–33, 42

reindeer, xix, 17, 18n1, 19–21, 48–49, 95–96, 174–75, 178–79; clothing and products made from, xxx, 99, 125, 152; draught reindeer, 7, 20, 94, 98, 116, 131–32, 142, 150, 160, 163, 165–67, 170, 181, 184, 212, 215; foraging and, xxviii; *gufihtarat* and, 97–98; herding and, xxix–xxxi, 89, 94, 98, 106–7, 116–17, 121, 142, 150, 176–77, 221, 224–26; in *joik*, 212; migration with, 94, 106, 121, 169, 221; in omens, 207–9; pastureland, xxvii, xxix, 106, 175; in proverbs, 183–84, 186, 191, 195–96; *sieidi* and, 102–4, 146; in songs, 6, 9–11, 14–15; wild reindeer, xxxii, 24–25, 29n7, 72, 83–84, 102–3, 110, 115, 144, 151–52, 163–64, 165–66, 170–71, 174–75, 179–88, 223, 226
riddles, 200–205, 231
rings, 36–38, 55, 62, 64, 177; in riddles, 202; in songs, 11
rivers, xxxiii, xliii, xlviii, 37–40, 66, 222–23, 225–29; animals and, 20–22, 28–29; drowning and, 123–24, 139; hunting and, 164–65, 167; *noaidi* and, 108–10; in proverbs, 189; rapids and waterfalls, xxxiii, 29, 89, 108, 130, 138–39, 202, 213, 227–29; in riddles, 201–2; in songs, 10; *stállu* and, 94–95
romanticism, xxv, 18, 154, 188
Russia, xxix, 81n5, 130–31, 136n6
Russian Orthodox Church, 108, 153, 155n2, 157, 220
Russians, 115, 130, 133, 137–39, 142, 220; in *joik*, 212; Peeivih-Vuáláppáž and, 148–49; *stállu* and, 88–89

Saariselkä (Suáloi-čielgi), 179, 224
sacrificial offering, 225; *sieidi* and, 102–5
sacristan, 176, 180; in proverbs, 189–90
saints, 85, 143; in songs, 14
salt, 11n16, 79, 206
Sandberg, Georg, xxvi, 222, 233, 238
Sápmi, xxv
Sarre, Anna Antintytär (Ison Antin Anna), xliii, 106

Sarre, Antti, xliv, 181, 232
Sarre, Matti, xxxi, xliv, xlv, xlviii, 18–19, 27, 89, 149–50, 232
Sarre, Yrjänä, xlv, 146, *146*
sauna, 58; in songs, 12
Schefferus, Johannes, 234
schools. *See* education
sea, 40, 43–44, 46–48, 108, 120 144, 148–49, 230n14; in riddles, 204; in songs, 3
settlers: Finnish, xxviii, xxix, xxx–xxxi, 10n11, 128, 130–31, 153, 226, 228; Norwegian, 148–49
sewing, 161; needles, 81; in riddles, 201, 205
sexism, xxxi, 4, 32–33, 58n1, 71, 153–54. *See also* feminist readings
sexuality, xxxi, xxxiv, 3–4, 31–33 56, 67–70, 129n11; *stállu* and, 87, 91–93; women and, xxxi 3, 12, 14–15, 58, 121, 153–54, 156, 158
shaman. *See* noaidi
shape-shifting, xxxi, 96, 110–14
sheep, 54–55, 77–78, 82, 160, 171, 176; lambs, 28, 198; *sieidi* and, 103–4; in songs, 9
sieidi, 102, 104–5, 226n10; Peeivih-Vuáláppáž and, 143–46
siida, xxviii, xxix, xxxvn3, 106, 109, 153, 169; Pååđár, 175; Suonjel, xxviii; Veskonjargå, 147
silver: courtship and, 128; in *joik*, 211–12; *noaidi* and, 116; *sieidi* and, 102. *See also* money; treasure, hidden
skiing, 114–15; Čuđit and, 142; hunting and, 109, 168 171; in proverbs, 196
Skolt Sámi, 72, 153–54; communities and, 53; haunting and, 116–17; hunting and, 83–84; language and, xxviii; *noaidi* and, 108–9; shape-shifting and, 11–14; *stállu* and, 89n6; tension with Aanaar and, xxxii; women and, xxxi, 154–62
smoking. *See* tobacco
snow, 168, 171, 179–80, 223–24; Čuđit and, 142; *gufihtarat* and, 97; in omens, 207–208; in proverbs, 196; in riddles, 201; Skolt Sámi and, 155; in songs, 213; *stállu* and, 95

Sodankylä (Soađigil), 177, 219, 223
soldiers, 47; animals and, 30; Čuđit and, 133; giants and, 100–102; *noaidi* and, 106–7
Sompio, 110, 114–15, 223–24, 226. *See also* Kemi Sámi
souls: death and, 122–23; *noaidi* and, 105, 109nn24–25
spears, 52, 93, 123, 171
spinning, 80–81; in riddles, 200, 203
spirits, 14, 85, 97–98, 99, 225; hauntings and, 114–17, 155; *joik* and, 4, 191; *noaidi* and, 105, 107, 109, 114; *sieidi* and, 102–4, 145, 226n10
springs, 74, 180
squirrels: hunting and, 171, 179; in proverbs, 190, 194; in songs, 12–13
stállu, 86–97, 100
starvation. *See* hunger
steel, 108; firesteel, 26, 117
Stenvik, G., 219, 22–23, 230
Stockfleth, Nils, 224, 231
St. Olaf (Olaf II Haraldsson), 143
storytelling, xix, xxxii–xxxv, 31
sucking straws: of *stállu*, 87, 92–93
Suenjel *siida*, xxviii
suicide, 10
sun, 79; names and, 143; in omens, 208; in proverbs, 194, 196; in riddles, 203; in songs, 5, 7, 15
Sundsvall, xxv, 220
Suomalaisen Kirjallisuuden Seura (Finnish Literature Society), xxxiii, 217
Suomalais-Ugrilainen Seura (Finno-Ugric Society), xxxiii, 217, 233n17
supernatural. *See* belief legends
swamps, 220, 223, 226, 228; hunting and, 103, 164, 181
swans, 209, 216
Sweden, 81, 136, 219; Swedish language, xxxviii, xxxvn1, xxxvii, 233
swords, 30, 68, 107, 142; giants and, 101–2

tall tales, 85
tar, 87–88, 95, 194; feathers and, 34–36, 77
taxation, xxvi, xxix
thunder, 46, 103n14, 204

tin, melting, 73, 140
tobacco, 118; in proverbs, 185, 193; in riddles, 203; in songs, 212
Tornæus, Johannes, 234
tragedy, xxxii, 119–24, 174, 177
trance, 105, 109n25, 217, 222
transgressive behavior, 18, 56–57, 97, 118
trapping, xxix, 75–76, 123, 174, 177–80, 187
treasure, hidden, 44–46, 75–76, 98–99, 199n10
trees, 6, 15, 57–58, 87, 113, 124, 150, 160–62, 164, 167–71, 201, 203, 205, 227; birch, xxviii, 6, 23, 88, 168, 170, 197, 201, 203; birchbark, 161, 186, 206, 207n1; birchbark baskets, 112, 172, 207; juniper, 144, 185; mountain ash, 204; pine, xxviii, 19, 22–23, 26, 73, 110, 116, 124, 135, 137, 140–41, 157–58, 169–71, 178; pine bark as food, xxviii, *xxx*, xlii, 140, 155, 161, 175, *189*; pine cones, 13, 197; roots, 19, 24, 26, 76, 82, 102–3, 116, 137, 150, 167–68, 172, 204, 215; spruce, 15, 116–17, 137, 160–61, 169, 215
tricksters, 18–28, 50–51, 56, 67–69, 72–73, 81
trolls. *See stállu*
tundra, xxvii, 72, 102, 141, 144–45, 223–24; *gufihtarat* and, 97; hunting and, 165, 179–81; in songs, 13
Turi, Johan, xxxii, xxxiv, 97, 167n6, 169n8

urination, 70, 159
Utsjoki (Uccjuuhâ), 124, 219, 221–22

Vaasa, xxv, xxxiii, 219, 231
Vadsø (Čácisuáloi; Čahcesuolu), xx, xxv, 10n11, 95, 149, 220
Valle, Martti, xlv, 28
Valle, P., xxxi, xxxvii, xlii, xlvii, 102–3, 110, 119, 127, 131–32, 135, 144, 214, 233
Valle, Paavali, xxxi, xlvi–xlviii, 53, 106, 108, 114, 154–57, 159, 232
Valle, Pekka, xxxvii, xlvi–xlvii, 25
Valle, Pietari, xxxvii, xlvi–xlviii, 139, 232
Valle, Santeri, xlvi–xlviii, *27*, 106, 108, 114–15, *136*, 154–57, 159, *189*
Varanger Fjord (Värjivuona), liii, 11, 95, 120, 149, 214, 220

Vardø (Várgáåh), 106, 127
Viklund, Karl Bernhard, 233
Virkkula, Viktor Alfred, xxv, 220, 232
violence, xxxii, 4, 8n8; Čuđit and, 74n1, 142; manipulation and, 71; sexual, 32, 33

wagers, 28, 50–51, 125; hauntings and, 117; *noaidi* and, 144; Peeivih-Vuáláppáǯ and, 151–52
war, 136n6; borders and, 81, 131; in omens, 209; threat of, 20, 25
washing, 6, 155, 199
weather, 62; controlling the, 105, 143, 145–46; predicting the, 163, 206–8; seasons and, 179n5, 216, 227. *See also* rain; thunder; wind
weaving, 137
whales, 198, 213
wind, 62, 138; in omens, 207; in proverbs, 191; reindeer and, 179; *sieidi* and, 145–46; in songs, 14–16, 15n21
winter camp, xxvi, 108–9
wolverines, 20
wolves, 17, 20–22, 24–25, 27–28; hunting and, 167n6; in proverbs, 188, 190; shape-shifting and, 110, 112; in songs, 10n10, 213
woman, elderly, from Juvduu (Juutua), xxxi, xlviii, 171
woman, unnamed, from Páččvei (Paatsjoki), xxxi, xlviii, 113–14
wool, 54
wrestling: bears and, 164, 168; giants and, 100–101; *noaidi* and, 109; over territorial borders, 124; Peeivih-Vuáláppáǯ and, 143–44, 149–51; in proverbs, 184–85, 198; in riddles, 203; *stállu* and, 88–96

yarn, 42–43

www.ingramcontent.com/pod-product-compliance
Lightning Source LLC
Chambersburg PA
CBHW050548160426
43199CB00015B/2581